CASTLEREAGH

Robert Stewart 2nd Marquess of Londonderry 1769–1822
by Sir Thomas Lawrence

CASTLEREAGH

C. J. Bartlett

MACMILLAN

London · Melbourne · Toronto

1966

MACMILLAN AND COMPANY LIMITED
Little Essex Street London WC2
also Bombay Calcutta Madras Melbourne

THE MACMILLAN COMPANY OF CANADA LIMITED
70 Bond Street Toronto 2

PRINTED IN GREAT BRITAIN

IN MEMORY
OF
PAUL

Contents

Note

To avoid confusion, I have referred constantly to the subject of this book by his best-known name, Castlereagh. He was, in fact, Viscount Castlereagh only from August 1796, and he succeeded his father as the 2nd Marquis of Londonderry in 1821.

To simplify the footnotes, and to facilitate easy reference, I have provided (see p. 282) an alphabetical list of the main works cited in this book.

List of Illustrations

Acknowledgements

My first debt is to Dr. Donald Southgate, who encouraged me to undertake this study of Castlereagh. Professor Asa Briggs very kindly read the whole typescript, and made many valuable suggestions. The style and format of the early chapters were greatly improved by Professor D. F. Macdonald, who throughout has taken an active and kindly interest in this project. I am heavily indebted to the library staff of Queen's College, Dundee, in the University of St. Andrews, and to the very efficient Inter-Library Loan Service. I have endeavoured in the footnotes and bibliography to acknowledge my debt to the many scholars who have laboured on the late eighteenth and early nineteenth centuries, and whose work throws light on the career of Castlereagh. Any academic merit the present study possesses is essentially due to them, and I can only hope that they will feel that this biography represents a useful synthesis not unworthy of their efforts. Any omissions in acknowledgement I trust they will forgive. My wife has nobly undertaken much of the mechanical work associated with this book, including the Index, and has, as always, proved a severe and invaluable critic, especially in matters of style. To the errors and omissions alone can I lay exclusive claim.

Queen's College, Dundee   C. J. B.
December 1965

1

The 'Mask' of Castlereagh

Of all British statesmen Castlereagh remains one of the most anonymous. To outward appearance his career should have proved attractive to at least one type of biographer. One, possibly two duels, a narrow escape from drowning in his youth, an active part in the suppression of an Irish rebellion, an intimate relationship with British and European royalty, attendance at some of the most glittering social occasions of the age, and the whole crowned by suicide — the most famous instance in all British history — the material for the romantic writer seems abundant. But just as Castlereagh repelled contemporary poets, so he has never attracted the imaginative writer to any great extent since that time.[1] His slowly growing band of admirers has numbered diplomats, or those interested in diplomacy, rather than any other readily identifiable group. Castlereagh, indeed, is frequently portrayed as the epitome of the nineteenth-century diplomatic profession — secretive, passionless, polished and aloof. When Shelley wrote, 'He had a mask like Castlereagh', was there not a second meaning behind the obvious one? Byron stressed Castlereagh's coldness even in the heat of his worst reputed crimes. Contemporaries who knew, but who were not intimately acquainted with him were fascinated by this characteristic. The handful of people who really knew him did indeed discover a warm and gentle person-

[1] Exceptions are Charles Lever's inclusion of some scenes of Castlereagh's early life in his *The Knight of Gwynne*, and Ione Leigh's *Castlereagh* (1951), though the latter also contains much valuable information, and is especially useful for Castlereagh's early career.

ality beneath the frigid exterior; many of Castlereagh's private
letters, especially to his wife, confirm this. But to the outside
world the mask rarely slipped. In time, instead of attracting as a
thing of mystery, it tended to repel inquiry. The study of
Castlereagh's career has consequently been confined to a handful
of devoted scholars. In contrast to the many biographies of
Wellington, born in the same year as Castlereagh, he has been
the subject of only one large-scale biography, two medium-
sized studies, and a few slighter efforts. There are only three
large monographs devoted exclusively to particular aspects of
his career, and for the rest one is dependent upon essays,
articles, and works devoted to problems with which Castlereagh
was connected.[1]

The scarcity of material with Castlereagh as the central theme
does not, however, mean that much has not been revealed
concerning his career. The evidence, though scattered, is
considerable, and a synthesis practicable. Fifteen years have
elapsed since the last biography of Castlereagh appeared, a
biography which incidentally devotes comparatively little
attention to his career after 1812. Some thirty years separate us
from the only truly comprehensive modern study, written by Sir
John Marriott, and historical studies have undergone many
changes since that time, even if this biography postdates the
monographs of Sir Charles Webster and Dr. Montgomery
Hyde. Castlereagh is so central a figure in British politics from
about 1797 to 1822 — far more so than Wellington or Canning
— that his life is always worthy of re-examination, and will
continue to be so just as long as historians are interested in this
period. Castlereagh was at the heart of British politics for
roughly twenty-five years. In that time he was a leading figure
in the highly controversial Union of Britain and Ireland, he was
connected with the great campaigns of the Wellesley brothers
in India, he was intimately associated with British planning and
preparation for war against Napoleon from 1803 to 1809, he
was Britain's Foreign Secretary during the critical years in the
overthrow of Napoleon and the period of European reconstruction thereafter, and he led the House of Commons during a
period of exceptional popular unrest in Britain. This was a

[1] See Bibliography.

strikingly controversial career for one whose political life was so often devoted to the removal or smoothing away of controversy.

For his part in the Act of Union, Castlereagh was fiercely denounced at the time by those who championed the Irish Parliament, and subsequently by Irish nationalists in quest of independence. As Secretary of State for War, he was deeply involved in the Walcheren disaster, and with several other setbacks to British arms in the struggle against Napoleon. *The Times* in 1812 thought him 'the very darling of misfortune'. Victories over Napoleon softened tempers in Britain, but found Castlereagh deep in controversy with his continental allies. The honeymoon period with his British critics soon ended as the pattern of the post-Napoleonic Europe began to emerge, and Castlereagh's continued association with his war-time allies in particular provoked hostility. As Leader of the House of Commons from 1812, Castlereagh was the most prominent of the cabinet in the defence of controversial measures against popular disturbance. For the Radicals he had become the personification of repression and reaction at home and abroad. His opponents at the time, and for much of the nineteenth century, possessed the bigger publicity guns. The Whig and Radical interpretations of early nineteenth-century events were not very effectively challenged, while Cobbett, Byron, Shelley and Thomas Moore had followings which no government 'scribbler' could challenge. Had Sir Walter Scott accepted the invitation to write a Life of Castlereagh, the picture might have been more favourable. As it was, Castlereagh's rehabilitation began as the mounting pile of *Memoirs, Lives, Diaries* and *Letters* of his contemporaries — not to mention the fifteen volumes of evidence on his own career published by his half-brother and by Sir A. Alison — provided increasing information concerning his conduct, character and intentions. Even some of his old opponents such as Brougham and Lord John Russell were beginning to acknowledge his possession of certain qualities. From such sources the future Lord Salisbury and still more Mr. Fyffe began to penetrate the secrets of his foreign policy. At the beginning of the twentieth century, Sir John Fortescue, the famous military historian, began to champion Castlereagh's

claims as a war minister, while Sir Charles Webster was
starting his monumental researches into Castlereagh's tenure
of the Foreign Office. He was able to confirm the conclusions to
which Fyffe had already been pointing, and so establish Castlereagh in his rightful place in the history of British foreign policy.
While Webster's work was in progress, British domestic
history in the early nineteenth century was not only being
subjected to detailed research, but was being approached from
new angles. Historians were asking new questions as to the
meaning of 'party', 'influence', 'nationalism' and 'liberalism' in
this period. The effect of all this new evidence and of these new
approaches was to draw much of the career of Castlereagh from
the gloom of prejudice — both for and against — and to
delineate it more clearly than had been possible in the nineteenth
century.

There have been many more dramatic ascents to eminence in
British politics, but Castlereagh's social background is still
worthy of note. In his lifetime his family passed from the ranks
of the untitled Ulster gentry to the status of an Irish marquisate.
The Stewart family first won a county seat in the Irish Parliament in 1769, the year of Castlereagh's birth, but it was
Castlereagh himself who first achieved political distinction for
the family. The great wealth for which the Stewarts (now
elevated to the Londonderries) became famous in the nineteenth
century was the work of Castlereagh's half-brother, the Sir
Charles Stewart of this book and subsequently the 3rd Marquis.
In 1819 he married the wealthy Vane-Tempest heiress, and
entered upon a successful career as a landowner and industrialist.
But all this lay in the future, and when Castlereagh first
entered politics it could not be said that his family were noted
for their wealth or status. The Stewarts had, however, already
demonstrated their ability to advance their fortunes by astute
marriages, Castlereagh's own father marrying successively into
influential English families, the Hertfords and Camdens. In
practice, the relations of his stepmother, the Camdens, proved
more helpful to the young Castlereagh than did the Hertfords,
but all connexions with the British aristocracy, such as with the
more distant Graftons and Somersets, were worthy of cultivation.
As will be seen in the next chapter, Castlereagh's all-important

first steps to political distinction were based upon his own talents, his family's position in Ireland, and the patronage of the Camdens in particular. By 1801, Castlereagh had gained sufficient political credit for his subsequent career to be largely of his own making. He had reached the take-off point for self-sustained growth.

Further interest attaches itself to Castlereagh's early years since the Stewarts' political loyalties in Ireland had long lain with the opponents of Dublin Castle. The Stewarts had supported those who had sought greater freedom for the Irish Parliament from British control and influence, and Castlereagh himself entered the Irish Commons in 1790–1 as a professed reformer and opponent of the government. He was, however, very quickly to break away from this line of conduct. He did so essentially because the ambition to tread a wider political stage persuaded him to think in a British rather than in an exclusively Irish context, and this tendency was reinforced by the growing threat from Revolutionary France. From the middle 1790s he was driven to work primarily for security and stability rather than for the domestic reforms which had first attracted his attention in politics. Personal ambition and harsh circumstances thus uprooted him from the Irish reform traditions of his youth; the security of British rule in Ireland, the security of Britain and of her empire, and finally the security of Europe as a whole commanded almost all his time and energies. Having become the least Irish of Irish politicians, it is not surprising that he later became the least British of British Foreign Secretaries. At the same time he became increasingly empirical in his political outlook. Admittedly he shared many of the prejudices of his class, but his continual preoccupation with the arts of manipulating and managing members of Parliament, foreign statesmen, and a host of other figures, softened some at least of these prejudices. Firm as he was in the defence of many causes, his flexibility in the face of intractable forces is equally impressive. It is this which makes it difficult to label him with any of the party tags of the time. Above all he was not one of the notorious ultra-Tories, yet he was hardly a Liberal–Tory of the Canning–Huskisson mould. Perhaps only that vaguest of terms, a British conservative (with a small 'c'), can do justice to him.

2

Irish Apprenticeship
1790–1801

No part of Castlereagh's career has evoked more hostility than that concerned with Ireland. In the gallery reserved for the oppressors of that country, Castlereagh occupies a special place.[1] Others might have been guilty of greater acts of cruelty or oppression, but Castlereagh had been born in Ireland, had, in his youth, shown great fervour for his country's rights, and had, finally, deserted his former professions to serve as the main agent of the British government in the Union of the kingdoms in 1800. Castlereagh himself had no illusions as to the feelings of many Irishmen concerning him.

> With respect to Ireland, I know I never shall be forgiven. I have with many others incurred the inexpiable guilt of preserving that main branch of the British Empire from that separation which the traitors of Ireland in conjunction with a foreign power had meditated.

Nor was the conscience of Victorian England unmoved by accounts of events in Ireland between 1798 and 1801. The future Lord Salisbury, who was subsequently to be associated with policies of 'coercion and kindness' towards Ireland, wrote in 1862 concerning Castlereagh's part in the Union.

> A certain admiration is due to skill in whatever occupation it is displayed and, therefore, we cannot refuse to admire the skill with which he effected the Irish Union. But still we should prefer to dwell on any other display of administrative ability than that which consists of bribing knaves into honesty and fools into Common Sense.

Castlereagh's political apprenticeship in Ireland consisted of a great deal more than 'bribing knaves . . . and fools', yet his

[1] Hyde, *Rise of Castlereagh*, pp. ix, 1–3.

6

Castlereagh as a young man by Sir Thomas Lawrence

success in these matters was a measure of his development in
one of the roughest schools of politics in Europe. By 1801,
indeed, he was being acclaimed as one of the most promising
young politicians of the time, and, unlike his distinguished
Irish contemporaries — Burke, Sheridan and Canning — he had
attracted notice through his work in the Irish Parliament. He
had gained considerable administrative experience, had learned
much concerning the management of men and parliamentary
business, and had established himself as an effective if rather
dull speaker. He had become an intimate of Pitt and other leading British politicians, and had shown his mettle both in the face
of rebellion and furious parliamentary opposition. Furthermore,
since 1790 his political ideas and principles had undergone a
profound change, and his vaguely reformist and essentially
parochial views had been displaced by a more pragmatic and
British — even imperial — outlook. The mature politician of
the Union is hardly recognisable as the young man, several
weeks short of his twenty-first birthday, who began his first
election campaign in 1790 to the roar from his opponents, 'Go,
boy, tarry in Jericho till thy beard be grown.'

Castlereagh's premature entry into politics was caused by the
death of his elder brother in childhood, and by the elevation of
his father, Robert Stewart, to the Irish peerage as Lord
Londonderry in 1789. His father had held one of the two County
Down seats from 1769 until his defeat in 1783 by the local
magnates, the Hillsboroughs, a defeat which the Stewarts were
determined to avenge. By judicious marriages and native wit
the Stewarts had steadily climbed the social and economic ladder
of Irish landlords in the eighteenth century, and, in so far as
these terms have concrete significance, the peerage of 1789
symbolised the Stewarts' passage from the upper ranks of the
squirearchy to the lower reaches of the aristocracy. The
recovery of the county seat in 1790 was badly needed to confirm
their advance, and it is this which explains why the Down
election of that year was one of the most sternly contested in the
whole history of the Irish Parliament. Polling was spread over
sixty-nine days, with both sides using every trick known to
Irish electoral campaigning. The cost for both sides was

B

staggering; the Stewarts alone spent £60,000, a fantastic sum which almost equals Wilberforce's election bill in Yorkshire in 1807.[1] Family properties in Dublin had to be sold, also books and pictures, while the grand projected country house at Mount Stewart had to be left in an unfinished state for some years. The election of 1790 was thus a tremendous gamble with the family fortunes, and a heavy responsibility rested upon Castlereagh, just twenty-one years of age, when he was declared elected as the second member for County Down.

The election, however, had been more than a family contest between Hillsboroughs and Stewarts. In the Irish Parliament there were two main streams of opinion at this time; there were those who supported the 'Castle' or Irish government, and there were those who detested this alliance between the English-appointed executive and many of the greatest borough-owners in Ireland. During the American War of Independence, those Irish politicians who aspired to greater political freedom for Ireland had been able to exploit Britain's embarrassments during that war to win legislative independence for their Parliament. But the Irish executive remained responsible to the British government, and through the power of patronage and influence and the existence of so many 'rotten' boroughs in Ireland this executive had been able to reduce the independence of the Irish Parliament to a very real degree. Consequently the agitation for further political change had speedily revived, and under the capable direction of Henry Grattan had centred upon demands for electoral reform, and for the reduction of placemen and pensions so that the capacity of the Irish executive to influence Parliament might be reduced. In this controversy the Stewarts and Hillsboroughs had taken opposing positions, with the former championing the reform or 'independent' cause. As a Presbyterian family the Stewarts had also won much sympathy and support from the numerous dissenters in County Down, and in the election of 1790 some of their strongest champions were to be found among future rebels or radicals. Their bitterness when confronted with Castlereagh's 'apostasy' is not surprising,

[1] Leigh, *Castlereagh*, p. 30 and n. Her researches in the Londonderry Papers have cleared up the obscurity surrounding the electoral costs. For the details of the election, see Hyde, pp. 54–65.

after the efforts they had made on his behalf and the faith which they had placed in him.

The beginnings of Castlereagh's 'apostasy' or enlistment as a follower of the Younger Pitt may be traced back even beyond the election. At first all the political pressures in his life had been family and local ones, and he had enthusiastically supported the anti-government cause. As a child he had proudly informed an uncle during the American Civil War and concurrent political excitement in Ireland, 'I am still a true American'. But his stepmother's relations, the Camdens, and especially her father, the first Lord Camden, had taken a great interest in Castlereagh's education, especially while at Cambridge in 1787–8. His years in England enabled Castlereagh to attend debates at Westminster, where he began to fall under the spell of William Pitt, a political allegiance which the Camdens encouraged. Castlereagh's hostility to the government of Ireland remained as strong as ever, but a few intimates soon became aware that a permanent career on the Opposition benches of the Irish Parliament held no attractions for him.[1] Paternal ambition was mainly responsible for his sudden entry into Irish politics in 1790; circumstances and negative rather than positive political convictions determined his party allegiance.

Nevertheless, whatever his inner doubts and uncertainty, Castlereagh speedily earned for himself a reputation as a 'not very moderate *patriot*'.[2] In 1789 he became one of the original members of the Northern Whig Club of Belfast, founded in imitation of Grattan's club in Dublin. The Irish radical, Dr. Drennan, dismissed it as mainly a dining club, and certainly much of its political activity took the form of uproarious toasts to 'President Washington and the United States of America', to 'A Happy Establishment to the Gallic Constitution', and to 'Our Sovereign Lord the People', all suitably preceded by feasting in the customary lavish style of the Anglo-Irish Ascendancy of the late eighteenth century. The club also promised its support only to those parliamentary candidates who agreed to subscribe to a 'test', which included promises to support various measures of parliamentary reform if elected.

[1] Leigh, pp. 26–32. Hyde, pp. 41–77.
[2] Sir J. Barrington, *Personal Sketches of his own Times* (1827), i. 321.

Castlereagh pledged himself in this fashion, and after the election
gave prominent support to these demands. The Irish executive
described him as 'a decided enemy', and in future years he was
frequently to be taunted by his opponents with reminders of his
reforming opinions in the early 1790s. A report reached the ears
of George III that Castlereagh had once drunk 'to the rope that
shall hang the last king'. Exuberance of this sort need not be
taken seriously; the Whig Club itself was eminently respectable,
with 12 peers and 2 bishops among its members, and counting
Burke among its admirers. Admiration for the French Revolution
was widespread and respectable in the British Isles at this time.
Furthermore, although Castlereagh was sincere in his Irish
reform beliefs, his thoughts were already turning to a wider
political stage, so that there was less inner unity than his outward conduct suggested.

Soon after his election Castlereagh explained his dilemma to
his grandfather, Lord Camden, Pitt's Lord President of the
Council. Castlereagh complained that he was 'thrown into a
situation where he was precluded from affording him [Pitt]
that support which his feelings inclined him to give'. Camden
felt that a British political career could not easily be opened to
him at this time; he pointed out that Castlereagh owed a heavy
obligation to his family, and that all his political assets lay in
Ireland. He was a little more encouraging a few months later, in
January 1791, when he asked Castlereagh, 'Would there be any
harm in professing yourself a friend of the Pitt administration
in England, though you are in opposition to the Castle?' This
was much to Castlereagh's taste, and Camden was soon going
further by interesting the Home Secretary, Lord Grenville, in
the possibility of some Irish employment for his young protégé.
But the Irish administration was adamant; the Chief Secretary
replied to Grenville that Castlereagh in 1792 was as 'uniform
in his encomiums on the English administration and equally
consistent in his opposition to us'.[1] But if Castlereagh could
secure no political advancement in Ireland, his admiration for
Pitt was imposing a strain on his relations with his old allies.
He was soon being described as '*quite too English*', and by
Drennan as 'a half-blooded fellow and one of those whom

[1] Hyde, pp. 41–78, 91.

Junius calls the meanest of the human race'. This uneasy intermediate position did not, however, impede his advancement in the exclusive sections of Dublin society.

Castlereagh continued to advocate parliamentary reform; he bitterly attacked an electoral system which he declared subjected the Crown to an 'aristocratic combination', and denied the people influence. But at the same time he urged that Ireland should see her problems in an imperial setting. In particular he warned that separation from Britain could only lead to domination by France. In his very first speech, delivered in February 1791, he argued that the admission or continued exclusion of Ireland from direct trade with India and the Far East should be resolved 'not with a spirit of local partiality, but as a member of the British Empire'. Such remarks were certain to make enemies. His separation from his former political friends was pushed still further in 1791 and 1792 by his changing views on the French Revolution. Visits to the Continent in those years coincided with the development of the extreme phase of the Revolution. Castlereagh continued to sympathise with and applaud the feelings which had accompanied and provoked the Revolution, and he saw that the old order could not be restored. But he castigated the latest developments as 'tumultuous pedantry tending directly to unsettle government and ineffectual in its creation'. The rights of personal liberty and property alike seemed inadequately secured. Tom Paine's *The Rights of Man* might be the most popular book in Belfast, but Castlereagh enthusiastically recommended Burke's *Reflections on the French Revolution*. As early as 1791 he was beginning to separate himself from the Northern Whig Club, and his denunciation of the execution of Louis XVI in 1793 earned him the retort, 'Robert Stewart will be the shadow of Burke against France.'

Meanwhile the political situation in Ireland, partially under the stimulus of events in France, was becoming more tense. Catholic pressure for political rights was increasing, and was supported by many Protestant reformers. Catholics numbered three-quarters of the population of Ireland, Protestant dissenters another one-eighth; to their dislike of paying tithes to an alien English Church had now to be added the aspirations and grievances of a growing number of tradesmen, merchants and

professionals in their ranks. From the Protestants in particular
there were emerging increasingly radical groups, notably the
United Irishmen of 1791, with their desire to unite Protestant
with Catholic in a common quest for drastic political change,
perhaps even to the point of an independent Hibernian republic.
Motives were mixed, and the numbers who were prepared to
follow the logic of their aims even to the point of revolution
were comparatively small. Perhaps only one-eighth of the
original membership of the Dublin society proved true revolutionaries.[1] But their capacity to cause trouble in a country so
permeated with religious, economic and social grievances was
immense. In much of Ireland, peasants enjoyed no security of
tenure against landlords whom they regarded as land-robbers.
If there were more good landlords than has normally been
supposed — and among them must be counted the Stewarts —
they were too few and the agrarian problems of Ireland too
great for them to exert much beneficial pressure. By the 1790s
they could not hope to deflect a tidal accumulation of the
grievances of centuries. To oppression in all its forms, to what
they did not understand, the traditional and inevitable response
of the mass of the peasantry was violence, however aimless and
ineffective in the long run.

Only a small minority of Irishmen understood and sympathised with the principles of the French Revolution; for the rest,
France was at war with Britain, and was therefore their natural
ally. Furthermore, the war raised rents, prices and taxes, and it
was no accident that agrarian outrages were on the increase by
1795. This was also a year of great expectations and greater
disappointment in Ireland itself, for the reformers of all kinds,
and especially the moderates, had been greatly encouraged by
the appointment as Lord Lieutenant of Earl Fitzwilliam, a
known sympathiser with the moderate reform party in Ireland.
Unfortunately his appointment had arisen out of the necessities
of political management in England, following the junction of
the Portland Whigs in 1794 with Pitt. No forward move in
Ireland was intended by the British government. The appointment of Fitzwilliam was unwise in the first place because of his

[1] R. B. McDowell, 'The Personnel of the Dublin Society of United
irishmen', *Irish Historical Studies*, ii. 12–18.

known sympathies, and secondly because he lacked the political skill and inclination to control the effect of those sympathies. The result was his recall after only three months in Ireland, a recall approved even by the Portland Whigs, but which left a shadow of demoralisation and disillusionment that no political skill could dispel from Ireland. For the first time, the United Irishmen began to make real progress in the recruitment of Catholics. If few were consciously planning rebellion, many were being driven in that direction by the logic of events.[1]

At the same time, the widely-held belief among Irish nationalists that the British government drove the Irish to rebellion so that a panic-stricken Ascendancy might be persuaded to accept the Union of the Irish and British Parliaments cannot be substantiated from the published evidence. It is true that many British ministers had expressed their dissatisfaction with the existing political relationship with Ireland upon many occasions, and had looked to some form of Union to remove the difficulties. Pitt himself had said as much in November 1792. It is also clear that Castlereagh, George III and Pitt, after the rebellion had broken out, perceived that here was a great opportunity to effect the Union while the confidence of the Ascendancy was shaken.[2] But to exploit a situation is not the same as to create it, and the student of the period can hardly fail to be impressed by the degree of alarm occasioned in government circles by the rebellion, and by the anxiety that it should be suppressed as soon as possible. As late as December 1798, Cooke, one of Castlereagh's intimates and ardent assistants in the struggle for the Union, was to lament the continuation of violence. Castlereagh himself was warned by an opponent of the Union that to seek its accomplishment would be the surest way to revive the United Irishmen.[3] It would also say little for the common sense of a supposedly Machiavellian government had it attempted to precipitate rebellion in the most vulnerable part of the British Isles within a year of the invasion scare of 1797, and the mutiny of the navy. At the time of the Irish rebellion,

[1] McDowell, *Irish Public Opinion, 1750–1800*, pp. 214–19.
[2] Holland Rose, *Pitt and the Great War*, p. 409. Barnes, *George III and Pitt*, p. 356. Lecky, *History of Ireland*, v. 151. Leigh, p. 108.
[3] C[astlereagh] C[orrespondence], ii. 49–52.

fears of a French attempt at invasion were still strong.

The explanation for this tenacious belief in a government plot is to be found in the rise of the Protestant Orange Societies and their attacks on Catholics, sometimes with the connivance of some Irish government officials, and the emergence of various irregular forces for the protection of the Ascendancy, who often acted on the principle that offence is the best means of defence. Ireland in the mid-1790s was rapidly succumbing to fear and suspicion, violence and counter-violence, in which each party viewed the other as the aggressor, and each was driven into actions beyond its original intention, or in which extremist minorities were able to come to the fore. By 1798 it would also be true to say that the Irish executive had reached the point where actual rebellion was almost preferable to secret conspiracy and terrorist tactics. Castlereagh himself defended exceptional government measures as forced upon it by a movement which acted 'in cowardly security of the principles and the dagger of the assassin', and shunned operations 'in open day'. The success of the government precautions early in 1798 drove the rebels to act before they were ready, and in particular before they could expect French assistance. Only in this sense was the rebellion precipitated by the government; only in this sense was Castlereagh in any way guilty of Dr. McNevin's charge that he, with others, had 'with cold-blooded artifice, stirred up an insurrection, that was to supply the necessary pretext for effecting their nefarious design'.[1]

Castlereagh had become persuaded as early as 1793 that a parliamentary Union with England was perhaps the only solution to Ireland's troubles. He had then separated himself from his former political friends by opposing the grant of the franchise to 40/- Catholic freeholders on the ground that 'it forces everything else'. He did not believe that the Catholic vote could be controlled indefinitely by Protestant landlords, as they had controlled their Protestant tenants, driving them, so Wolfe Tone noted bitterly, like so many sheep and bullocks to 'their octennial [electoral] market'. Castlereagh feared that ultimately the Catholic vote must overthrow the Protestant Ascendancy, and in 1793 he cast around for new political

[1] Lecky, v. 144–5.

solutions to the Irish question, and among them, though a very distant one, he perceived the possibility of Union. There is no evidence as yet that his ideas on the Union crystallised until after the rebellion, and from the outbreak of war with France in 1793 until 1798 he was deeply preoccupied with the defence of Ireland, whether against French invaders or Irish rebels. He was actively involved in government measures against possible rebellion in Ulster in 1796; at the end of that year he was hurried south with 500 militia as part of the defence measures taken against the unsuccessful French attempt to land at Bantry Bay. He supported those who insisted that the local gentry should be allowed to organise their own yeomanry, arguing that without such forces for their own protection the gentry might lose confidence and fail to aid the government in a crisis. In July 1797 he was appointed to a junior post in the Irish government, and was soon in the centre of discussions concerning the security of Ireland. Ulster had by now been disarmed, but the threat of rebellion was spreading rapidly to other regions. In the opinion of General Sir John Moore the increasing disaffection was due in no small measure to the indiscriminate military violence permitted, and even encouraged by the government during the winter of 1797–8. Like General Abercromby, who had thrown up his command in disgust, he was shocked by the attitudes and conduct of the majority of landlords and those in authority.[1]

Of Castlereagh's industry and enthusiasm during these months there can be no doubt; but it is far from clear whether his actions were tempered with the same discretion and restraint as in the later stages of the struggle. Certainly he made his mark, and to such an extent that when the Chief Secretary of Ireland, Thomas Pelham, fell ill in March 1798, Castlereagh was asked to act for him. Admittedly his uncle, the second Lord Camden, was now Lord Lieutenant, but nepotism alone does not explain his temporary appointment to the most important post in the Irish government after the Lord Lieutenant himself. Within two months of his appointment he was confronted by the great Irish rebellion, which ravaged much of south-eastern Ireland until the government victory at Vinegar Hill on 21 June. French assistance was fortunately too little and too late, but unorganised

[1] Sir J. Maurice, *The Diary of Sir John Moore* (1904), i. 309.

fighting and violence continued for some time, while the fear of
a further rising and of a second French landing remained very
strong. Dublin and London reflected uneasily concerning the
vulnerability of Ireland, both from its internal condition, and on
account of the prevailing south-westerly winds which favoured
the French fleet at Brest at the expense of the British navy in any
operations in Irish waters. The country was too open for forti-
fication to provide much security, and it was with no little relief
that it was learned soon after the outbreak of the rebellion that
French forces under General Bonaparte were operating in the
Mediterranean, and were no longer threatening the British
Isles.

Yet the long-term problem of Irish vulnerability remained.
Castlereagh was among those who perceived that more than
military measures would be needed to meet this threat. At the
political level he was convinced, as we shall see, that only a
Union could safeguard British interests in Ireland, but he also
saw the need to conciliate as many of the Irish people as possible
in the interval. Though disagreement will necessarily exist as
to the adequacy and wisdom of the policies he attempted to
pursue, the evidence is abundant that he favoured greater
leniency to the rebels than all but the most reforming of the
Protestant landlords. His outlook and ideas made him immediately acceptable to the new Lord Lieutenant, Cornwallis, who
arrived in the summer of 1798. Within three weeks the latter
was declaring that Castlereagh was equal to any office, and was
one of the very few of the Irish upper class to earn his respect
and commendation. Cornwallis never took kindly to Ireland or
its people; in particular he lamented the absence of good
landlords whom he regarded as the key to any satisfactory and
stable society. There were perhaps more of this breed in Ireland
than Cornwallis noted, but if he exaggerated a little he was
right in his main point that too many of the Ascendancy thought
in terms of continual coercion. As de Tocqueville subsequently
noted, there existed a striking contrast between the British
aristocracy in England and Ireland; in the former they were as
valuable socially and politically as they were maleficent in the
other. In Castlereagh Cornwallis discovered a rare kindred
spirit, while the whole district around Mount Stewart and the

neighbouring town of Newtownards bore testimony to two generations of model landownership by the Stewart family.

One of Castlereagh's fiercest English critics, Henry Brougham, later admitted that 'to him, more than perhaps anyone else, was to be attributed the termination of the system stained with blood'. In 1799 Cornwallis and Castlereagh, faced with continuing disturbance in Ireland, began to wonder whether they had been too lenient.[1] Admittedly, not all would describe the execution of some one hundred rebels as conciliation, and it is true that Castlereagh's moderation extended rather to those whom he chose to call the 'deluded' rank and file than to the leaders. Instances might also be cited when he failed to live up to his own standards, in particular when he failed to persevere with the case against that peculiarly sadistic High Sheriff, Thomas J. Fitzgerald, or when his intervention was ineffective. But history is supplanted by myth and legend when Castlereagh is portrayed as 'the Robespierre of Ireland', or as the villain who 'has left a memory that smells of hot blood', or as he was described by Byron,

> Cold-blooded, smooth-faced, placid miscreant
> Dabbling its sleek young hands in Erin's gore

To argue against such charges it is not necessary to proceed to the other extreme. But it is necessary to remember that civil wars are not fought according to the rules of chivalry, that so honourable a figure as Sir John Moore found himself justifying certain cruelties lest he should be driven to worse tortures,[2] and that it was an American veteran of the Civil War (1861–5) who told a Prussian officer that the war against France in 1870–1 was not being fought with sufficient ruthlessness. As for Castlereagh himself, it is a mistake to concentrate on his crimes against the rebels, real or imagined, since he constituted a greater threat to them in his political capacity. As a gendarme he might make martyrs, but as a politician he strove to make a

[1] Lord Brougham, *Historical Sketches of Statesmen who flourished in the Reign of George III* (1839–43), ii. 126. Ross, *Cornwallis*, ii. 371–2, 405–6, iii. 90. Hyde, pp. 237–77, 418–28. Lecky is more critical, iv. 461–9. See also *C.C.* ii. 174.

[2] Maurice, i. 288–90.

people — if not loyal — at least acquiescent and apathetic.

As official thoughts both in London and Dublin in the summer and autumn of 1798 turned more and more to the question of Union, so it also became necessary to settle the matter of the Irish Chief Secretaryship. The holder of this office was the main government spokesman in the Irish House of Commons, and was in many ways the Prime Minister of Ireland. In 1786 it was described as 'the most troublesome office in the British empire, comprising every department in the church, law, state, army and revenue, and both houses of parliament'. Henry Dundas, more bluntly, said that nerves and bad taste were particularly required in that office! The health of the present occupant, Pelham, would not permit his return, but, unfortunately for Castlereagh, no Irishman had ever held the post, and there was much prejudice in London against his appointment.[1] He had the support of the last and present Lords Lieutenant, and much was made of the fact that he was so unlike 'an Irishman'. He had sufficiently attracted the attention of the British cabinet — or some of its members — for him to have been given the Treasury borough of Tregony in Cornwall as early as 1794, while his marriage in the same year to the Lady Emily Anne Hobart had added the Buckinghamshires to his family's important connexions in England. His support of Pitt and his role in the defeat of the Irish rebellion were well known, but it was probably of vital importance that no strong English candidate was forthcoming at this time. Thomas Grenville was approached, but he felt that the status of the office was beneath him. Lord Grenville himself added, nevertheless, 'In point of real utility and scope for displaying the powers of his mind, God knows, it is difficult, extensive, and important enough for the talents of the greatest man this country ever saw.' He agreed that Castlereagh was 'a man of parts and character', but at first he feared he lacked the 'weight' which the situation demanded. Within a few months, however, he was writing, 'I am better satisfied than I had expected with his manner of doing business, which I found both

[1] R. McDowell, 'The Irish Executive in the Nineteenth Century', *Irish Historical Studies*, ix. 265–6. A. and E. Porritt, *The Unreformed House of Commons* (1909), ii. 470–1. Johnston, *Great Britain and Ireland*, pp. 34–44.

ready and clear. . . .' Portland was still more impressed.[1]
Castlereagh became Chief Secretary of Ireland in November
1798, and for the next two years his thoughts were to be given
over almost entirely to the question of the Union, and problems
associated with it. By 1801 few doubted that he possessed the
necessary 'weight', while his political mentor, the late Lord
Camden, would have noted with satisfaction that Castlereagh's
political assets were no longer confined to Ireland.

In the second half of 1798 both the English and Irish executives
became persuaded that a Union of the Parliaments was desirable
and practicable, and by the end of the year planning was
proceeding apace. To some the difficulties still seemed immense,
but it was recognised that the Irish rebellion had shaken the
nerve of the Ascendancy, while it had also confirmed the belief
of many British politicians that Ireland would never be peaceful
and secure so long as it possessed an independent parliament to
encourage centrifugal tendencies or present obstacles to the will
of Westminster. Pitt and his most enlightened colleagues also
saw that through the Union it might become possible to eradi-
cate one major grievance, the exclusion of Irish Catholics from
Parliament and from other high offices. Whereas the numerical
weight of the Irish Catholics in an Irish Parliament must
ultimately have swamped the Protestants, in a Parliament for
the whole British Isles the Catholics would always be a small
minority, and therefore harmless. Castlereagh and Cornwallis
conceived the problem in the same light, the former advocating
Catholic Emancipation in the context of the Union as forcefully
as he had opposed the grant of the Catholic vote in the Irish
circumstances of 1793. As he informed Pelham in October 1798,

I see with you its [the Union's] difficulties and dangers in a strong
point of view, but am discouraged by neither from looking to it as the
only measure that can ever enable this country to act either upon a
Protestant or Catholic principle with safety to the Constitution itself.
As a distinct Kingdom our present system is not reconcilable to any
principle upon which the human mind can or will rest quiet, which does
not condemn our Establishment in principle, and consign them

[1] Hyde, p. 288. Buckingham, *George III*, ii. 399, 411.

inevitably in a course of years to certain destruction. Whether the
pride or good sense of the country will triumph it is difficult to
calculate.[1]

Any hope of proceeding with the Union and Emancipation
simultaneously, however, was wrecked by the lack of support in
London, while in Ireland it would have cost the support of many
of the small group who were deeply in favour of the Union. In
particular, Lord Clare, the Irish Lord Chancellor, a powerful
Unionist, was determined to frustrate Emancipation.[2]

Visits to London by Clare and Castlereagh in October and
December 1798 enabled plans for the Union to be swiftly
finalised; most of the pressure for haste came from the Irish
ministers, and in this they would seem to have miscalculated
badly. Castlereagh was convinced that any delay could benefit
only the French and the disaffected, and would lead to further
armed clashes.[3] He was aware of the great hostility that existed
towards the project in Ireland, and of the still greater apathy,
but he put his faith in the effect which a display of unshakeable
resolve on the part of the British government would have upon
the doubting and the waverers. He also underlined the Irish
dependence upon Britain for protection, writing in September
1798,

I consider it peculiarly advantageous that we shall owe our security so
entirely to the interposition of Great Britain. I have always been
apprehensive of that false confidence which might arise from an impression that security had been obtained by our own exertions.
Nothing would tend to make the public mind impracticable with a
view to that future settlement without which we can never hope for
any permanent tranquillity.[4]

There was in Castlereagh's conduct at this time a little too much
of the impetuosity and over-confidence of youth. In general he
had not miscalculated, for past experience had shown that on
most issues the British government had been able to impose its
will on Ireland. But it had also shown that this often required

---

[1] Hyde, p. 281.

[2] Hyde, pp. 278–370; Porritt, ii. 469–529; Lecky, vol. v, provide
valuable accounts of the Union.

[3] *C.C.* i. 442–3.   [4] Hyde, p. 280.

patience and skilful management, and it was here that Castle-reagh failed to make adequate provision.

Castlereagh underestimated the time that would be required to secure a majority in the Irish House of Commons for what was, after all, the most momentous issue that had ever come before it. He also miscalculated, or so he claimed afterwards, the tactics of the staunch opponents of the Union. This does not seem very convincing, as the first reports of an impending proposal of Union had created a furore in Dublin; a press and pamphlet war was in full swing by the end of 1798 in all the main urban centres of Ireland, although the countryside by and large remained quiet. Castlereagh's private secretary, Alexander Knox, remarked, 'Surely all Bedlam . . . is let out.' Most of the legal profession, the bankers, the leading interests in Dublin and Belfast, many of the aristocracy and gentry, and even some members of the administration itself were furiously opposed. Government dissidents could soon be weeded out, but the phalanx of opponents in the Commons could only be overcome by superior voting strength. For this task government placemen, pensioners and other dependants would not suffice, and it was necessary to turn to the large number of members who had not yet firmly committed themselves to either side. But these were not to be stampeded into the government lobby by Castlereagh's generalities concerning the resolve of the British cabinet, or the threat from France and future rebels; most of them required persuasion of a more substantial and precise nature.

Castlereagh himself was conscious that many members were undecided when the Irish Parliament met in January 1799, but lack of time and late arrivals prevented him from seeing as many members privately to present his case as he would have wished. Even so, he hoped for a majority of 40 or 50. A vague remark in the King's Speech on the opening of Parliament that means should be found to consolidate the connexion between England and Ireland was the only warning given, but it was a vain hope that a rampant Opposition would allow this to pass unchallenged. An impassioned debate followed; it lasted 21 hours and was carried by the government by only a single vote. The next day the House voted by a majority of 5 to erase the controversial paragraph from the royal speech. Castlereagh could draw some comfort from the fact that many members had abstained, while a motion to pledge the House to preserve its independence was withdrawn. The Irish House of Lords meanwhile voted in favour of Union. Briefly, however, Castlereagh was so discouraged by his defeat that he was tempted to leave Ireland to discover for herself where her true interests lay. Within four days his self-confidence had returned, and on 1 February he was ready with proposals for the government's counter-attack, and he was soon busy endeavouring to restore the faith of his less resilient chief, Cornwallis.[1] He also reviewed the reasons for the government's defeat with considerable candour and realism, and the resultant memorandum was described by the British Home Secretary, Portland, as 'a masterly outline'.

Undoubtedly some Irish members had been deterred by the strength of anti-Unionist feeling in Dublin; others had been impressed by the hostility to the measure of so many of the country gentry, who enjoyed something of the reputation for independence of their famous counterparts at Westminster. The respected Speaker of the House, John Foster, was another powerful opponent; the absence of the influential Lord Downshire and many of his supporters, the abstention of the great borough-monger, Lord Ely, from the vote in the Irish House of Lords had all been matters for comment, and had had a disastrous effect upon many members of the Lower House who had no strong convictions in the matter, or who perceived that here was a measure for which votes might be sold at a high price. Ely had already told Pitt that he was unbiased concerning the question of Union, but he was 'open to conviction'. The subsequent promise of an English peerage proved most convincing. Again there had clearly been insufficient time in which to sound figures of importance, and further alarm was caused by garbled reports concerning the nature of the intended measure. Finally, although most supporters of the Union applauded Castlereagh's efforts to that end, there was considerable dissatisfaction with the conduct of the Lord Lieutenant. Buckingham remarked that Castlereagh had 'really worked like a horse, but his principal is a dead weight that bears down on everything'. Edward Cooke grumbled in December 1798, 'If we had a more able, active, conciliating

[1] *C.C.* ii. 142–53.

The Irish House of Commons by Francis Wheatley

Chief, we might do; but the *vis inertia* is incredible. There is an amazing disgust among the friends of Government. The tone of loyalty is declining for want of being cherished.' Clare made similar complaints, while Grenville in England began to regret his appointment.[1] But Cornwallis continued to go his own way, disliking Ireland and most things Irish; limiting his confidence to Castlereagh and few others; nauseated by political jobbery, and anxious to doze away the remainder of his days at his Suffolk farm at Culford. Only his sense of duty sustained him, but his outlook made the task of Castlereagh and Clare more difficult.

Castlereagh's analysis of the character, composition and suspected motives of the opposition to Union led him to some important conclusions in February 1799, and provided him with the basis for a second, and this time more carefully prepared campaign. Above all, his analysis impressed him with the 'private' nature of so much of the opposition; opposition which he believed could be removed 'within a reasonable time' by compensating advantages of various kinds. To a considerable extent this was to be the case, but he was guilty of an injustice to the Irish county members when he thought their majority against a Union could be destroyed by permitting the counties to retain their present number of seats when the Parliaments were united. A majority of county members continued to oppose the Union to the very end.[2]

Castlereagh calculated the degree to which private interests would suffer in the event of Union, and found that approximately £1,500,000 of private property, in the eighteenth-century sense of that phrase, was at stake. There was the cash value of the parliamentary seats to be abolished under his revised scheme, 200 in all, as the British cabinet were insistent that no more than 100 Irish members should be added to Westminster. It would be necessary to compensate both the owners of these seats, and those who had purchased seats in the expectation that the Parliament would last its full term. One might also have to consider the probable fall in value of certain properties in

[1] Hyde, p. 308. Rose, p. 405. Lecky, v. 181. Buckingham, *George III*, ii. 429.

[2] Lecky, v. 289–90.

c

Dublin when it ceased to be the seat of the Irish Parliament.
There were, too, some fifty barristers to be considered, whose
parliamentary seats were regarded as the best means of personal
advancement in their profession. Direct monetary compensation
in the end was confined to the suppressed seats, and was paid to
supporters and opponents of the Union alike. But a wide range
of other rewards and inducements were offered to procure the
support necessary for the passage of the measure.[1]

This forms a chapter in Irish history which has been bitterly
criticised by opponents of the Union as one of the most cynical
and flagrant examples of bribery and corruption of all time.
Certainly Cornwallis, and even Castlereagh himself, felt that
they were sometimes overstepping the generous bounds of
eighteenth-century practice in such matters. Castlereagh had
no illusions as to the nature of his task; it was, as he told the
Lord Lieutenant, 'to buy out, and secure to the Crown for ever,
the fee simple of Irish corruption, which has so long enfeebled
the powers of Government and endangered the connection [with
Britain]'.[2] Several times after the completion of his work he was
to admit that the government had been obliged to make
promises which were not strictly in accordance with the merits
of the claimants. A new Irish Lord Chancellor, Lord Redesdale,
thought in 1802 that 'Lord Castlereagh's ideas of making men
"amiable" must be forgotten'. The next Lord Lieutenant,
Hardwicke, however, seems to have been less disturbed, despite
the degree to which the outstanding claims from the passage of
the Union ate into most of his own patronage.[3] It would be
difficult, however, to improve upon Castlereagh's own summing
up of his conduct.

The Irish Government is certainly now liable to the charge of having
gone too far in complying with the demands of individuals; but, had
the Union miscarried, and the failure been traceable to a reluctance on
the part of Government to interest a sufficient number of supporters in
its success, I am inclined to think that we should have met with, and,
in fact, deserved less mercy.[4]

As to the methods employed, it is difficult to particularise.

[1] Porritt, ii. 365.   [2] *C.C.* iii. 333.
[3] M. MacDonagh, *The Viceroy's Postbag* (1904), pp. 42–53, 67.
[4] *C.C.* iii. 328, 339–40. Hyde, p. 365.

Many charges of actual bribery exist against Castlereagh and others, but this is not a matter which can be dealt with in blanket terms. Reliable evidence, in any case, is unlikely to be found in such matters, while the distinction between bribery and rewards for services rendered is not always easily drawn. The amount of cash at the government's disposal was limited, and it would appear that apart from compensation for the abolition of seats and offices, and from which the arch-opponent of the Union, Lord Hillsborough, was the chief beneficiary, only some £50,000 was paid out by the government itself, mostly to pay pamphleteers, to seek press support,[1] to buy parliamentary seats for government supporters in the customary way, or as pensions. Cornwallis, perhaps without full knowledge of the facts, commented, 'The enemy to my certain knowledge offer £50,000 for a vote; if we had the means and were disposed to make such vile use of them we dare not trust the credit of Government in the hands of such rascals.' The government was certainly short of money following the insurrection and it is significant with what relief even small sums of 'the needful' were received from England. Cash, therefore, as far as the government itself was concerned, seems to have played a very small part.

There remained the considerable store of government patronage, political, military, ecclesiastical, legal and administrative, together with the enticement of promotions to or within the peerage, and the other honours at its disposal. This 'refined species of seduction', as Alison described it, was the determining factor, especially at the level of peerages. The hesitant Marquis of Ely, who was worth six or more seats, was secured with the promise of an English peerage. It has been estimated that eighteen individuals controlled seventy of the 234 borough seats with influence in several other constituencies, and only thirteen boroughs were not under the control of a single interest. The main assault to win votes for the Union could therefore be directed against a comparatively small number of powerful figures, peers receiving no less than three-fifths of the compensation granted for the suppression of 200 seats in 1800.

[1] A. Aspinall, *Politics and the Press*, c. *1780–1850* (1949), pp. 136–8. B. Inglis, *The Freedom of the Press in Ireland, 1784–1841* (1954), pp. 52–112.

Several more seats were controlled by the Anglican hierarchy in Ireland, and the wily Archbishop of Cashel assured himself of the premier see of Dublin before making up his mind on the great question. Many minor rewards had also to be found for the protégés of these great figures, while the consistent supporters of the government could not be forgotten. Thus William Wickham, the next Chief Secretary of Ireland, noted concerning Lord Longueville that he 'had very considerable Parliamentary influence in Ireland, always voted with the Government, and strongly supported the Union, for which services he obtained, among other things, a promotion in the Peerage, a seat here in the House of Lords, a seat at the Revenue Board, and what is called the patronage of Cork, jointly with Lord Donoughmore'.[1]

In all, about forty individuals were promoted to or received promotions within the peerage, and there was a host of minor rewards, not all of which could be fulfilled at once, and some of which, being still outstanding when the Ministry of All the Talents was formed in 1806, were never fulfilled. The net result of these promises by Castlereagh and others in 1799–1800 was an increase in the government's paper strength in the Irish House of Commons from 148 in May 1799 to 180 in December. This was according to Castlereagh's own calculations, though he admitted that this was a 'lukewarm, and, in some instances, an unwilling majority'. In practice the largest government vote was 162. Cornwallis agreed as to the character of many of their supporters, and noted that strong, firm leadership, displays of government resolve and strength, as well as 'reasonable expectations' were needed to keep them loyal. This underlines the importance of the hard bargaining that occupied so much of Castlereagh's time in 1799. Nevertheless, although government influence was exerted on an unparalleled scale — this, after all, was an issue of unparalleled importance — it should not be forgotten that patronage played an important part in Irish life long after it had begun to decline in England. Two recent important studies of Irish politics of this period have both revealed the vital place of patronage in Irish life at this time, and have noted that some English politicians, such as Robert

[1] MacDonagh, pp. 19, 94.

Peel, when confronted with Irish conditions, failed to appreciate the difference between the two kingdoms. Professor Gash notes with reference to the period after 1812, 'In England the greater wealth and solidity of the nation had emancipated society from undue dependence on court and administration. In Ireland the Protestant caste had been permanently conditioned to look almost solely to the state for support and nourishment.'[1] Edith Johnston adds that 'Most Irish politicians felt that they had an inherent right to suitable recognition from the "Castle", and consequently the Irish House of Commons abounded in pensioners and placemen.' So important, so indispensable was patronage to the management of Irish politics that even some of those 'economical' crusaders, the Rockingham Whigs, hesitated to attack it in Ireland.[2] A determination to sell votes dearly was therefore inevitable over so great an issue as the Union, especially when it was feared that future opportunities might sharply diminish.

Even the British government was somewhat shaken by the size of the commitment when the promissory bills began to fall due, especially those for English peerages and Irish marquisates. Cornwallis and Castlereagh protested furiously against all efforts at reduction in the summer of 1800, and only slight modifications took place. Nor did promises and rewards on this scale enable the Irish executive to relax in Parliament, where both management and debating skill were called for. The Opposition, at the beginning of 1800, numbered some 120, including more than half the county members and several leading debaters. They were backed by several vociferous and powerful Dublin interests. Popular feeling in that city compelled some Unionist supporters to go about armed, while at least one member refused to support the Union because of the apparent strength of feeling against it. The government could boast the support of property in the ratio of three to one in favour of the Union, but it was perhaps fortunate that the heated anti-Union atmosphere of Dublin was exceptional. The mass of the population was apathetic; many of the disturbances of this period

[1] Gash, *Peel*, i. 120–1.

[2] Johnston, pp. 227–8. McDowell, *Irish Public Opinion*, pp. 27–32, and *Public Opinion and Government Policy in Ireland*, p. 48.

were economic in origin and totally unrelated to the question of
Union; improving economic circumstances kept many towns
quiet, while some interests, especially in the north, saw good
export prospects to England as a result of the Union. The bloody
memories of the rebellion cooled many hearts, especially the
better-off Presbyterians and Catholics, and the political excesses
of some representatives of the Ascendancy were a further
inducement for them to turn towards the rather more liberal
atmosphere of Westminster. Both, as will be shown later, had
reason to hope for certain concessions as a result of Union.
Castlereagh's fear that the anti-Unionists might endeavour to
win Catholic support with a promise of Emancipation was unreal,
since such an appeal would have split their ranks.[1] The Unionist
camp would have been similarly split had his own intentions been
prematurely divulged, though he was able to offer sufficient
secret inducement for most Catholic leaders to support his cause.
The mass of the Catholic population, however, remained passive
and indifferent, and even the popular excitement in Dublin was
in many ways superficial. The city remained very quiet when the
Act of Union received the royal assent on 1 August 1800;
pickpockets, not political agitators, gave the police their only
trouble. At least one anti-Unionist admitted to a feeling of
having been deserted. The general election of 1802 was very
quiet; the Emmet rebellion of 1803 was a tragic farce.

Castlereagh, as the main government spokesman, faced a
stiff task in both 1799 and 1800. He acquitted himself com-
petently, if not brilliantly, against the debating talent on the
opposite benches. The latter made a desperate resistance in the
early months of 1800, fighting on every conceivable ground
against the bill — one member even quoted from the books of
Daniel and Revelation. One parliamentary duel passed beyond
the oratorical stage, and Castlereagh himself came near to
challenging his arch-opponent, Grattan. But by the early
summer of 1800 the steam was going out of the attack; the
British and Irish governments were clearly unshakeable in their
resolve; their majority in the Irish Parliament was holding
firm; the numerous anti-Union petitions, despite all their

[1] T. D. Ingram, *A History of the Legislative Union of Great Britain
and Ireland* (1887), p. 105.

signatures, represented neither the mass of property nor the mass of the population. For this victory, Castlereagh has rightly received the main credit, from friends and enemies alike. Not only did he conduct the measure through the one chamber where serious resistance was to be encountered (Clare had a relatively easy task with the Irish House of Lords), he was also one of the most active in the complex business of procuring a majority for the measure behind the scenes. Cornwallis, Clare and many others were similarly engaged, and Cornwallis indeed rated his Military Under-Secretary, Lieutenant-Colonel Littlehales, the most skilled of all in 'the private management of mankind'. But Castlereagh's part also extended to many of the major decisions concerning the character of the measure, the compensation to be offered, and the inducements to be offered to potential supporters. In particular, his memoranda prepared immediately after his parliamentary defeat of January 1799 provided the main departure point for the second effort to launch the measure, and stood in sharp contrast to the pessimism of Cornwallis at this time. Whatever Castlereagh's debt to Cornwallis, the latter was heavily dependent upon him for local knowledge, for tactical advice, and for a steady resolve to see the business through.

Cornwallis wrote in May 1800 of his young Chief Secretary's progress. 'Lord Castlereagh has improved so much as a speaker as to become nearly master of the House of Commons; and the gratification of national pride, which the Irish feel at the prospect of his making a figure in the great political world, have much diminished the unpopularity which his cold and distant manners in private society had produced.'[1] Pitt and his cabinet were also well aware of their debt, but it is not clear whether Castlereagh's father was refused an English peerage because George III felt that enough Irish peers had received that honour for their part in the Union, or whether, as Cooke was told, the British cabinet were anxious to fortify their front bench debating talent in the English House of Commons, and feared the loss of Castlereagh to the Lords in the event of his father's early death. They perhaps made a virtue of necessity, and sweetened the father's disappointment with an assurance that an English

[1] Ross, *Cornwallis*, iii. 235.

peerage would be granted at any time in the future, at the family's request, as a reward for Castlereagh's services. But Castlereagh's immediate hopes of distinction on the government front bench at Westminster were to be shattered early in 1801 by the fall of the Pitt ministry over a matter of unfinished business in connexion with the Union, the controversial question of Catholic Emancipation of which Castlereagh was now one of the strongest advocates.

Even Ireland had experienced a little of the relaxation in religious conflict that had developed in eighteenth-century Europe. Some Irish Protestants, and especially the followers of Grattan, had come to believe that the spiritual obedience of Catholics to an international potentate no longer constituted a political threat, and that they might safely be admitted to all, or almost all, of the offices of state. Castlereagh, when he first entered politics, had shared this feeling only to the point of extending all civil liberties to Catholics, and had firmly held in 1793 that political concessions would ultimately endanger the Protestant Ascendancy. Since then he had been impressed by the loyalty to the state of most leading Catholics, lay and ecclesiastic, who dreaded the social and intellectual consequences of the triumph in Ireland of admirers of the French Revolution. Few Catholic priests had spontaneously supported the rebellion; the day of the radical Irish priest lay in the future. By 1800, if not before, Castlereagh saw leading Catholics as allies in the defence of the existing social and economic order,[1] whilst any remaining divisive tendencies on their part would be swamped by the passage of the Act of Union. This would leave any Irish Catholic politicians in a small minority at Westminster. Emancipation would thus do much to reduce dissension in Ireland, to strengthen the forces of law and order, and at no risk to the existing structure. There was a further inducement in that Catholic sympathy, or at best neutrality, would be of immense

[1] Castlereagh declared that the safety of the state was dependent on the support of the 'great mass of its proprietors', *C.C.* iv. 392–400. See also V. Harlow, *The Founding of the 2nd British Empire* (1952–64), ii. 631–9.

advantage in the forthcoming struggle to secure the passage of the Act of Union.

Cornwallis was fully in sympathy with these views, but it was necessary to proceed with caution. The British cabinet was divided and was not anxious to hurry the question of Emancipation, while strong feelings would be aroused among powerful Protestant forces in Ireland at the first hint of Emancipation; to do so prematurely might jeopardise the Unionist cause. One of the crucial figures in the Irish executive, Clare, the Lord Chancellor, was violently anti-Catholic, and Castlereagh had to take great care to keep him in the dark concerning his negotiations with Catholic leaders in 1799–1800. Even to the historian little has been revealed concerning these talks, and this obscurity has contributed to the controversies that have subsequently arisen as to the nature and extent of Castlereagh's promises and assurances. Castlereagh and Pitt always insisted that no pledge was ever given to the Catholics that Emancipation would follow from their support of the Union. It was, indeed, seriously considered during Castlereagh's visit to London in the autumn of 1799, when Catholic sympathies appeared to be wavering. It was finally decided to try to win the support of the latter by all means short of a definite pledge, but that if necessary Castlereagh should refer back to the cabinet should this prove inadequate. Castlereagh did not refer back to the cabinet, and always contended that he gave the Catholics no pledge. This has been disputed, and one historian has recently written, 'The treatment of the Catholics was a piece of sharp practice, equalling in its dishonesty and the polish of its execution the finest diplomatic manœuvres of the classical era of Cabinet diplomacy, which fitted its hero for his future distinguished tenure of the British Foreign Office.'[1] Such conviction is hardly sustained by the evidence; the question is not proven one way or the other, and is likely to remain so. In negotiations of this sort, even the inflection of the voice is all-important, and this cannot be recaptured by the historian. Equally, Catholic expectations may have led to misconceptions: a wink or a nod imagined where none was intended.

Further possibilities might also be explored, but the crucial

[1] E. Strauss, *Irish Nationalism and British Democracy* (1951), p. 64.

point is that the charge of 'polished dishonesty' has not been established, while the concrete evidence that exists shows that Castlereagh fought a sincere battle on behalf of the Catholics in 1800–1. His anger, with that of Cornwallis, at the first hint that the cabinet might not be able to initiate legislation on behalf of the Catholics is unmistakable. He reported that without Catholic support the Act of Union could not have been carried in Ireland; more than that, he believed that a Union not followed by Emancipation might possibly prove more disastrous than the continuance of the old Irish Parliament. He wrote,

If the same internal struggle continues, Great Britain will derive little beyond an increase of expense for the Union. If she is to govern Ireland upon a garrison principle, perhaps, in abolishing the separate Parliament, she has parted as well with her most effectual means as with her most perfect justification. . . . The Union will do little in itself, unless it be followed up. In addition to the steady application of authority — support of the laws, I look to the measure which is the subject of the above observations [emancipation of Catholics], to an arrangement of tithes, and to a provision for the Catholic and Dissenting clergy, calculated in its regulations to bring them under the influence of the State, as essentially necessary to mitigate if it cannot extinguish faction. . . .[1]

In pursuit of the above objectives, Castlereagh had been in close and apparently cordial communication with both Catholic and Presbyterian representatives. In January 1799 he had persuaded some at least of the Irish Catholic hierarchy to agree that 'a provision through Government for the Roman Catholic clergy of this kingdom, competent and secured, ought to be thankfully accepted', and 'in the appointment of the Prelates . . . to vacant sees within the kingdom, such interference of Government as may enable it to be satisfied of the loyalty of the person is just, and ought to be agreed to'. The bishops were also attracted by offers of state assistance for the support and education of clergy. The Catholic college of Maynooth had received a small state grant since 1795, and it appeared to the advantage of all parties to increase this. Hitherto most Irish priests had received their education in France, but this was no longer possible. The British government hoped that Irish-

[1] *C.C.* iv. 392–400.

educated priests would prove less bigoted than their predecessors; the Irish bishops hoped that in Ireland they would escape infection from new and radical ideas. These two streams of conservatism were not incompatible, and it was the young priests who rejected them. In vain the college authorities struggled against the resolute identification of the young priests with the impoverished and oppressed peasantry from which they were sprung, and among whom they returned to work. Where the French colleges had taught political non-resistance, at Maynooth the students gained — even if they were not taught — a knowledge of British theories concerning the rights of the individual. They emerged more politically conscious and radical than their predecessors, though they did not begin to exert a significant influence until shortly after Castlereagh's death in 1822. It is possible that, had some state provision for all priests followed, their relationship with the peasantry might have been a little different, but this is highly speculative.[1]

Castlereagh was pursuing a similar policy towards the Presbyterians, who had been receiving a small state grant, the *regium donum*, since the late seventeenth century. This was now increased. Castlereagh hoped to encourage the present 'quiescent loyalty', and to add another section of the Irish community to the defence of the British cause in Ireland. He was also interested in the establishment of a Presbyterian 'Maynooth' in Ulster, but this institution did not begin to emerge for another decade, and when it did Castlereagh was soon disturbed by its radical tendencies. He strove to reduce its status in 1816, and to compel all Presbyterian ministers to hold the degrees of recognised British universities alone on pain of forfeiting their share of the *regium donum*. In the end only the state grant to the Belfast Academical Institution was withdrawn, but this failed to prevent the recognition of its certificates as qualifications for entry into the Presbyterian ministry by the Synod of Ulster.[2] Castlereagh's efforts to purchase men's minds in Ireland therefore enjoyed

---

[1] McDowell, *Public Opinion and Government Policy in Ireland*, p. 31. J. H. Whyte, 'The Influence of the Catholic Clergy on Elections in Nineteenth Century Ireland', *English Historical Review*, lxxv. 239–40.

[2] McDowell, op, cit. pp. 55–56.

much less success than his recent efforts to purchase their votes in favour of the Union.

More rewarding would have been the implementation of his desire to introduce some form of tithe commutation to meet the grievances of seven-eighths of the Irish people, who resented paying tithes to an alien Church. Prejudice in British politics would not permit this, and it was not until 1822 when Ireland was suffering from acute distress and agrarian disturbances that the question was taken up by the cabinet. A tithe composition bill followed, which effected only limited changes, and tithes were not commuted until 1838. Castlereagh therefore had little to show for his efforts on behalf of dissenters in Ireland. Even his two successes, a permanent grant to Maynooth and an increase in the *regium donum* did not have the results he expected; yet no attempt at an assessment of Castlereagh's relationship with Ireland can escape a consideration of such acts and hopes as these. It helps to explain how even his great enemy, Grattan, relented a little towards him in old age, and told his son, 'Don't be hard on Castlereagh, for he loves Ireland.' Castlereagh's visit to London towards the end of the sweltering summer of 1800 underlines his anxiety, within his limitations, to conciliate Ireland. He pointed out to the British cabinet that if they wished to avoid governing Ireland on 'a garrison principle', if they wished Ireland to 'prove a resource rather than a burden . . . an effort must be made to govern it through the public mind'. He left again for Ireland, convinced that the question of Emancipation would now be taken up in earnest. Indeed, so convinced was he of the political security afforded by the Union that he opposed those cautious souls who felt that some offices of state should still be denied to Catholics, even in the Act of Emancipation. But all this was to remain of merely academic interest, for hardly had the cabinet begun to discuss the matter than the suspicions of George III were aroused, and his obdurate opposition finally drove Pitt and his cabinet to resignation in February 1801. Castlereagh and Cornwallis resigned at the same time.

Pitt's resignation has been a matter of some controversy. Many have speculated whether Pitt could have taken a stronger stand against the King; others have questioned whether he really resigned over the question of Emancipation or was merely seeking for an excuse to escape the responsibility for negotiating an unpopular peace. Others, again, have been impressed by his sincerity, and his impossible position. Castlereagh's own reaction was also confused. On the one hand, he doubted the value of Pitt's persistence against a royal veto, not to mention strong cabinet and popular opposition; in such circumstances the measure would lose its necessary character as an act of grace, and would prove of doubtful political utility. At the same time there occurs a hint of regret that Pitt had not proved more obdurate, and he certainly regretted Pitt's encouragement of his supporters to join the new Addington ministry. This, he feared, would weaken the party of Emancipation. These doubts lasted little more than a year, when he both joined the Addington ministry and bowed to the King's wish that his ministers should promise never to raise the question of Emancipation again during his lifetime. He always believed that politics were a matter for the head rather than the heart, though he perhaps eased his conscience by pleading — unsuccessfully as it proved — within a month of his re-entry into office, for the state endowment of the Irish Catholic Church. Five years later he had no difficulty in joining a ministry which owed its installation to the quarrel of its predecessor with George III on an Irish Catholic question, and it was not until 1812, when the old King was hopelessly insane, that he refused to enter the Perceval ministry without the right to vote on Catholic issues as he pleased.

Castlereagh, therefore, in an essentially opportunist manner, remained faithful to the Irish Catholics. After 1812 he was a strong supporter of bids to secure Emancipation, though with all his customary circumspection. He pitched the tone of his speeches as low as possible, and did his best to illumine the practical reasons for the concession. He argued, for instance, on 9 May 1817 that he believed Emancipation would be of advantage to the state rather than to the Catholics themselves, since it would remove a cause of dissension within the empire without increasing the influence of the Catholics.[1] The House of Lords in particular, however, was not yet in a mood to respond

[1] *Hansard*, xxxvi. 396–404.

to such argument, so that the measure failed to reach the statute book in Castlereagh's lifetime, despite the growing support of the Commons. Even if it had done so, there is little reason to suppose that it would have brought about a dramatic improvement in Anglo-Irish relations, as there was, unfortunately, no single solution to the outstanding problems. Grey and Grenville and other Whigs have been criticised for 'Fingallism', a short-sighted belief that with such measures as Emancipation a firm alliance could be concluded with the moderate Catholic leaders of Ireland, of whom Lord Fingall was a leading representative, and that through such an alliance with Catholic landlords and prelates, Ireland would be broadly pacified.[1] Castlereagh was a more cautious exponent of the same policy, believing, as he once said, that the safety of the state depended upon the support of the 'great mass of its proprietors'. But, as we have already seen, the rebellion of 1798 had shown how easily control of the Catholic masses could pass from the Catholic conservatives, while the subsequent history of Maynooth was to demonstrate the inability of the Catholic bishops to produce an acquiescent priesthood. Long before the 1820s there occurred other warnings of a militant Catholicism which the traditional leaders would be powerless to suppress; a militant Catholicism which, with Irish nationalism, was to provide the main rallying point for Irish radicals and for the mass of inarticulate discontent.

This is not to assert that the policy of Catholic Emancipation was useless or unwise; clearly it was an act of statesmanship to attempt its implementation in 1801.[2] But there was a dangerous tendency to see it as a panacea. In particular with Castlereagh and others there was this concentration upon an alliance of property, with insufficient recognition that so many of the landlords were a prime cause of social and economic discontent, and therefore of political and general disturbance. Admittedly their role cannot be isolated from the legacy of the past, the limited resources of Ireland, and the population explosion. Similarly, although many schemes were put forward in the early nineteenth century for the economic regeneration of Ireland,

[1] Roberts, *The Whig Party*, p. 57

[2] Some United Irishmen feared in 1797 that Emancipation would wreck their plans, Lecky, iv. 216.

most respected the current theories of *laisser faire*. Whig reformers went no further than exhortations to the Irish country gentry to act against poverty on their estates, even if the basically Whig ministry of 1806–7 showed a greater awareness of the need for positive measures to meet the problems of Ireland than its basically Tory successors.[1] It required acute distress in 1817 and 1822 to persuade the Liverpool government to provide some public money to relieve the situation and to begin the amendment of tithe payments. Throughout this period Castlereagh differed from his colleagues, and then not all of them, only over the question of Emancipation.

At the time of the Union, Castlereagh had not neglected certain Irish economic interests, notably the incipient industries of Ulster. He responded quickly and effectively to demands from cotton and calico interests for protection from English competitors, and he was able to persuade the British government to postpone for seven years the reduction to 10% of the import duties on these goods. The Irish linen industry also continued to receive some protection, and Castlereagh was assisting at the same time in the improvement of the River Shannon and Dublin harbour.[2] But fundamentally it would appear that his social and economic outlook was dominated by the family experience at Mount Stewart, in County Down. Here the Stewarts had made the most of a region of great natural beauty and fertility, where the peasantry enjoyed certain tenant rights unknown in most of Ireland, and where religious dissension was comparatively limited. Lord Henry Petty indeed described the whole county as 'the Yorkshire of Ireland'. The Stewarts built many solid houses in the local town of Newtownards and around Mount Stewart; they even built a Catholic church; rents were often reduced in bad times, and soup kitchens provided for the needy. True, the troubles of 1795–8 did not pass them by, and for a time troops were needed to guard the family property, while Castlereagh

---

[1] Lord Holland as late as 1822 confined his Irish reform proposals to Emancipation, tithe reform, legal reform, and, more vaguely, the discouragement of absentee landlordism, *Hansard*, new series, vi. 206–8.

[2] See also E. R. R. Green, *The Industrial Archaeology of Co. Down* (1963), p. 67.

himself was busy in the district combatting disaffection. His
mask of aloofness and reserve lifts briefly as he describes some
good-humoured banter between himself and one group of the
discontented. Again the region was one of the more fortunate in
Ireland, and in the late 1830s, although the head of the family
was now an absentee, visitors to Newtownards found 'only
admirably constructed farmhouses, well furnished with barns
and byres, cornfields and pasture lands, the natural richness of
which has been enhanced by industry and well-applied science;
every dwelling bore numerous tokens of comfort; every peasant
looked cheerful'.[1] Although it would be difficult to document
such a conclusion, it is hard to believe that Castlereagh was not
profoundly influenced by this striking example of the success of
enlightened landlordism. For one who was so profoundly
concerned with practical matters, it must have seemed a magnificent demonstration of the efficacy of a model landlord in Irish
conditions.

If such were his conclusions, they were, of course, as superficial as they are understandable. The number of model landlords
in Ireland may have been underestimated in the past, but they
were still too few to grapple with the problems of early nineteenth-century Ireland. An indefinite number would probably
have found it beyond them. But without entering into the realm
of the hypothetical, it is necessary to try to demonstrate where
exactly Castlereagh and his ideas stood in relation to the whole
tragedy of Ireland. He put his faith in an alliance of all property,
an alliance which he hoped would transcend all religious divisions,
and he intended to supplement this by a measure of state control
of dissenting Churches. Tithe commutation would appear to be
the limit of his positive ideas to meet the discontents of the
masses.[2] The Union he felt to be necessary to increase British
security, to simplify the task of administering Ireland, and also
to facilitate the task of conciliating wealthy and influential
dissenters. Only in the matter of the Union was he wholly

[1] S. C. Hall, *Ireland: its scenery and character* (1844). J. Stevenson,
Two Centuries of Life in Down (1920), pp. 241–4.

[2] Later he was to be a member of a British government which
altered the law heavily in favour of Irish landlords against their
tenants.

successful in his lifetime; the fulfilment of his other aims would have eased, though they could not have solved the problems of Ireland. Yet even without the complementary effect of his other schemes, the Union in the short-run proved a successful and practical policy from the British point of view. At least one of the United Irishmen, Edward Lewins, expected the Union to strengthen Britain politically, financially and economically,[1] while some Catholics already feared that Emancipation would draw those of wealth and influence away from the mass of their co-religionists and into alliance with the British state and society.[2] With all their limitations, the policies with which Castlereagh was associating himself therefore had much to offer the contemporary Irish scene, and in the process Castlereagh was making for himself a British reputation as a practical politician of great promise. In the detail of the Union itself he had shown some originality, he displayed a mastery of complex problems, a dogged parliamentary skill, and many of the other qualities required by a front-bench politician. Above all, Pitt was now proclaiming him to be a first rate talent for the defence of the British empire against Jacobinism.[3]

[1] Lecky, v. 335.
[2] Maureen Wall, 'The Rise of a Catholic Middle Class in Eighteenth Century Ireland', *Irish Historical Studies*, xi. 91–115.
[3] *Colchester Correspondence*, i. 257.

D

3

---◆---

India and the War against Napoleon 1802–9

In the leisurely manner of the early nineteenth century, several weeks elapsed before the transfer of power from Pitt to Addington was completed. Castlereagh was able to use this interval to make a favourable impression as a government spokesman; when he subsequently spoke as a private member he was already a marked man, and few were surprised when Addington offered him the Presidency of the Board of Control in June 1802. Although Pitt was still encouraging his supporters to assist the government, Castlereagh's acceptance represented a considerable change from his original attitude to the new ministry. With Pitt committed to the postponement of the Catholic question during the King's lifetime, Castlereagh was not disposed to waste time in idle opposition on behalf of distant and speculative objectives.[1] He did propose state endowment of the Catholic clergy of Ireland to Addington, but did not press the matter.

The Board of Control was not an easy office. It had been established by Pitt in 1784 in an endeavour to form a working relationship between the British government and the East India Company in the management of British interests in India. Some state intervention had become necessary to meet the growing discontent with the Company's conduct in India, and also in recognition that the extent of British involvement in the subcontinent had passed beyond the competence of the Company to

---

[1] Ziegler, *Addington*, p. 157, draws attention to a story that Castlereagh was indebted to Addington for assistance with debts incurred during the passage of the Union. Addington apparently hoped that Castlereagh would become his right-hand man in the Commons.

manage on its own. Pitt had intended the Company's Court of Directors to be subordinate to the Board of Control, but political considerations had prevented him from making this explicit in his Act. In practice, with cabinet and parliamentary support, this could be achieved, and until the war with France from 1793 had absorbed so much of Dundas's attention, his Presidency of the Board of Control had been successful. He relinquished the office in 1801 to a weak successor, and the Company's Court of Directors were quick to exploit their opportunity. When Castlereagh himself became President in 1802, he found that the Addington ministry believed itself so heavily dependent upon East India votes in the Commons that the ultimate weapon of an appeal to Parliament against the Court could not be used. The more devious method of undermining opposition in the Court from within, by the management of new elections, also failed, and Castlereagh found much of his time devoted to the thankless task of acting as mediator between the influential Court in London and its formidable Governor-General in India, the irascible and autocratic Richard Wellesley. For Castlereagh it was to prove a valuable experience in the art of managing men, but on the whole he did not relish his years at the Board of Control.

Wellesley had been Governor-General since 1797. Steeped in the spirit of imperial Rome, he was determined that India should be 'ruled from a palace, not from a counting house; with the ideas of a Prince, not with those of a retail-dealer in muslims and indigo'.[1] Five years had been more than sufficient time for this 'sultanised Englishman' to fall foul of the 'mercenary mind' of Leadenhall Street. Wellesley's superb self-confidence had been further inflated by his great victories and conquests in India. He had defeated Tipu Sultan in 1799, and thereby destroyed the most powerful ally of the French in India at a time when Napoleon's eastward thrust had only recently been frustrated by Nelson and Sidney Smith. All southern India was now in British hands or subject to British influence; the East India Company's territory had been increased by half. But the

[1] Lord Curzon, *British Government in India* (1925), i. 71. For Castlereagh at the Board of Control see especially C. H. Philips, *East India Co.*

Court seemed more impressed by the vast increases in the
Company's Indian debts which had accompanied these campaigns.
Wellesley, flushed with victory, found the Court's rewards and
praise niggardly. Furthermore the incompatibility of tempera-
ments was now extending to a clash of authority, not least in
that most delicate of eighteenth-century matters, patronage.
The Court was also trying to interfere with the administration
of Madras by Lord Clive, one of Wellesley's allies, and there
was a major clash concerning the ships to be employed on the
India route. The Court was dominated by certain London
shipping interests which held a monopoly in the building and
managing of the Company's ships, 'the system of hereditary
bottoms' as it was called. But there were other shipping interests
who were anxious to enter the trade, and there were many who
supported their claim, including Wellesley himself, on the
ground that the 'hereditary bottoms' provided insufficient cargo
space for all concerned in the Indian trade. Finally Wellesley and
the Court were disputing the future of his newly established
college of Fort William, Calcutta. Castlereagh entered office to
find Wellesley demanding a vote of confidence from the Court
under threat of his resignation.

This was the first of several crises between Wellesley and the
Court that were to tax Castlereagh's skill and tact as a politician
to the utmost. What he had learned in the hard Irish school was
to be of immense value, but he was to gain no comparable
reputation at the Board of Control, and indeed he was to leave
with a reputation for vacillation and unhappy compromises.
Decisive conduct, however, was an impossibility, unless he
threw in his lot with the Court. The political situation would
not allow him to challenge it, as the Fort William college
question at once demonstrated. The Board of Control and Court
of Directors each claimed the authority to establish new
educational institutions for the Company's servants destined for
service in India. The Law Officers of the Crown recommended
an appeal to Parliament to decide who had the better right under
the ambiguities left by the Act of 1784. The Addington cabinet
decided against such a move, in the knowledge that, although
Parliament would almost certainly have supported the Board
against the Court, East Indian supporters of the government in

the Commons would have been antagonised, and the government's majority endangered. For Castlereagh the fate of the college itself had been a minor matter; for him, it had been essentially a question of the respective spheres of authority of Court and Board. It was not difficult to reach a compromise concerning the college, but on the essential point he had been defeated because of the government's parliamentary weakness. This was to be the pattern for the future. As Henry Wellesley informed his brother in July 1803,

> The Board of Control has . . . actually been transferred from the Board to the Court of Directors; . . . Castlereagh approved of all your measures, but . . . it is perfectly evident that he cannot obtain what the Court of Directors has resolved not to grant. That nothing could be more disagreeable than the situation in which he was placed.[1]

Not surprisingly, Grenville learned soon afterwards that Castlereagh was not averse to vacating so thankless a post.

Castlereagh did his best to master the unfamiliar problems of India. He reinforced his reading by consulting such notable experts as Dundas and Cornwallis, and he was well served by some of his staff. His first notable success was to effect a temporary reconciliation between Wellesley and the Court. This entailed submission to the Court's demand that Indian expenditure and debts should be sharply decreased. Such reductions, however, could only be achieved if peace were maintained in India, and if bullion were sent out from Britain to pay off part of the debt Some four millions were in fact despatched, but this bullion arrived most opportunely to help sustain Wellesley's credit during his next series of wars. The Indian debt was almost to double between 1802 and 1808. This outcome has contributed to the suggestion that there may have been a plot by the Board to so reduce the funds of the Company in England that it would be driven to Parliament for assistance, which in turn would enable Parliament to increase the powers of the Board of Control. This is interesting, but a little speculative. In September 1802, for instance, when there was still a prospect of a long peace with France, Castlereagh appears to have been genuinely intent on economy.[2] Shortly afterwards he

[1] Philips, p. 132.

[2] Cf. Philips, pp. 124–5, 143, and Marriott, *Castlereagh*, p. 103.

was rewarded with a seat in the cabinet for his part in mollifying Court and Governor-General.

There could, of course, be no permanent peace between the Court and Wellesley; the Court was soon trying to provoke the latter's resignation. Wellesley was indifferent to such pin-pricks, as long as he possessed power enough to pursue his policies. His imperial eye roved from the Cape to the Philippines, from Ceylon to Persia, but it rested most often upon the confused affairs of central India. There the Maratha princes intrigued and fought among themselves, creating a state of affairs which Wellesley interpreted as a threat to good order in British India, and as a standing invitation to the French. But Castlereagh in London, with his eye on Parliament and the Court, was anxious to avoid further conflict, and he warned Wellesley in September 1802 that enough was enough, and that 'solidity' should now replace 'brilliance'. He cautiously supported Wellesley's assumption of the administration of the Carnatic and his treaty with Oudh; at first he opposed the extension of the Company's authority near Surat, but later withdrew it when no outcry resulted in England. He welcomed Wellesley's Treaty of Bassein of 31 December 1802 with Baji Rao, the nominal head of the Maratha confederacy, and pooh-poohed the idea that it would lead to war with those Maratha princes who challenged Baji Rao's authority. But war broke out in August 1803, and a dismayed Castlereagh began to enquire more carefully into the matter, and to seek a means of escape from a long and costly war.

Pitt became Prime Minister again in May 1804, retaining Castlereagh at the Board of Control. For a month or two Castlereagh became more bellicose, apparently because he hoped that Pitt would be able to take a stronger line with the Court, and also revealing his preference for Wellesley's forward policy, providing British politics would permit. But the Pitt ministry proved barely stronger than its predecessor, and Castlereagh was finally driven to take a stand against Wellesley by the news that arrived from India in the autumn of 1804. The successful war against the Marathas had been followed by yet another war, this time against Holkar, the most determined of the Maratha princes. Wellesley himself had penned several letters, replete with savage criticism of the Court and thus effecting the breach the Directors had desired for so long. Castlereagh examined the correspondence of Court and Governor-General in December 1804, and sadly concluded that 'every chance of our case being improved is exhausted'. The policy of tacking and trimming was at an end. Meanwhile, some friends of Wellesley had described Castlereagh in 1804 as one who,

with studied coyness, hesitated and paused, and appeared desirous to approve, but his candour it seems stood in his way; he had not, forsooth, made up his mind, he had not weighed all the causes of the war, he was not prepared to give a detailed opinion on its justice and policy.

This was both accurate and a little unfair. Castlereagh's position with the Court, even under Pitt, had been too weak to do otherwise. But now a decision had been made, and it was Wellesley who was to go. The veteran Cornwallis was chosen as his successor, an appointment that was popular with the Court, and one that represented a decisive swing in favour of a policy of consolidation in India. Castlereagh was soon to become Secretary of State for War as well as President of the Board of Control, and his interest in the affairs of India was rapidly waning. Until his loss of both offices in January 1806 he was a continual advocate of caution, restraint, even retreat from the advanced position in central and northern India which Wellesley had sought.

Wellesley's successors, Cornwallis — until his early death in 1805 — and Sir George Barlow, were admirable executors of such a policy. Many of Wellesley's Maratha policies were reversed, some conquests were relinquished, and British influence was much reduced. What followed, however, proved to be no more than an uneasy truce, and this has led many historians to argue that Wellesley was right, and that his successors merely postponed the day of reckoning until the Governor-Generalship of Lord Hastings in the following decade. The Indian historian, V. B. Kulkarni, for instance,[1] has claimed that as a result of Wellesley's conquests, the British had no option but to go on. He had made 'the paramountcy of British rule in India certain and inevitable . . . it was no longer possible to halt the march towards the goal'. Wellesley had

[1] *British Statesmen in India* (1961), pp. 91–93 especially.

eliminated the French threat, he had weakened the already
anarchic Maratha confederacy, while a British retreat simply
left a region of confusion and disorder on the frontiers of British
India, a situation which could not be tolerated in the long run.
The preoccupation of Castlereagh and others with retreat and
consolidation is thus said to have been short-sighted and
mistaken.[1]

To have continued Wellesley's Maratha wars would certainly
have been more logical, and would have tidied up the pages of
Indian history for this period. Both Britons and Indians might
have gained, but the considerations on the other side cannot be
ignored. From the standpoint of the Court in England, a
standpoint which Castlereagh was coming to share from the end
of 1804, the struggle seemed endless, with no obvious conclusion.
The expense was colossal, one of Cornwallis's first acts being to
detain two millions of bullion destined for China in order to
meet immediate war charges. As Secretary of State for War in
the second half of 1805 Castlereagh was reluctant to see many
more British troops added to the army of India, especially as the
prospect of offensive action in Europe seemed once more to be
presenting itself. Castlereagh, it is true, never apparently
formulated any principles for his overall guidance in Indian
affairs; his approach always seems to have been *ad hoc*. Nor is
this surprising when the weakness of his position is recognised,
and when the Court was determined to avoid all unnecessary
expense. The Directors of the Court thought as traders and
shippers, not as empire builders. Add to this the immense delays
in communication, and the difficulty of understanding the
problems of India at so great a distance, and the decisions of
1805 become less surprising. The opinions of Arthur Wellesley
are also worth recording at this point. His doubts concerning
some of his brother's objectives have already been noted. It is
true that he poured scorn on Castlereagh's ideas of March 1804
for a defensive strategy against the Marathas, but after the
intensive campaigning and victories of 1803–4 he agreed that
British India was no longer in danger, that there had been
enough war and the time had come to see what good faith,

[1] *Cambridge History of the British Empire*, iv. 375. Philips, pp. 175,
235.

moderation and the judicious exercise of indirect influence could achieve.[1]

Castlereagh was therefore associated with a decision which is not wholly indefensible, at least in contemporary terms. On the whole, however, his impact on the affairs of India was slight, and his main contribution indirect; he averted the resignation of Wellesley and enabled him to begin, if not to complete the task of subduing the Maratha confederacy. Wellesley later warmly thanked Castlereagh for his aid.[2] But Castlereagh probably gained more from the office than he was able to give to it; he learned much concerning the art of politics and the management of men, and he also received much useful administrative experience. Indeed, some of his best work at the Board of Control was achieved in the unspectacular field of administrative reform. Although Dundas had made a start in trying to organise the work of the Board's four departments, the division of business between them had been left vague. On the basis of a report by two investigators, Castlereagh introduced a proper cataloguing system, and divided business among the departments according to subject matter, Madras, Bengal and Bombay, and the secret correspondence relating to the general external policies of the Company in the East. A general index of all the Board's correspondence was also begun. If Castlereagh had not made much history at the Board, he had at least facilitated its writing.

Pitt had retained Castlereagh at the Board of Control on his return to office in May 1804, and had appointed him to the office of Secretary of State for War as well in July 1805 when the impeachment of Dundas (now Lord Melville) compelled him to recast his ministry. This new office was far more to Castlereagh's taste than the Board. He had taken an enthusiastic interest in military matters in Ireland, and had devoted increasing attention to the affairs of Europe. At an early stage of the French Revolutionary Wars he had perceived, as Pitt had

[1] P. Guedalla, *The Duke* (1931), pp. 109, 114. S. G. P. Ward, *Wellington* (1963), pp. 32-33, 42-43.
[2] *C.C.* i. 100.

not, that financial weakness would not necessarily cripple the French war effort. He had welcomed the experiment of peace with Napoleon's France in 1802, though he had done so with a wary eye to the future. The conduct of the First Consul soon after the peace of Amiens speedily disillusioned him, and as a member of the cabinet from October 1802 he had followed with great interest the Anglo-French negotiations which led up to the resumption of war in May 1803. During this period he wrote a number of able, if at times rather academic memoranda, but it is difficult to see on what evidence the claim is founded that he profoundly influenced British foreign policy at this time.[1] His interest in good Anglo-Russian relations was no novelty; Hawkesbury, the Foreign Secretary, had been courting Russia from the Peace of Amiens itself.[2] Similarly on the question of the renewal of the war with France, Castlereagh was less anxious for such an eventuality than has been suggested, and, in so far as his memoranda reveal his thoughts and arguments between October 1802 and August 1803,[3] they indicate a very flexible and wide-ranging approach to the problem. He was greatly influenced by several considerations; in particular by the need to weigh the nature of the threat from France to British interests against British readiness for war and the likelihood of foreign assistance.

He wished to check the aggrandisement of France, but he wished also to be free to choose the diplomatic option for as long as possible. He agreed that a point might be reached where the French threat to British interests was so great that a war could not be avoided; at this point Britain must fight, regardless of other considerations. But short of that point, Britain should recall the need to recoup her financial strength; she must recall that, great though her resources were, she was a constitutional state, and that the granting of the requisite means for war was dependent upon public morale and support. Castlereagh himself was to be driven to a reluctant retreat on the Orders in Council in 1812 in just such circumstances as these. He argued that it

[1] A. Bryant, *Years of Victory* (1944), pp. 36 ff. Marriott, pp. 98–99.
[2] H. Beeley, 'A Project of Alliance with Russia in 1802', *English Historical Review*, xlix. 497–502.
[3] *C.C.* v. 29–82.

was imperative not to jeopardise morale and support by a premature renewal of the war. Equally it was vital that Britain should fight if possible as a member of a European coalition, since, unaided, her efforts must be confined to the sea or to a colonial war, neither of which would seriously injure France. 'A maritime war in itself is incapable of rescuing any usurpation France may make on the Continent from her: the most it can effect is to strip her of those Colonies she either possesses or wishes to acquire.' Colonial warfare was 'a species of attack which but remotely affects her present power, and is in itself inadequate to shake the source of her authority and the stability of her military empire, whilst it bears much more severely upon our resources than it does upon hers'. This line of thought was to have an important effect upon much of his future war and foreign policy. He concluded that as it was desirable that Britain should fight with continental allies, so she must see many issues in their European perspective, and try to fight on questions which would ensure her the support of European friends. Again one sees an early hint of his future role as the most European-minded of all British Foreign Secretaries. The Irish member of Parliament had become a British politician; the politician was beginning his long growth to the stature of a European statesman.[1]

In the spring of 1803, as Napoleon's ambitions in Italy, Egypt, the Netherlands, Switzerland and elsewhere became clearer, so Castlereagh became reconciled to the necessity for counter-action. Above all he argued that Britain must possess Malta, or some adequate alternative Mediterranean naval base. But no acceptable compromise over Malta or in Anglo-French relations in general could be found, and Britain declared war on 18 May 1803. Castlereagh could find reassurance in the massive parliamentary and public support for war,[2] but August 1803 saw him almost hoping that Napoleon would attempt an invasion of the British Isles, since he believed that only the catastrophic defeat which Napoleon would suffer in making the attempt

---

[1] Not that his opinions were unique; many were everyday topics of conversation; e.g., see *Malmesbury Correspondence*, iv. 156–7, 207–8, 227.

[2] Napoleon's restrictive commercial measures, and his 'betrayal of the Revolution' did much to unite British feeling against him.

would persuade him to agree to a compromise peace. It was not
until later that Castlereagh's single-mindedness concerning the
conduct of the war was to develop, and even then some of the
ideas which are to be found in these memoranda continued to
influence his thinking. In August 1803 he was still giving much
thought to a compromise peace, and on the 19th he submitted to
the unfortunate Hawkesbury the following involved analysis of
the situation.

Were I even warranted in forming more sanguine expectations of
Continental co-operation than present appearances justify, my
decision would be the same, inasmuch as I think it unwise to risk
what may continentally be called the last stake, where there is neither
vigour nor concert to oppose to the power of an enemy impregnable
at home, and, in opinion, irresistible abroad. Whatever may be the
destiny of France, I do not see that there is anything which should
tempt us to select the present moment, if it can be avoided, for pushing
the question to an issue. If it can be waived, not only without further
loss, but with some advantage gained, if the mischief can be circumscribed, I had rather leave the rest to time, placing our own security
beyond the reach of attack, which, in the present temper of the
country, may be effectually done, than prosecute the war in the hope
of keeping Malta, which seems to depend on our means of reducing
France.[1]

The compromise peace which he envisaged would have included
the transfer of Malta to Russia in return for Corfu.

   The Addington ministry survived the renewal of the war by
less than a year. Recent historians have tended to give it more
credit than their predecessors, even for its war policies, but its
long-term chances of survival were slender unless it could
produce some great naval or military victory, and so lessen the
lustre of the great parliamentary figures who attacked it. An
alternative possibility was to seek new allies in Parliament, and
clearly the most desirable acquisition would be that of William
Pitt. Castlereagh himself acted as the bearer of one proposition
from Addington whereby Pitt was offered the Premiership
provided he would guarantee to exclude Fox and Grenville from
the new ministry. The offer was proudly declined, and in April
1804 Addington was driven to resign. Castlereagh was one of
the old cabinet who gladly accepted office under Pitt, the

                     [1] *C.C.* v. 81–82.

relationship which he had established with Pitt during the Union surviving without difficulty the growing friction between the latter and Addington. Although there are some signs that Castlereagh favoured the inclusion of Addington in Pitt's ministry in 1805, there is no doubt where his real loyalties lay.[1]

Pitt's second ministry was never a strong one; there was much internal friction; its parliamentary strength was uncertain, and the reconciliation with Addington in 1805 proved short-lived. The impeachment of Lord Melville not only cost Pitt his right-hand man, but contributed to the resignation of Addington and his supporters in July 1805. These setbacks, however, benefited Castlereagh. Pitt, shuffling desperately with the limited talent at his disposal, made Castlereagh Secretary of State for War. The appointment obliged him to seek re-election, and it is possible that his role in the Union now recoiled on his head and contributed to his defeat in County Down in September.[2] He did not regain Down until 1812, and sat for a Yorkshire and later a Devon borough in the interval. But under Pitt, he was now the only member of the cabinet to sit with the Prime Minister in the Commons. His ministerial responsibilities placed him in continual contact with his revered leader, and it is known that among the important matters which Pitt discussed with him at this time was the famous peace memorandum which Pitt drafted in his negotiations with Russia, and to which Castlereagh himself was to refer when embarking upon the European peace settlement from 1813.

Castlereagh's first spell as Secretary of State for War lasted for only six months; far too short a time in which to make his mark, but perhaps long enough to learn at first hand how much was wrong with the direction of Britian's military effort, and what mistakes he must try to avoid in the future. More than ten years of war had produced no notable British success on land — save in India — and though this was largely attributable to circumstances beyond the control of Britain through the defeat or submission of her allies, it was only too apparent that from the heights of strategic direction and thought to the humbler

[1] *Sidmouth Correspondence*, ii. 325, 355–6. D. Marshall, *The Rise of Canning* (1938), pp. 251–2, 259. Ziegler, pp. 210–11, 226.

[2] *Creevey Papers*, i. 42–43.

tasks of recruiting, training and equipping the troops there had been much mismanagement. It is true that in some important particulars major reforms were already in progress, inaugurated for the most part by the conscientious Commander-in-Chief, the Duke of York. But these reforms needed time to take effect, and some important deficiencies remained, above all that of recruiting sufficient men to serve with the regulars, a problem which was not to receive satisfactory treatment until Castlereagh's second period in office from 1807.

One of the main obstacles to the satisfactory conduct of the war was the chaotic distribution of authority and responsibility; even the creation of the office of the Secretary of State for War in 1794 left the direction of the war very much at the mercy of the strongest personalities in the ministry. Canning, as Foreign Secretary between 1807–9, proved particularly anxious to secure greater control of strategy for himself, and at one point considered a redistribution of the responsibilities of the Secretaries of State to achieve this. The Home Secretary added a further complication by his control of the Militia and Volunteers. The Secretary of State for War was supposed to plan the campaigns which had been agreed upon by the cabinet, but to execute them he had to secure the co-operation of the Commander-in-Chief, himself normally a member of the cabinet, but responsible to the Sovereign rather than to Parliament. He had also to try to work with several authorities who enjoyed great independence, and most of which were of doubtful efficiency; namely, the Board of Ordnance, the Transport Board, and Commissary General. The Secretary-at-War, the parliamentary watch-dog over military expenditure, was also responsible for troop movements within the British Isles. This office was lamentably administered until the appointment of the energetic Palmerston in 1809.[1]

Castlereagh faced certain problems in the running of his own department. He had no military experts to assist him, and his exiguous staff of thirteen had to be deployed in the management of colonial as well as military problems. The colonies had been

[1] Fortescue, *History of the British Army*, iv, pt. 2, 871 ff. For this problem, and the following paragraphs on military reform, see R. Glover, *Peninsular Preparation*, *passim*, and S. G. P. Ward, *Wellington's Headquarters* (1957).

entrusted to the Secretary of State for War since 1801, but until Bathurst succeeded to the office in 1812 no Secretary appears to have paid much attention to colonial problems. Indeed, in 1806, William Windham added a second Under-Secretary so that the first might concentrate upon colonial matters.[1] The department was housed in a decaying Restoration house in Downing Street, with the River Thames occasionally washing through its basements. Even this building was a slight improvement on that occupied by the neighbouring Board of Control.

It was no easy matter to keep the cumbrous machinery for the conduct and management of the war in motion, and to synchronise its working for the speedy equipment and despatch of British expeditions to the Continent or overseas. It was not surprising that delays and deficiencies in equipment frequently occurred, though on the whole expeditions were assembled and despatched with a fair degree of promptitude while Castlereagh was in office — once the cabinet had made up its mind to act. To the more efficient conduct of the war Castlereagh's mastery of detail, his industry, his readiness to take professional advice, and not least his diplomatic touch made a major contribution. Inevitably he was indebted to the work of others, such as the Duke of York, the Commander-in-Chief, and to the fact that earlier reforms were beginning to pay off. For instance, it was not until 1804 that the supply of British small arms became adequate; by 1807 they were abundant, and Britain could now supply some of her allies. The forces sent abroad were more efficient in many respects than those of the 1790s. The Duke of York had begun to tighten up the very lax discipline over officers; by careful regulation he had begun to check some of the worst abuses attendant upon their promotion, so that although promotion by purchase continued, certain age and military qualifications were now required as well. Matters were a little better than in 1793 when an adjutant-general had complained,

There is not a young man in the army that cares a farthing whether his commanding officer, his brigadier or the Commander-in-Chief himself approves his conduct or not. His promotion depends not on their smiles or frowns — his friends can give him a thousand pounds with which he goes to the auction room in Charles Street and in a fortnight he

[1] *Cambridge History of the British Empire*, iii. 711–12.

becomes a captain. Out of the fifteen regiments of cavalry and twenty-six of infantry which we have here, twenty-one are literally commanded by boys or idiots — I have had the curiosity to count them over.[1]

At long last, too, the military education of officers was receiving some attention from a central authority; hitherto it had been left to individual officers or their regiments, often with disastrous results. Regimental instruction was obligatory by 1800, the Royal Military College was opened in 1802, while a small staff college, after some vicissitudes, was finally established in June 1801.[2] So little had hitherto been done by way of theoretical instruction or in the form of manœuvres that few senior officers were competent to handle more than a battalion on the battlefield.

Hard as it is to conceive from descriptions of a soldier's life in the nineteenth century, pay, rations, barracks and clothing had all been somewhat improved since the 1790s.[3] The training of troops had also been taken in hand, especially of light infantry. Early experience against the French in the Revolutionary Wars had demonstrated the British deficiency both in quality and quantity in this arm. The Duke of York pressed hard for action against political indifference, and had finally carried his point. The 95th, the future Rifle Brigade, began training with the new Baker rifle and in the new light infantry tactics. Later Sir John Moore was to win high praise for his training of light infantry at Shorncliffe camp. This new light infantry was to be one of Wellington's main weapons in the Peninsula.

Equal progress was not made in all branches of the army. The cavalry, for instance, had plenty of dash, but much less sense of order, and Wellington used them sparingly in set pieces. They approached battle too much in the spirit of a fox-hunt. British artillery remained below the best continental standards, especially the French, and Wellington's forces in the Peninsula were to be under-gunned compared with their opponents until after Vittoria in 1813. The artillery corps was too small; the field artillery was often poorly organised, while it has been estimated that in only three of Wellington's eight sieges could

[1] E. S. Turner, *Gallant Gentlemen* (1956), pp. 118–19.
[2] Glover, pp. 198–210.   [3] Fortescue, vol. xi. chap. i.

the siege train be described as adequate. The engineers, another responsibility of the Board of Ordnance, were hardly recognisable as such by continental standards. In technical skill and equipment they were very deficient, and these defects added to the British casualty lists in Wellington's sieges. They were too dependent upon hired transport, even for their bridging materials. The commissariat was another essential service that provoked bitter criticism from Wellington in the early stages of his Peninsular campaigns. In 1808 he dismissed the heads of the commissariat, all nominees of the Treasury, as incapable of managing anything outside the counting-house, and even the establishment of the new office of Commissary-in-Chief in the same year had little effect until it gained a strikingly efficient occupant in 1810. In the interval Wellington had virtually to be his own Commissary-in-Chief to ensure that his offensives should not stall for want of regular supplies.[1]

Another great deficiency in the army was the poorness of its intelligence service, and its lack of even such obvious items as reliable maps. Castlereagh made great efforts to procure reliable information, but even so the major expedition against Antwerp in 1809 — the ill-fated Walcheren landing — was sent with information as to its fortifications no newer than 1794. As for maps, there were few of these even for southern England, and in 1805, in anticipation of operations in Hanover, a map had to be borrowed from George III and a copy taken. In Spain and Portugal Wellington soon had his officers at work mapping the countryside to avoid the dangers of fighting blind in an unknown land. These, then, were some of the important weaknesses in the armed forces which Castlereagh found at his disposal in 1805–6, and again in 1807–9, weaknesses which had some effect upon the outcome of the expeditions of the period, weaknesses which he was not always in a position to correct even when he was aware of them. There remains one further deficiency to be discussed, the defective and inadequate system of recruitment of regular troops, the problem to which Castlereagh particularly turned his attention, and in the solution of which he made considerable progress.

Troops had been expended with reckless prodigality in the

[1] D. Gray, *Spencer Perceval*, pp. 324–30.

E

1790s; the years 1793–6 alone cost 40,000 dead and as many more lost to the service from various causes — twice the numbers that were to be lost by Wellington in his Peninsular campaigns.[1] Only the minimum of inducements existed to attract recruits. Apart from bounties on enlistment, soldiers' pay was only seven or eight shillings a week at a time when an artisan might earn nearly one pound, perhaps more. The poverty and ignorance of Ireland and some British agricultural districts could be exploited, and there were always criminals or young men who, having sown their wild oats, were now threatened with a less pleasurable harvest, and were willing to take the King's shilling. But the regulars were handicapped by severe competition for recruits from the Militia, and other auxiliary forces for home defence. The Militia was normally raised by ballot, but substitution was allowed, and many who might otherwise have joined the army, seized the opportunity to serve at home, with the added attraction of an allowance for a wife which was not paid to the regulars. The Militia itself was handicapped by the existence of Volunteer forces, which gave little training, and exempted their members from the Militia ballot. The renewal of the war with France in 1803, and the ensuing invasion scare had led to a tremendous expansion of these auxiliary forces, far beyond the numbers which the country could arm, and to the detriment of the concurrent efforts to expand the regular forces.

The years 1802–3 alone witnessed the passage of twenty-one Acts of Parliament and two codes of regulations on recruiting as the government grappled with the problem. There was much confusion and contradiction, and those measures which gave good results tended to do so at the expense of other modes of recruiting. Pitt followed these with his Volunteer Consolidation Act, which certainly improved the efficiency of the Volunteers, but his Additional Force Act which tried to raise second battalions for home defence by imposing quotas of men — with fines for deficiencies — on the parishes produced only 13,000 men over two years instead of the expected 20,000 within two months. The legislation itself was defective, but the parishes were unsuitable and unwilling agents of the government. The

[1] Fortescue, iv. 496.

death of Pitt in 1806 removed Castlereagh from office for one year, and in the interval William Windham tried a new approach. He hoped to attract regulars with better pay, pensions, and with the offer of seven-year periods of service in place of the normal life commitment. He suspended the ballot for the Militia, hoping to attract sufficient volunteers with modest bounties, and embarked upon ambitious schemes for training the whole able-bodied population in annual batches of 200,000 for periods of 24 days. An armed peasantry would thus be available to assist the regular army in the event of invasion. In practice, Windham weakened the Militia, and almost destroyed the Volunteers, whose fighting value had greatly improved since 1803. Windham proved to be a poor administrator, and his year in office left matters in greater confusion than ever before. It is difficult to take very seriously a Secretary of State for War who objected to military training on Sundays.

Castlereagh therefore returned to office in 1807 to find the regular forces 35,000 below strength, and the auxiliary forces in a state of confusion. He had shown some interest in these problems during his previous spell in office, but he lacked the time, and perhaps the opportunity under Pitt's dominating personality, to take action himself. But in 1807 he was free to make a thorough review of the situation, and this he undertook with his customary industry, mastery of detail, and open-mindedness. He turned down an ambitious plan to reorganise the army proposed by the Duke of York, possibly out of a feeling that Parliament would object, while his own schemes had often to be watered down in practice as too expensive or too far-reaching. Nevertheless, in the course of the next two years, and despite some changes of plan *en route*, notably in his scheme for universal military training, he was able to devise an effective structure for recruitment both to the army and to the auxiliary forces. There were few real novelties in this structure; essentially it was a synthesis of previous schemes which had enjoyed a measure of success, and it owed its strength to careful formulation and to the imposition of a logical and coherent relationship between all the aspects of recruitment which had hitherto been lacking. The various forces became complementary rather than competitive.

The Volunteers he at first tried to revive and reform, but

ultimately he encouraged their disappearance into a new Local Militia. This force, nearly 200,000 strong by 1809, was intended for local defence save in the event of rebellion or invasion. Recruited by ballot, this force received 28 days' annual training, and also served as a recruiting ground for both the Militia and the regular army. All weaknesses were not eliminated, but it became the best force of its type in the Napoleonic period.[1] The Militia, with a strength of 120,000 for the whole of the British Isles, was recruited both voluntarily and by ballot. It was designed to release much of the regular army for foreign service, save in times of gravest emergency, but it was also now used as never before as a recruiting ground for the regular army. Recruitment from the Militia by means of bounties was not a new idea, but hitherto it had been attempted only on a very small scale. In 1807 and again in 1809 Castlereagh authorised the recruitment of 28,000 men from the Militia with excellent results. The links between the regular and auxiliary forces were drawn tighter by giving the latter the uniform, colours and equipment of the local county regiments, and it was hoped that these connexions would increase efficiency and encourage recruitment. Great reliance had still to be placed in the traditional methods of recruitment, and at no time were the army's continual demands for more troops fully met. But Castlereagh had set himself in December 1807 to raise the army to 220,000; he surpassed this total in less than a year, and since his return to office he had in fact increased the army by one-quarter. Furthermore, although the Militias remained under the direction of the Home Office, Castlereagh's schemes had brought greater uniformity and systematic control, the sum total of which greatly facilitated Wellington's Peninsular campaign.[2]

When Castlereagh became Secretary of State for War in July

[1] Fortescue, vi. 183, 'two hundred thousand men, who could be compelled to undergo training and to do what they were told, were substituted for an uncertain number who after great expense to the country, still claimed the glorious privilege of doing as they pleased.'

[2] Glover, pp. 214–54. *C.C.* viii. 113–27, 194–7. Fortescue, x. 185, however, points out that by 1814 the scheme was breaking down, as the growth of substitution in the Local Militia was impeding recruitment to the Militia and Regular Army.

1805, Napoleon's army was still massed at Boulogne, and the outcome of Nelson's pursuit of Villeneuve to the West Indies unknown. Britain's military preparations were, however, well-advanced, and already the foundations of the third coalition against Napoleon were being laid. Soon came news of Calder's action with the French fleet, and of the latter's resort to Ferrol. On 26 July, a month before Napoleon broke camp to march against the Austrians, Castlereagh was beginning to consider the problems associated with the renewal of land warfare against the French, and to plan the collection of a force of 45,000 troops with a transport fleet for 10,000 men permanently at their disposal to operate from Cork, Portsmouth and the Kent coast.[1] Castlereagh made this 'disposeable force', ready for speedy offensive action, one of the main features of his policy as Secretary for War, and it stood in sharp contrast to Pitt's reliance upon improvisation, and Windham's short-sighted passion for economy which had led to the dispersal of invaluable transports in 1806–7.

When Napoleon marched from Boulogne to meet the assembling Austrian and Russian armies in central Europe, Castlereagh estimated that between forty and sixty thousand British troops had been released for continental operations. How could these be used to best advantage in the service of the coalition? From early September various operations in northern Europe were contemplated. Boulogne, the Dutch coast, Walcheren, and a landing in north Germany on the River Weser were all considered; the last-mentioned was finally accepted as the most practicable. Gradually in September and October the scale of the intended operation mounted from a cautious probing manœuvre into the ultimate hope of a major allied offensive. At first no more than Prussian neutrality was expected, but news of Napoleon's infringement of Prussian neutrality reached Britain in mid-October, and this raised hopes of direct aid from Berlin. Russian and Swedish troops were expected in the same theatre, and the liberation of Hanover, perhaps even Holland, seemed possible. Castlereagh soon collected a large number of ships to transport infantry, but horse transports were more difficult to find. However, the main delays arose from adverse winds. By the end of the year, more than 20,000 troops had been sent to

[1] *C.C.* viii. 6–8.

the Weser, and more were to follow. The whole expedition was, of course, dependent upon Prussian intervention, as Britain could not mount a major offensive unaided, and the British forces were designed in the first instance to remove all Prussian doubts as to British seriousness, and to encourage them to act. They were to fail by a narrow margin.

On 3 November the Prussians had agreed with Austria and Russia that they would intervene if, after a month, the French had refused their terms, and if the allies would promise Hanover to Prussia. Here was the first stumbling-block; Pitt could not concede Hanover, the patrimony of George III; it would have driven the old King out of his mind again. As the diplomats negotiated and bargained, Napoleon struck; Austerlitz was a shattering defeat for the Austrians and Russians, and as it became clear that the Austrians were seeking peace, so the uncertain pendulum of Prussian policy swung back to Napoleon, and left the British force poised aimlessly and dangerously on the Weser. Wisely and promptly the cabinet decided on its recall. This expedition has been much criticised, especially by Sir John Fortescue. He argues in his most forceful style that no trust should have been placed in Prussia, who had been subservient to France since 1795; that Pitt was obsessed with Holland; and that the best region for a British offensive would have been Italy, where their forces might have been linked with those of Russia and Austria, and could have continued the struggle independently of the fate of the allies.

The question of a Mediterranean versus a northern strategy will arise again, and several authorities will be found lamenting the feebleness of British efforts in Italy. As Castlereagh was one of the main participants in the direction of the war, these charges must be carefully considered. In 1805 only 4,000 reinforcements were sent to the Mediterranean, and Craig's landing in Naples with 7,000 troops was totally ineffective. The critics of Pitt claim that had the Weser expedition been sent to Italy the result might have been different. Fortescue is an impressive authority to question, but as presented his arguments leave room for certain doubts.[1] In contrast to his careful analysis of the logistic

[1] Fortescue, *British Statesmen of the Great War* (1911), pp. 177–80. Barnes, pp. 464–6.

difficulties confronting Wellington in Spain in 1809, Fortescue makes no reference to the immense task of transporting and maintaining a large force in the Mediterranean. The battle of Austerlitz would have been fought before the reinforcements could have reached Italy. It seems unlikely that the transport fleet was equal to the movement or supply of many more than 20,000 troops in the Mediterranean, and Castlereagh was indeed to conclude in 1809 that this region 'is too remote to admit of our acting with the gross of our army in that quarter'; the army would be 'removed from all its resources'.[1] On logistic grounds alone there would seem to be good reason to question Fortescue's premises, and given the limited size of the army that could be supported in this region it seems equally unlikely that Fortescue's second claim — namely, that a British army could tie down large French forces irrespective of the conduct or existence of any British allies — can be substantiated. General Sir John Moore, for instance, believed that Britain could act 'with great effect' in Italy, but only if there were a coalition in the field against France. He later noted that 'Bonaparte knows that the fate of Italy will be decided on the Vistula', and that therefore he would not sacrifice troops from his main operations in central Europe in order to contain diversionary moves in Italy. Napoleon had certainly no intention of committing so elementary a strategic mistake at this stage in his career, and was indeed disposed to run considerable risks with his troops in Italy both in 1805 and 1809 in order to gain victory in the central theatre. British forces in the Mediterranean could attain useful, but limited objectives.[2]

The claims of a Mediterranean expedition were therefore open to doubt, yet at the same time it must be admitted that the Weser expedition was a gamble against long odds. The Duke of York, the Commander-in-Chief, and with personal experience of much of the intended field of campaign, underlined the weaknesses of the British force, and the difficulties it would encounter. He concluded, 'The first supposition, that Prussia will enter heartily into the cause . . . is a *sine qua non* without which the

[1] *C.C.* vi. 404, vii. 126.

[2] P. Mackesy, *The War in the Mediterranean, 1803–10* (1957), especially pp. 56–58, 68–73, 89–93. Maurice, ii. 134–5.

whole plan must at once be given up.'[1] Arthur Wellesley also
felt that the politicians were too optimistic, but Castlereagh was
perfectly clear in his own mind as to the importance of Prussia.[2]
Despite Prussia's past record, the possibility of her intervention
was real, and it required all Napoleon's audacity, skill and good
luck to defeat the Austrians before the Prussian resolve had
crystallised. Pitt may have been over-optimistic, dreaming idly of
'Bonaparte's army either cut off or driven back to France', but his
instinct was sound. He saw, as did Castlereagh, that Napoleon
could only be defeated by a coalition, not by inspired side-shows.

Pitt died on 23 January 1806, and his already weak ministry
possessed no hope of survival without him. His successors, a
coalition of Foxites, Grenvilles and Sidmouth, inherited a
difficult situation, and it is easier to criticise their conduct
than to point to alternative policies. Nevertheless, some
specific charges must be made against them. Windham's
disastrous experiments with home defence have already been
noted; likewise his dispersal of Castlereagh's transport fleet for
the use of the 'disposeable force'. The force itself had declined
between Castlereagh's departure from office and his return in
March 1807 from 30,000 troops to 12,000. If the Talents' Mediterranean strategy has recently been presented in a more sympathetic light,[3] their South American adventures, and the ultra-
cautious assistance which they had given to their allies, Russia,
Sweden and Prussia (the latter had at last entered the war in
1806, only to meet early disaster at Jena) must still count against
them. The new Pittite ministry under Portland was determined to
recover the confidence of Russia and Sweden, but time was against
them. It took time to collect a new transport fleet, and troops
could not be promised for service in the Baltic until June 1807.
Stores and specie had to suffice in the interval. Castlereagh had
serious doubts as to the military wisdom of committing a large
force of British troops to so distant a theatre as Swedish Pomer-
ania, but he agreed with Canning, the Foreign Secretary, that a
British gesture was needed to restore allied confidence in Britain.[4]

[1] A. H. Burne, *The Noble Duke of York* (1949), pp. 256–7.
[2] *C.C.* vi. 53–54.   [3] Mackesy, pp. 154–99.
[4] *C.C.* viii. 66–68. R. Carr, 'Gustavus Adolphus and the British
Government, 1804–9', *English Historical Review*, lx. 36–66.

Unfortunately on 14 June, two days before the first British contingent sailed from Yarmouth, Napoleon had won the decisive battle of Friedland against Russia. In less than a fortnight the Russians had agreed to make peace, and Britain's only allies had been reduced to Sweden and Sicily. The former was soon to become more of a liability than an asset, as the eccentric Swedish King expected British aid in the continuance of a war which could only lead to disaster for Sweden and embarrassment for Britain without other allies. In vain, in 1808, Britain offered to release Sweden from the alliance, and later reluctantly sent further subsidies and troops. This chivalrous farce ended only when the mad King tried to imprison the British Commander, Sir John Moore, who then had a legitimate excuse to withdraw from an intolerable situation, and return to Britain in time to join the Peninsular campaign in the late summer of 1808.

The intervention in the Baltic in the previous year, however, had not been a total waste, as the British contingent despatched in June 1807 was on hand to assist in one of the speediest, If one of the most controversial, British operations in the era of sail. News of a Franco-Russian peace began to arrive in London in the middle of July, but other hints had already reached the government that Napoleon's interest had begun to turn towards Denmark, the closing of the Sound, and the seizure of the Danish fleet. Howick, Foreign Secretary to the Talents, had remarked in December 1806 that Britain could never allow France to secure the Danish fleet. With the volatile Canning at the Foreign Office, with a force already in the Baltic, and with Castlereagh's massive efforts to rebuild the 'disposeable force' and its transports achieving rapid results, the government was ready to act. If its information as to Napoleon's intentions was not complete, no great measure of insight was required to guess the whole truth. An ultimatum backed by Gambier's battle fleet and 30,000 troops was promptly despatched. The British demanded the surrender of the Danish fleet into safe custody, and a Danish alliance with Britain. Similar moves by Napoleon came about a week to a fortnight later. Already, however, most of the Danish army was in Holstein to guard the frontier, and the British landing on the island of Zealand was opposed mainly by the Militia. A three-days' bombardment of Copenhagen was needed before the Danish submission on 7 September, when fifteen ships of the line passed into British hands.[1]

Castlereagh's secretary boasted, 'There never was an expedition of such magnitude so quickly got up; so secretly sent and which was conducted from the beginning to its termination with greater ability or success.' Without a similar indulgence in hyperbole, it must be agreed that the expedition had been prepared and despatched with remarkable speed. The troops which left England, two-thirds of the total force, were ordered to sea in less than a fortnight. The expedition was roundly condemned by most of the opposition in Britain, and it was claimed that the ships captured were unseaworthy. But even unseaworthy ships can sometimes be repaired, while Napoleon's anger at the success of the expedition would appear to be good evidence as to its wisdom. Less wise was Canning's desire to retain the island of Zealand as a base against the French, a policy against which the commanders on the spot strongly protested, and a protest in which they were finally upheld by Castlereagh after he had studied their reports and the British strength available.[2] Later in 1807 the British won a second important race against Napoleon, this time to Lisbon where the Portuguese fleet and royal family were the prizes. These useful naval and political assets were removed almost under the nose of the advancing French army commanded by Junot. This was another operation in which Castlereagh took a deep and active interest.

Despite these displays of strength and resolution, the overall British position in the struggle against Napoleon was far from satisfactory by the end of 1807. Britain had no ally, save the embarrassing Swedes, and the unreliable Neapolitan Bourbons in Sicily. She was wholly excluded from the European mainland, and even Sicily was viewed as a point she must hold rather than as a base for offensive operations against Naples. Even with the

---

[1] A. N. Ryan, 'The Causes of the British Attack upon Copenhagen in 1807', *English Historical Review*, lxviii. 37–55. R. Ruppenthal, 'Denmark and the Continental System', *Journal of Modern History* (1943), p. 8. Britain was anxious to keep the Baltic open to British trade.

[2] *C.C.* vi. 179–87.

Russians in the field earlier in 1807, Castlereagh's hopes of a
Mediterranean offensive had been disappointed. His suggestions
on these lines of May 1807 had been greeted with ridicule by
Sir John Moore, the ablest military mind in the British forces in
Sicily. Any British offensive would be dependent upon support
from Sicily and Naples. This presupposed reform of the Sicilian
government. At the moment the Sicilians were ineffective
militarily and a liability politically. There could be no hope of
sympathetic risings in Naples so long as the Bourbon government was unreformed. Castlereagh had allowed himself to be
over-impressed by Sir John Stuart's victory at Maida in 1806;
this was a tactical success with no long-term strategic prospects.
Castlereagh was to commit a further mistake from his reading
of the Maida accounts by reappointing Stuart to the Mediterranean in 1808; as Commander-in-Chief he was to be unpopular
and indecisive, as well as ineffective in his dealings with the
wayward Bourbon court.

Circumstances, quite apart from the reaction of his officers in
Sicily, soon drove Castlereagh to a defensive strategy in the
Mediterranean. After the defeat of Russia, the threat from
Napoleon — and perhaps also Russia — was so great, and could
be directed to so many different points, that the main British
forces had to be redeployed. Britain herself might even be
threatened. British troops in Sicily were beyond the effective
control of London, and so Moore was ordered to Gibraltar in
August 1807 with 7,000 troops to act as a mobile reserve. Sicily
itself was left in a vulnerable condition until the spring of 1808,
so great was the danger elsewhere, and indeed for much of the
winter of 1807–8 British strategy and troop movements were in
a state of confusion, as Castlereagh and his colleagues tried to
anticipate Napoleon's moves, and to provide for the most vital
points. Moore himself arrived at Gibraltar in December (it had
taken three months to order and accomplish that limited move)
only to find that he was not wanted there, and in the end he
returned to England, passing troops on the way whose complex
orders, by a process of elimination, finally carried them to
Sicily. This apparently absurd exchange only makes sense if one
understands the slowness of sea-borne communications with the
Mediterranean, the uncertainty as to Napoleon's intentions, and

the partial improvement to British security effected by the successes at Copenhagen and Lisbon.

By December 1807 the problems were becoming clearer; Napoleon had no fleets for the invasion of Britain, though his range of choice in Europe and the Mediterranean was still large. On the other hand, Britain could now develop a defensive strategy in the latter region based primarily upon Collingwood's fleet, and with this fleet based on Sicily, Malta and Gibraltar. Canning, indeed wanted to resume the offensive there with an attack on Corfu, but Castlereagh and Portland clung to the defensive. In January 1808 Castlereagh was able to fix the British strength in Sicily at 16,000, so that only limited expeditions with about 8,000 men could be attempted. If Napoleon struck eastward, Britain could do no more for the moment than harass him from the sea, and try to improve her relations with the Ottoman empire, Persia, and also Afghanistan.[1] The adoption of this defensive posture, inevitable as it was, left Britain in exactly that position which Castlereagh had foreseen and dreaded in 1802–3, a position in which she was without continental allies, and would find it impossible to strike any damaging blows against France. This situation compelled Castlereagh to reflect upon his former attitude to colonial and maritime warfare. If the war was to continue these were the only instruments at the disposal of Britain, apart from the quest for new allies by diplomatic means. Though he did not neglect colonial and extra-European operations, Castlereagh rarely showed much enthusiasm for them save when he was convinced of their necessity, or of the existence of no alternative. If Britain had to rely on her maritime power, it should be directed wherever possible against the continent of Europe. Not surprisingly, he became one of the strongest advocates of economic warfare against Napoleon's empire. As he wrote to Perceval on 1 October 1807.

The more I have had time to reflect on our future prospects in this war, the more impressed I am with a conviction that neither peace nor independence can be the lot of this nation, till we have found the means of making France feel that her new anti-social and anti-commercial system will not avail her against a power that can, for its own pre-

[1] Mackesy, pp. 216–66.

servation, and consequently legitimately, counteract at sea what she lawlessly inflicts and enforces on shore.[1]

Britain and France had been using economic weapons against each other since 1793, but it was only with Napoleon's triumph at Tilsit, which brought almost all Europe under his direct control or in alliance with him, that he was in a position to apply the so-called Continental System with full rigour. By a series of Decrees, beginning with those issued from Berlin in November 1806 and climaxed by those from Milan in December 1807, Napoleon endeavoured to prevent British trade with Europe. Britain, before the autumn of 1807, had been content to apply her Orders in Council to contraband trade with enemy ports, and to coastal traffic between enemy ports, including that conducted by neutral ships. This policy had irritated neutrals rather than embarrassed the French, and both Castlereagh and Perceval had criticised it as ineffective. By the autumn of 1807 it had become a question of retaliation, as British trade with Europe was declining sharply and was passing into the hands of neutral shipping. Many mercantile interests in Britain demanded government assistance and protection, and the government was obliged to keep a wary eye upon its powerful supporters in the City of London. According to Lord Erskine, the government was besieged until it met their demands. But apart from such interests, it was impossible to overlook the fact that all the determination in the world could not continue the war unless the British economy was in a position to sustain it, unless it was able to provide sufficient employment to avoid mass discontent and uprisings, and unless it was able to provide a reasonably satisfactory income for the well-to-do. As Castlereagh had remarked earlier, Britain was a constitutional state, and the fight could be continued, not for as long as the resources existed, but only for as long as the public were prepared to support the war.

Before new Orders in Council were issued in November 1807, there were several keen debates within the cabinet as to the extent of Britain's retaliatory measures. Castlereagh, with Westmorland, was an advocate of the strongest possible line. He warned the cabinet that this was no longer a war for territory or a point of honour, 'but whether the existence of Great Britain

[1] *C.C.* viii. 87–88.

as a naval power is compatible with that of France'. Britain must
destroy or be destroyed by the Continental System; there could
be no peace until France ended 'the social and commercial
warfare between the two states, as well as the contest in arms'.[1]
The debate in the cabinet turned essentially on how far Britain
could afford to offend the neutrals, especially the United States,
with whom there were various outstanding questions quite
apart from American resentment at British treatment of neutral
shipping, and with whom there had recently been a brief threat
of war. Canning was the main spokesman of the moderates, and
he wished to meet some at least of the American complaints, to
avoid so open a British effort to monopolise all trade with the
continent as the most extreme version of the new Orders in
Council would have asserted, and to concentrate the blockade
against France and French-occupied territory, rather than against
all supporting the Continental System. For the most part,
however, the extremists prevailed. Castlereagh himself appreciated the importance of striving to divert the hostility of
neutrals to France, and some small concessions were made to
them. But otherwise all harbours from which British ships were
excluded were declared to be in a state of blockade, and all
neutral trade with these harbours had to pass through certain
British ports, paying a duty in the process. Above all, neutrals
could no longer trade direct with France from colonial or
American ports.

These Orders in Council had several objects in view; it was
hoped to cause a superabundance of locally produced goods on
the continent, with a shortage of overseas products, and so upset
the economy of the Napoleonic empire. Neutrals were to be
prevented from capturing the trade of Europe from Britain;
neutral efforts to export non-British colonial goods to Europe
were to be impeded by British duties, and these duties should
aid both the British revenue and British colonial re-exports.
Although these were the main objects of the Orders, it cannot be
said that they achieved any consistent results, so great were
vagaries of international politics between 1808 and 1812.[2] At

[1] Gray, p. 170.

[2] F. Crouzet, *L'Économie Britannique et le Blocus Continental,
1806–13* (1958), provides the best full analysis.

times it seemed as if Britain's policy was designed to add to her enemies, and to provoke the world against herself by the extremity of her maritime claims. At others it seemed that her opponents were at the greater disadvantage in this struggle. In the first half of 1808 British exports fell by one-quarter, and Lancashire in particular experienced acute distress under the combined effects of the Continental System and the United States' imposition of an embargo on trade with belligerents in protest against the treatment meted out to neutrals. Doubts began to develop in the minds of some British ministers, but Castlereagh and Canning were adamant. They did not believe the Americans would fight, and they believed that American mercantile interests would insist on the early resumption of trade with Britain. There was something to be said for this argument, but the really decisive relief for the British economy in the second half of 1808 arose from the beginning of the Peninsular War, and the increasing demand from South America. A good harvest in Britain was another valuable stimulant.

Distress returned to many parts of Britain in the winter of 1808–9, but failed to provoke a serious outcry against British policy, and the response of the mercantile interests was too varied to give much encouragement to the Whig critics of the Orders. In 1809 Napoleon's difficulties on the continent began to mount, while the United States government abandoned the embargo under pressure from east-coast merchants. It proved to be a record year for British exports, especially re-exports; many of Napoleon's subjects would not forgo their taste for tropical luxuries, which were smuggled into Europe through Holland or the Baltic. Official corruption and inefficiency, Napoleon's own need for British goods, provided more openings for exports, and if the defeat of Austria at Wagram began to reverse this trend, exports to the United States continued to boom well into 1810. Indeed, in 1809 and the early part of 1810 one of the basic weaknesses in the British economy was over-confidence; there was too much speculation, too many grants of credit, too much inflation. British imports rose very rapidly, and with heavy government spending overseas to promote the war, an adverse balance of payments situation was developing. But at the time when Castlereagh left office in September 1809 there seemed no reason to question the efficacy of the Orders in Council as an instrument of policy, and only minor concessions had been made to the United States at the behest of Canning. These concessions were insufficient to appease the Americans, and the continuance of the Orders in Council was to be a major cause of the Anglo-American War of 1812. This development, and Castlereagh's part in it, can be more conveniently discussed in a later chapter.

If Castlereagh had supported the Orders in Council as the main weapon whereby Britain might hope to injure France following the disasters of 1806–7, he had also, despite his earlier doubts concerning the utility of colonial warfare — save to acquire strategic bases such as Malta and the Cape of Good Hope — begun to ponder the desirability of some extra-European operations. In particular he was moved by the fear that Napoleon's hold upon the continent might become so complete, his Continental System so effective, that Britain might be obliged to base her trade upon regions outside Europe. His reactions to developments in Latin America during these years admirably illustrate this point.

He was called upon to define his attitude immediately upon his return to office in 1807, as a considerable force of British troops had been committed by his predecessors to the recapture of Buenos Aires. That city had originally been seized by Admiral Sir Home Popham in 1806, who had acted without any authority from the British government. The seizure had, however, whetted the appetite of certain commercial interests, and the Talents, after some hesitation, had decided to follow up this venture. Other expeditions to Spanish America had been planned, but the expulsion of the British from Buenos Aires had led to the concentration of all British reinforcements in La Plata under the command of General Whitelocke. Castlereagh himself was prepared to send a further 5,000 troops if necessary, but he also drew up a lengthy memorandum on 1 May 1807 in which he strove to clarify his thoughts concerning this region. Although he expected Whitelocke to recover Buenos Aires, and was in fact disappointed when he learned in September of the latter's disastrous failure, he saw that such expeditions, unless directed with great political discrimination, would do more harm than good.[1] The Talents had vetoed any incitement of the local population to rebel against Spanish rule, and Castlereagh agreed with this policy, since Britain could give the potential rebels little assistance, and in particular could give no guarantee as to the future when peace should be restored between Britain and Spain. Britain could certainly not conquer territory for herself. In addition, a policy of irresponsible meddling might injure British political or commercial interests through the replacement of the existing 'bad government' with 'revolutionary' or 'democratic' government, or no government at all. Castlereagh seems to have perceived that the first British expulsion from Buenos Aires had been the work mainly of the Spanish Americans themselves, and that unless Britain could offer them independence, her military intervention might well antagonise them, and even strengthen the Spanish position. Far better, therefore, was the 'silent and imperceptible operation of our illicit commercial intercourse', whereas the policy of direct interference would 'be productive of little commercial or political benefit, and must be felt as a great waste of our military means'.[2]

But already Castlereagh could not ignore the possibility of an overwhelming French victory in Europe. What if the French began to impose indirect control on Spanish America by way of Spain? To meet such an eventuality Britain might have to act more positively. A possibility that strongly appealed to him was that of a new Bourbon monarchy in Spanish America, erected by the colonists themselves, and perhaps with the French Duke of Orleans as King. He could be relied upon to resist Bonapartist influence, and also restrain democratic tendencies among the South Americans. The British role should be confined to that of 'auxiliaries and protectors'. As British prospects in Europe darkened in the second half of 1807, it is not therefore surprising to find Castlereagh's interest in Spanish America mounting. With other ministers and generals, he discussed, planned, and even began preparations for several Spanish American expedi-

[1] *C.C.* viii. 83-86.

[2] *C.C.* vii. 319-24. See Harlow, ii. 615-61, for British debate on policy towards Spanish America.

F

tions. La Plata, Venezuela and Mexico were the regions of most economic and political interest to Britain. Castlereagh busily collected information for the guidance of the expedition commanders; he consulted the Venezuelan patriot, Miranda, who had vainly sought British intervention for many years; he received the advice of the French military adventurer, Dumouriez. He was also in close touch with Arthur Wellesley, who had been placed in command of one of the intended expeditions. For a time it seemed that Castlereagh might be able to divert troops from the Mediterranean to La Plata, but these were finally sent to defend Sicily and other important points. Castlereagh had plans to seize Montevideo even if Britain should decide against a policy of encouraging Latin American independence. From Montevideo British trade could be protected and developed, and French influence in La Plata and Brazil combatted. It was not until the revolt in Spain against Napoleon's overthrow of the Spanish Bourbons began to appear well-established in June and July 1808 that references to Spanish American independence as a counterpoise to French influence in Spain disappeared from Castlereagh's correspondence. At the same time Wellesley and his Spanish American expedition were diverted to the Iberian Peninsula.[1]

Castlereagh had therefore taken the possibility of operations in Spanish America very seriously; he had made preparations both for limited intervention to seize certain vital points, and for assistance to a colonial revolt against Spanish rule, should European conditions make it necessary. But always the Spanish American scene had been viewed within the European context, even the export of British goods to and imports of specie from that continent having relevance to the struggle against Napoleon. He showed great awareness of the necessity to avoid the dispersal of British troops in side-shows which could not influence the main issue. Latin America should become a British battlefield only if Napoleon made it so. Castlereagh's caution here was repeated in the West Indies, those fever-ridden islands which had so often destroyed whole British armies. This was not a new policy, since the cabinet had tended to reduce the British effort

[1] *C.C.* vi. 364–8, 375, vii. 332–44, 385–90, viii. 96–100. *W[ellington] S[upplementary] D[ispatches]*, vi. 38–74. Maurice, ii. 217, 219.

in the West Indies since 1798, while Castlereagh himself did not advocate total inaction. He approved expeditions against the French islands of Martinique, the Saints, and Guadeloupe; as privateer bases they were a considerable source of injury to British shipping in the Caribbean, but he was careful to add in the case of Guadeloupe that it should only be attacked if there were a good prospect of early success. He had no wish, certainly once the possibility of European campaigning had returned, to pour troops into that open grave. Castlereagh, and still more his successor, provided few reinforcements, and encouraged the use of Negro regiments.[1]

The Spanish revolt flared in Madrid on 2 May 1808. It was suppressed, but soon much of Spain was in turmoil, and French conceptions of warfare as a straightforward conflict between armies with defined areas of power was thrown into confusion by the upsurge of provinces and localities — if not a nation in arms. It took time to restore discipline and organisation so that they might begin to limit the effects of the fanaticism of such numbers in such a terrain. Before this could take place, British forces had also entered the fray. The Spanish revolt had at once provoked great excitement in Britain, and there was soon over-whelming support in favour of British intervention. Even so, the development of British policy in practice is worth a little study. Castlereagh had been watching for signs of a Spanish revolt as early as December 1807.[2] He had received further encouraging reports since then, and was well prepared when definite news arrived on 25 May. He at once cancelled preparations for an attack on Minorca, and prepared to move troops from Gibraltar and Cork, though the latter (under Wellesley) could still go to Spanish America if Spanish resistance crumbled. British opti-mism was not confined to Spain at this stage; high hopes existed that similar outbreaks might occur in Naples, and that Britain might be able to take the offensive from Sicily also. Other parts of Italy might rise too, and inspire Austria and Russia by their example. This was building castles in and out of Spain with a vengeance, and even in Spain Britain was to experience dark disappointment. But it led first to the retention of the Mediterranean transport fleet, and then when Italy failed

[1] Fortescue, vii. 1–20.   [2] Mackesy, p. 266.

to rise, Castlereagh unsuccessfully tried to move 8,000 troops from Sicily to Spain, a transfer which Sicilian circumstances would not permit.[1]

While Castlereagh was clarifying his mind as to the real potentialities in Europe, he contributed to — was indeed perhaps mainly responsible for — one decision of the highest significance for the future, the choice of Wellesley to command the vanguard in the Peninsula. The latter was too junior to receive the supreme command of a large expedition, but in the intrigue that accompanied the subsequent appointments, Castlereagh tried hard to defend Wellesley's interests, going so far as to write to Sir Hew Dalrymple when he was finally chosen as Commander-in-Chief that he would do well to 'make the most prominent use [of Wellesley's services] which the rules of the service will permit'. Castlereagh also informed Wellesley that he had 'made every effort to keep in your hands the greatest number of men, and for the longest time that circumstances would permit'. But three generals senior to him were following in his wake, and he had just time to land in Portugal and win the decisive battle of Vimeiro on 21 August as one senior officer landed from his ship, and the Commander-in-Chief approached. Matters now passed out of Wellesley's hands, and the new commanders, having prevented a pursuit of the enemy after Vimeiro, entered into negotiations with the French, and finally concluded the Convention of Cintra on 30 August 1808. This Convention ended their careers, and nearly ended Wellesley's.

By its terms the French troops were permitted to leave Portugal, with all their equipment and their 'legitimate property', an interesting euphemism which included their plunder, and were to be transported to France in British ships. The outcry in Britain was immense; Castlereagh when he received the first intimation of the terms thought it must be a 'base forgery'. Historians have sometimes described the outcry as exaggerated, and felt that there was much in Wellesley's plea that, though he disagreed with some of the terms, the general principle of withdrawal was correct, as it spared the British forces in Portugal many tedious sieges which would have been inevitable

[1] Mackesy, pp. 266–71.

following the failure to exploit the victory of Vimeiro to the full. But Wellesley himself at first shared the public displeasure, and had to appear before a court of inquiry in November. Canning, unlike Castlereagh, had not yet recovered from his initial disappointment at the Convention, and attacked Wellesley in the cabinet. Castlereagh, however, quietly supported him whenever possible, while Wellesley required no advocate for his defence before the court. He also continued to act as Castlereagh's private military adviser, and when events in the Peninsula took a new turn in the early months of 1809, and another Commander-in-Chief was required, Castlereagh in his turn was to assist nobly in the gradual restoration of Wellesley to favour. He was much encouraged in this line of conduct by the appeal from his half-brother, Charles, in the Peninsula, 'Would to God we had the hero of Vimeiro at our head now'. Wellesley sailed again for the Peninsula in April 1809.

Much had happened in his absence. Through the recall of three generals following the Convention of Cintra, the cabinet had been obliged to appoint as Commander-in-Chief the independent-minded Sir John Moore, whom they had vainly tried to prevent sailing to the Peninsula in the first place by a series of calculated insults.[1] Moore was not one to allow bad personal relations with leading ministers to interfere with his career. From the Peninsula he was able to establish a satisfactory working relationship with Castlereagh, and when his winter campaign of 1808–9 ended in the retreat to Corunna, and in his own death, Castlereagh steadfastly defended Moore's conduct before a hostile House of Commons. He refused to find a scapegoat for the disaster in Moore himself. Some of his opponents were impressed in spite of themselves.[2]

Castlereagh must take the main responsibility for the inception of this famous campaign. In the middle of August 1808, and even before the battle of Vimeiro had been won, the news from Spain was so encouraging that Castlereagh expected that Britain would soon be in a position to extend her operations from Portugal to Spain. His optimism doubtless sprang in part from wishful thinking; his desire to wrest every possible advantage from a European opening, and so prevent Britain

[1] Maurice, ii. 273, 331–5.   [2] Buckingham, *George III*, iv. 308–9.

from slipping back into the position of isolation and alarm that had followed Tilsit. If his subsequent thoughts on strategy often appeared over-sanguine and naïve, they should be balanced against this anxiety lest any offensive opportunity should be neglected, and by his fear lest Britain should again find herself excluded from the continent of Europe. Consequently he was increasingly attracted to the idea of striving to strike a decisive blow in company with the Spaniards in northern Spain. Perhaps some 30,000 British troops could be concentrated there from Portugal and Britain herself. Problems of supply and communication would be less difficult than in the Mediterranean, but his amateur enthusiasm betrayed him when he suggested that such a force might menace the French flank and rear, and endanger any French retreat through the western Pyrenees. As Wellesley subsequently explained to him, any major British force would act as a magnet, and draw overwhelming French armies against itself, especially near the French frontier. Moore was more caustic, and dismissed it all as 'plausible, verbose nonsense', and spoke of this enveloping strategy as 'a sort of gibberish which men in office use and fancy themselves military men'. He later excused some of Castlereagh's mistaken optimism on account of the misleading information he had been receiving from Spain.[1]

The British entry into Spain in the autumn of 1808 was based on three misconceptions : that the armies of Spain were united and efficient and stood some chance of beating the French, that the French could not speedily reinforce their armies in Spain, and that the British forces would be able to fight far from the sea. Wellesley warned Castlereagh to distrust each of these calculations, and urged that either a smaller British force should be sent, or absolute priority should be given to a safe communication with the sea. Moore found himself expected to lead an ill-prepared army from Portugal into northern Spain, with little information as to Spanish roads and conditions — and much of that information was unreliable — and with little time in which to try to improve matters. If he delayed, the autumn

[1] Maurice, ii. 261, 281. Moore had had earlier experience of Castlereagh's optimism and superficial understanding of military problems when in Sicily in 1807, Mackesy, pp. 206, 294, 387.

rains would render impassable such roads as existed; not that he was even certain which roads would bear his artillery into Spain. He was dismayed by the ignorance and easy-going attitude of many of his officers. 'They talked of going into Spain as of going into Hyde Park.' In mid-October he began his painful advance across 300 miles of barren, mountainous country. One officer subsequently likened it to travelling on the bare outside of the world, 'bordered by the chaotic beginning of things'.

Moore reached Salamanca on 13 November. At the same time further British forces from England were beginning to land at Corunna, and a junction of the two was planned at or near Valladolid. Castlereagh, meanwhile, was making great efforts to send out more equipment and reinforcements, but there was the usual shortage of horse transports, and there was little specie to enable the army to purchase supplies in Spain. But both he and Moore continued to receive encouraging reports from the uncritical and impressionable British agents with the Spanish forces, though it must be added that the Spaniards seemed as misinformed as the British observers. It is true that Castlereagh learned on 4 November that Napoleon had massed no less than 120,000 troops on the Ebro, but matters were now out of his hands, and in the middle of the month the Spaniards, with Moore still 200 miles distant, recklessly shattered their main armies against the French. This almost wholly eliminated the forces upon which the British intervention had been founded, and Moore, upon hearing the news, at once contemplated a retreat to Portugal. He was checked by reports of a rising in Madrid against the French, and so embarked upon his diversionary campaign in the north. The subsequent complex manœuvres and flight to Corunna need not delay us. The British moves had the fortunate result of drawing the French after them, and afforded a valuable breathing-space to the Spaniards in the south. The battle of Corunna ensured a safe embarkation for the tattered remnants of the British army. Castlereagh imperturbably faced the parliamentary and popular outcry, and commenced the unspectacular task of re-equipment. Wellesley pondered the lessons of the campaign, and with Castlereagh and the Duke of York, turned his mind to the future. Castlereagh's great hopes of August and September 1808 had been shattered; Moore was dead; but much of southern Spain was still in arms, and the British still held their base in Portugal.

For a time, however, it seemed as if the British might try to make Cadiz their main point of entry into the Peninsula. Canning favoured this policy, but could make no progress against the suspicious Spaniards who held the port. The Portuguese, on the other hand, were willing to place their troops under British command in return for British pay and supplies, while Wellesley impressed upon Castlereagh the possibility of defending Portugal with no more than 25,000 or 30,000 British troops, aided by 70,000 Portuguese against at least an equal number of French. Should the Spanish resistance continue, diversionary British operations from Portugal might be possible, but on the other hand he admitted that if the French were free to launch a major, concentrated attack on Portugal, he believed that the Portuguese frontier would be indefensible, and that even Lisbon might prove untenable. Lisbon was a long way up the Tagus, and Wellesley feared that it might be impossible to hold all the river bank below the city, so that if a British army were driven to embark, the retreat down river might be some-what hazardous. Wellesley, therefore, in his comprehensive way, was determined to leave the cabinet with no false illusions as to the prospects of the strategy he recommended. With Cadiz closed to them, his proposals offered the best prospects of useful employment to 30,000 British troops, about the largest number of troops that Britain could afford to supply with specie for permanent continental operations at this time.

Wellesley sailed for Portugal for the second time in April 1809. By the middle of May he had cleared the country of the latest French invaders, and was in a position to contemplate offensive operations in Spain. On 11 June he received permission from the British government to cross the frontier if he felt it safe to do so. There followed the abortive campaign in Estremadura and New Castile, a campaign marked by the victory of Talavera on 27–28 July, but chiefly remembered for its setbacks and misfortunes. Wellesley was still learning the art of war in the Peninsula. In the first place he had put too much faith in the Spanish armies; they had proved unreliable both at the tactical

level in the field, and in strategy. For Wellesley's small forces
to achieve any success, they depended upon the Spaniards to
keep the French scattered and distracted; when they failed to do
this the British had been forced to retreat. Until these French
concentrations could be prevented, Wellesley intended to
refrain from deep penetrations into Spanish territory. He was
also deterred from such penetrations by the failure of the
Spaniards to keep his forces supplied with food, and it was indeed
lack of supplies which actually determined the date of his retreat
to Portugal. His first experience of war in company with the
Spaniards persuaded him that they were 'children in the art of
war', and he concluded,

Till the evils of which I think I have reason to complain are remedied;
till I see magazines established for the supply of the armies, and a
regular system adopted for keeping them filled; and an army upon
whose exertions I can depend, commanded by officers capable and
willing to carry into execution the operations which may have been
planned by mutual agreement, I cannot enter upon any system of
co-operation with Spanish armies.[1]

But there was much that he found wrong with his own forces
as well. He was handicapped by the shortage of specie; the
commissariat and transport service were exceedingly inefficient,
and Admiral Berkeley noted the arrival of ample food and
medical supplies in the Tagus from England, only for the chain
of supply to break down badly at that point. Wellesley dismissed the commissariat officials as unequal to the management
of anything outside the counting-house, and it is true that for too
long this service had been the refuge of Treasury nominees, of
decayed merchants, even outright rogues, and little real reform
was effected until 1810. In the interval Wellesley did much of
the work himself. Not surprisingly he informed Castlereagh
that even with more than 30,000 troops he could have achieved
no greater success in Spain as problems of supply would have
prevented them from even reaching Talavera, and certainly from
returning. Wellesley had to overcome major logistical problems
before he could hope to grapple successfully with the French.

Defects in the British artillery and engineer corps have
already been noted, while Wellesley was especially alarmed at

[1] Gurwood, *Wellington Dispatches*, v. 258.

the ease with which gross indiscipline developed among his troops, and of the lax attention of so many officers to their duties. He complained to Castlereagh that the lack of patronage at his disposal was a major cause of disobedience among officers, for they looked to other quarters for advancement, and had little or no reason to seek his good opinions or to fear his displeasure. The Duke of York's reforms had clearly not yet gone far enough, or taken full effect. This, then, was the state in 1809 of the Peninsular army which Castlereagh had helped to forge. As we have already seen, responsibility for the various components of the British army was so divided that this statement of its weaknesses is less a criticism of Castlereagh's failings as Secretary of State for War, than a partial explanation for the failure of several of the campaigns he had helped to plan. The main weakness in the Peninsular army for which he was directly responsible was the shortage of reinforcements in the early part of 1810 as a result of the heavy losses sustained by the British in the Walcheren expedition. Although one famous historian of the Peninsular War, Napier, was sharply critical, Wellesley himself wrote to Castlereagh after the latter's resignation from office in September 1809,

If I had been your brother, you could not have been more careful of my interests than you had been in late instances, and on every occasion it has always appeared to me that you sought for opportunities to oblige me and to mark your friendship for me.[1]

The Peninsula was not the only scene of British operations in 1809. The possibility of raids or even more serious operations against the north coast of France and her allies had been kept almost continually in mind, and with Austria stirring against Napoleon early in 1809 the cabinet was anxious to strike a useful diversionary blow. Various possibilities were considered, but the destruction of the menacing French naval base at Antwerp was finally settled upon as the objective. There were four main reasons for this choice. The capture of the island of Walcheren and an attack on Antwerp would impose the least strain on British reserves of specie of all seemingly worth-while continental expeditions; as it was, the British force was to some extent handicapped by lack of specie. In the second place, the

[1] *W.S.D.* vi. 401–2.

Admiralty were anxious to destroy the great French naval base at Antwerp, which they argued was a major threat to Britain. Hopes also existed that disaffection in the Netherlands might be exploited, and that the expedition might develop into a full-scale field operation.[1] Fourthly, it was believed that the garrison at Antwerp would be much weakened by Napoleon's commitments in central Europe and in the Peninsula, but on this possibility the British government could secure no precise information. Even the intelligence concerning the fortifications around Antwerp dated from 1793, which is all the more surprising as expeditions to Walcheren had been considered on at least four occasions since 1797, three of them while Castlereagh was Secretary of State for War. But this objection, if it was sufficiently considered, was outweighed by the presence of the Austrians in the field, by the value of the objective itself, and by the lack of specie for alternative operations.

Critics of the Walcheren expedition have asked why the main British diversionary effort was not made in the Mediterranean, where there were already 20,000 British troops in Sicily. The long Italian coastline has exercised a peculiar fascination over the enthusiasts of amphibious warfare, and Castlereagh himself, as we have already seen, showed an occasional if fleeting interest in such possibilities. But a large proportion of the 20,000 British troops in the Mediterranean were tied to defensive responsibilities; more troops would have been needed for serious operations, and these would have added to the already almost intolerable shortage of specie. It is possible that the troops in Sicily might have been used more aggressively and purposefully than they were, but owing to problems of communication over so great a distance, such decisions had largely to be left to the discretion of commanders on the spot with intimate knowledge of current local conditions. Here Castlereagh's choice of the victor of Maida, Sir John Stuart, was a bad one, for as Commander-in-Chief in Sicily he displayed little energy or perception. But at best, it seems that any Italian offensive must have been on a small scale, while Napoleon at this point in his career showed no disposition to be diverted from his main

[1] L. A. Thiers, *Histoire du Consulat et de l'Empire* (1845–69), xi. 218.

objectives by mere pinpricks. He was prepared to run great
risks in Italy in order to win the critical battles in central
Europe. Therefore, although Castlereagh displayed some
interest in a Mediterranean offensive in May 1809, he soon put
his main trust in the Walcheren expedition and the war in Spain,
and shortly before his resignation he began to reduce the
Mediterranean to a defensive theatre once again.[1]

To establish doubts as to the wisdom of an alternative policy
is not, however, to remove doubts concerning the policy actually
implemented. The margin between military success and failure
is often a narrow one — one has only to consider Napoleon and
the battle of Marengo or some of the episodes in the career of
Nelson to appreciate this — and whereas failure tends to
compound every error, success tends to obscure them. Walcheren
was a disaster, and all associated with the expedition suffered in
consequence, perhaps more than their just deserts. Napier
condemned it as the largest, the worst-planned and worst-
conducted of British expeditions. Fortescue, more restrainedly,
concluded, 'The Cabinet, therefore, finally decided to devote all
their strength to an operation so difficult and delicate that the
slightest mishap must wreck it. . . .'[2] Wellington and Napoleon,
however, criticised the tactics of rather than the idea behind the
expedition, whilst the French general in command at Flushing,
Monnet, insisted that at the outset of the expedition, the locally
available French forces were so weak and badly organised that a
rapid advance on Antwerp must have been decisive.[3]

All authorities, whether for or against the expedition, are in
agreement on one point — the need for speedy action against
Antwerp before the French could collect reinforcements. Likewise all are broadly in agreement that speed was not the keynote
of the British expedition, even if they disagree over the
distribution of blame for its absence. The expedition sailed later

[1] Mackesy, especially pp. 333, 357, 389, 394. As we have already
seen, the Iberian Peninsula, according to Wellington, could absorb no
more British troops, *C.C.* vii. 112–16.

[2] Fortescue, *British Statesmen*, p. 229.

[3] *C.C.* vi. 328. Thiers, xi. 200 ff. Napoleon declared that Britain 'la
manqua par la impéritie', La Comte de las Cases, *Le Mémorial de
Sainte Hélène* (1948), i. 104.

than it should have done; it was handicapped at some points by bad weather, but more so by the lack of drive and dashing qualities on the part of the military commander, 'the late Lord Chatham'. There were some tactical errors, and the expedition steadily fell behind the necessary time schedule until not only was Antwerp unassailable, but half the army was falling or would fall victims to the Walcheren fever. Thereby a military defeat was turned into a military disaster on a scale hitherto unknown.

Castlereagh's share of the responsibility for this catastrophe needs careful examination. Although he was the strongest and most persistent advocate of the expedition in the cabinet, the responsibility for the decision was not solely his. In particular, he was not to blame for the long delay before a firm decision was taken, a delay which contributed to the ultimate failure. He was opposed by most of the professional experts at the Horse Guards, and was further handicapped by the fact that the Duke of York had recently been driven to resign, and the new Commander-in-Chief, Sir David Dundas, was a cautious veteran still introducing himself to his work. The opposition of the military was finally overborne by political and financial considerations — this was the best and cheapest way to aid the Austrians; but there remained the task of assembling 40,000 troops and some 600 ships. That so many troops were available is ample testimony to the impressive work of reconstruction which Castlereagh and others had achieved since the return of the ragged remnants from Corunna, and in the training of new recruits. Unfortunately the press was full of reports of a great expedition to the continent from the beginning of July, and its destination was known from the 17th, eleven days before it sailed.[1]

The insufficiency of intelligence on which the expedition was based has already been noted, though Castlereagh in general seems to have been active in its quest. It was more unfortunate that his instructions to Chatham were not more precise and emphatic, for the latter lacked the instinctive perceptiveness of a Nelson or Wellesley in a given military situation. Consequently, although Castlereagh included the need for haste, and

[1] Gray, pp. 278–81.

wrote of the desirability of proceeding at once with 'a considerable force against Antwerp, which may be reinforced as soon as Flushing is invested, if not actually reduced', he failed to make it clear that the capture of Antwerp would alone justify the expedition. Indeed, the instructions suggested that secondary objectives might offer some consolation to the government should Antwerp hold out, and Chatham was told to use his 'utmost endeavours . . . to secure as many of the objects above pointed out as the circumstances of the moment will permit . . .'. This was perhaps a necessary discretionary power, but as expressed the instructions allowed the leisurely and methodical Chatham to think too much in terms of lesser objects, and too little in terms of reaching Antwerp in the shortest possible time. Only the capture of Antwerp could really justify the government's decision to undertake so ambitious and dangerous an enterprise.

The favourite criticism of the tactical opening of the operation is that the British failed to make a determined effort to seize the island of Kadzand, which forms the southern shore of the West Scheldt. This was lightly protected, and a much easier proposition than Flushing on the opposite shore, which soon attracted the bulk of the British forces. With Kadzand in British hands, it would have been sufficient to mask Flushing, and to have used the Weiling Channel to Antwerp. This failure to secure Kadzand, and the consequent delay before Flushing, robbed the expedition of whatever chance of success it possessed. Castlereagh, with the commanders on the spot, failed to appreciate the significance of this failure. Flushing did not fall until the middle of August; sickness was already beginning to appear among the British troops; bad weather and a lack of co-operation between the naval and military commanders added to the troubles, and every day saw the French strengthening their hold on Antwerp. On 27 August Chatham abandoned all hope of taking that city, a correct decision in the circumstances, but the only justification for the continuing effort to hold the island of Walcheren could now be the hope that it would encourage the Austrians to renew the struggle. Before the expedition had even sailed, news had reached London of the decisive French victory over the Austrians at Wagram, and of the subsequent Austrian request for an armistice. But British hopes lingered on until the end of October that the Austrians would not conclude a peace treaty, and only when that prospect was finally disappointed was the evacuation of Walcheren approved.[1] By then Castlereagh had been out of office for more than a month.

There remains the question of Walcheren fever, apparently a combination of malaria, typhus and typhoid, and caused by an inadequate diet and heavy drinking among the troops, reinforced by too much fruit and general dampness. It cost the expedition 20,000 dead and sick. Castlereagh had been made aware of the sickliness of the area in the late summer during previous discussions of a possible landing on the island. Before the expedition sailed, one of the naval advisers, Sir Home Popham, spoke of the dangers of sickness through delay. Yet the army medical board was not warned of the expedition's destination beforehand, a strange obeisance to security in the light of the press publicity of July. Had the expedition been a success, much of the sickness might have been avoided, but confinement to the island of Walcheren was fatal. The fever there soon reached proportions far beyond the capacity of even a forewarned medical organisation, or indeed a much more efficient medical organisation than existed at this time. Castlereagh made great efforts to send what aid he could during his last days in office, but immediate evacuation was the only method open to the government which could lessen the disaster, and this it declined to do for the political reasons already mentioned. In this way was human error and incompetence compounded to bring about the final tragedy.[2]

Castlereagh resigned his office in September 1809 for reasons to be explained in the next chapter. But without his famous quarrel with Canning, his position in the cabinet could well have been jeopardised by the Walcheren disaster, and by the bad news that was arriving from the Peninsula. Wellesley was retreating to Portugal, and with Austria seeking terms with

[1] Yonge, i. 280–4.
[2] T. H. McGuffie, 'The Walcheren Expedition and the Walcheren Fever', *English Historical Review*, lxii. 191–202. There is no evidence of any real effort afterwards to avoid a repetition of a disaster of this type.

Napoleon, Britain's war fortunes were once again at a low ebb, almost as low as at the time of Tilsit. Briefly, British and Austrian victories had raised unreasonable expectations in the public mind, and now the reaction was as unreasonable in the opposite direction. In such circumstances Castlereagh was an obvious scapegoat, and his quarrel and duel with Canning may even have been a blessing in disguise. They removed him from office before the Walcheren disaster had run its dreadful course; they removed him in highly dramatic circumstances which not only won him sympathy, but also diverted attention to some extent from the failures with which he was associated. From the backbenches he was able to stage a considerable come-back early in the New Year as a defender of the Walcheren expedition, and to begin the process of restoring his reputation far earlier than he might otherwise have done.

Modern historians have gone further, and have begun to ask whether his tenure of the office of Secretary of State for War was so disastrous as contemporaries believed. Fortescue and Glover have indeed rated him among the greatest British ministers of war.[1] This may seem surprising in the light of the Walcheren expedition, the failure of two Spanish campaigns, and the reduction of Britain's position in the Peninsula to a toe-hold. One recalls also the criticisms of Moore, Wellington and Dundas of his efforts at strategic planning. Castlereagh in fact had no military experts in his department to assist him in such matters, and his correspondence with Wellington in 1808 shows his concern to find at least an *ad hoc* substitute. It should also be clear that some of his undoubted errors were compounded by those of others, especially in the Walcheren disaster. Furthermore, conditions were not right for major British victories at any point on the continent; Britain could not fight without allies, and even the Spaniards had much to learn in the art of guerrilla warfare. In a sense, almost any major British military move was foredoomed to failure at this time simply because no other continental army could keep the field against the French. Yet what would have been Britain's reputation in Europe had she refrained from intervention because she was not guaranteed certain success? To act was necessary for her own moral position

[1] Fortescue, *British Statesmen*, p. 228. Glover, p. 13 n.

Disciples catching the Mantle

and influence; she had to act to encourage her allies, for all their weakness. At times even defeat was not all loss, as both Spanish campaigns demonstrated. Continental campaigning had more point than the conquest of French colonies, and, despite the current disappointments, the Iberian Peninsula was to prove the most rewarding battlefield of the war for British arms. Time would vindicate Castlereagh's decision to fight on the defensive in the Mediterranean. In the long run his improvements to the transport service, and in the recruitment of Britain's land forces, were to contribute to the final victory. Castlereagh had certainly proved himself an abler Secretary of State for War than any of his predecessors.

4

The Pittites without Pitt
1806-12

The military campaigns in the summer of 1809 had ended in disappointment or disaster; this situation in itself might have brought about a ministerial crisis in the autumn, and perhaps driven Castlereagh from office. As it happened, these circumstances did no more than strengthen the arguments of George Canning that the ministry should be recast in order to achieve a more efficient direction of the war, and — it is not unfair to add *sotto voce* — to promote the interest of George Canning himself. The crisis precipitated by Canning was to drive himself and Castlereagh out of the ministry, and though Spencer Perceval and Liverpool were able to reconstitute it, there was to be a continual quest for reinforcements, and its long-term prospects were often in doubt. Repeatedly the years 1806–12 were to underline the problem of maintaining the party or government of Mr. Pitt without the leadership of Pitt himself. Indeed, only the fortuitous quarrel of George III with the Ministry of All the Talents in 1807 may have saved the Pittites from disintegration, or at least from a very real diminution of strength. Thereafter their survival in office owed much to equally fortuitous circumstances, such as the failure of any other combination of politicians to possess the confidence of the King, or later of the Prince Regent, and also of Parliament. These shifts of fortune were of vital consequence to Castlereagh's future career, for it was only in a ministry dominated by Pittites that he was likely to hold a leading place. As a result of the political developments of these years, he not only found high office open to him in 1812, but through the personal misadventures of his old colleagues the

lead in the House of Commons devolved upon him. He was not
Prime Minister, but for the last ten years of his life he was to be
the most important member of the government. The six years of
uncertainty following the death of Pitt were to be finally resolved
in favour of the ascendancy of Castlereagh and Liverpool. It
is the purpose of this chapter to try to show how this came about.

When Pitt died in January 1806 he left no heir-apparent; only
several pretenders. Nor did he leave, as he would have done
thirteen years earlier, something in the nature of a set of unifying
political principles. Almost all his energies in his last years had
been devoted to the defeat of France. Pitt, in any case, resembled
his father in that he believed he should and could transcend
parties; his own followers rarely numbered more than fifty.
Pitt thought in terms of governing as the King's minister,
supported by the 'King's Friends' and those who normally
supported any government that had not palpably lost the public
confidence. He aspired to attract as wide a range of talent in
support of his ministry as possible. The intangibles that
cemented his ministry were the name of Pitt, and the fact that he
governed as the King's minister. Even his ministers were far
from being a team, as Pitt's preference for conducting business
through individuals encouraged rivalry between them for his
favour and notice. It is not surprising, therefore, that on his
death his ministers at once recognised that there was no one
among them to fill his place, nor did the ministry possess
sufficient cohesion and influence to continue in office on a col-
lective basis. Resignation was a matter of course; some Pittites
expected the disintegration of the party to follow as naturally.

The group had four leading personalities, Hawkesbury,
Perceval, Canning and Castlereagh. Of these Castlereagh had
only a minute following, nor was he popular or well known in
Parliament. He did not try to emulate Canning's famous dinners,
or his roaring progress through the social high-spots; he had
few close friends, and his future political advancement was to be
achieved by administrative competence, by his obvious mastery
of many subjects, and by his influence in the inner counsels of the
Pittites.[1] His power over the House of Commons was to come

---

[1] One of the few to be convinced of Castlereagh's promise was the
famous ex-diplomat, Malmesbury, iv. 270, 278.

much later, and was to grow out of his success elsewhere. But
clearly he had no claim to the leadership in 1806; on the other
hand, no more had any of his colleagues. Canning, in particular,
despite all his outstanding gifts, was too volatile to command
proper respect for his judgement and dependability, and in
1806–7, of all the Pittites, he seemed the most convinced that
they had no future. Indeed, had the Talents lasted a little longer,
he might have been admitted to their ranks. As for Hawkesbury
and Perceval, their claims to the leadership were no more self-
evident than those of Castlereagh himself. Of the Pittite
predicament Romilly remarked, 'It is not very encouraging to a
party to have no leader but one who is dead'.

The Pittites were as divided on the question of parliamentary
tactics. In any case there existed in the early nineteenth century
no consensus as to the proper conduct of parties out of office; the
idea of 'formed opposition' was unpopular with many. Among
the Pittites themselves at this time, some wished to oppose the
Talents as little as possible, others favoured opposition on all
issues. Castlereagh adopted a middle position, reserving his
main criticisms for Windham's military policies, and for the bill
to abolish the slave trade. Not surprisingly the normal parliamentary impact of the Pittites was negligible, and Grenville
remarked that from their benches in the Lords he heard grumbling rather than 'formed opposition'. Often their backbench
attendance was so desultory that the party dared not divide the
House. On the whole their position was deteriorating, especially
after the death of Fox in the Autumn of 1806. His death removed
one feeble unifying force — that of a common antipathy — but
more important it opened the possibility of the Leadership of the
Commons to Canning. Fox's successor, Howick, seemed likely
soon to succeed his ailing father in the Lords.[1] The Pittites had
maintained their unity in the face of Grenville's overtures in the
summer of 1806 — they were unlikely to do so a second time.
With the failure of the Talents' peace negotiations with
Napoleon in 1806 the question of war and peace no longer
divided them, and the Pittites' common principles were reduced
to little more than a dislike of Sidmouth — one of the components of the Talents — and the veneration of their dead leader.

[1] Cf. Rolo, *Canning*, pp. 81–82, and Gray, pp. 58–71.

By the beginning of 1807 it seemed to Castlereagh and Perceval that the only course open to the party was to accept the leadership of an aristocratic figurehead — in this case the aged Portland, who was sustained by heavy doses of laudanum — and to preserve their unity in the hope that the King and Grenville might seek a new ministerial combination at the expense of the Foxites. The main incentive for unity was thus reduced to the hope of using it to gain office. This policy was not to be tested in practice, for soon afterwards a Catholic relief measure divided the King from his ministers, and also separated Sidmouth from the rest of the cabinet. In the ensuing government crisis the Pittites were able to present themselves to the notice of the King as an alternative ministry. They duly returned to office under Portland, giving a firm pledge to the King that under no circumstances would they propose any measure of Catholic relief in his lifetime. There followed an election in which the new government made considerable use of the 'No Popery' appeal, although Lord Holland — not usually a favourable witness on Castlereagh's career — makes the interesting comment that he suspected that both Castlereagh and Canning worked to lessen the Protestant fanaticism of their colleagues.[1]

Portland kissed hands on April Fool's Day, 1807. It might have been an omen, for many of the ministry's subsequent difficulties were of its own making. Its initial parliamentary strength surprised even the cabinet; an election added perhaps 60 new supporters, while the government could rely on those who normally supported the King's ministers. Wilberforce and Sidmouth and their friends would be found in the government lobby on many issues, and the ministry also benefited from the prejudice against 'formed' opposition. Finally, although government electoral influence and patronage were in decline, they were still important. There were perhaps 16 Treasury boroughs; more could be won in alliance with local interests. About 75 members of Parliament were office-holders, or in receipt of pensions and sinecures. George III, however, was reluctant to grant honours on the lavish scale practised by Pitt, while the strength of parliamentary and public feeling against government 'influence' was such that its remnants had to be utilised with

[1] Holland, *Memoirs*, ii. 216.

great discretion. Indeed, in 1809, Thomas Grenville was to comment that 'the influence of what they call corruption is, for practical purposes, too small rather than too great'.[1]

Castlereagh was to gain personal experience in the spring of 1809 of the dangers of arousing public suspicion in these matters. The East India patronage committee revealed in March 1809 that he had planned to place a Company writership at the disposal of Lord Clancarty to help him win a parliamentary seat in 1805. Nothing had come of the plan, and the Speaker thought that though there was a prima facie case of breach of privilege, it seemed as 'slight' an instance as was possible. A Commons' majority of 50 accepted Castlereagh's apology, Wilberforce grudgingly agreeing that an adverse vote would have been 'too severe for such an offence'. A second charge of electoral corruption against both Castlereagh and Perceval was so general and mismanaged that it was easily defeated amid one of the noisiest scenes ever witnessed at Westminster.[2] The charges did, however, injure Castlereagh's reputation in general, and weakened his position in the cabinet, even with his uncle, Camden. The incidents were a warning of the intensity of feeling against government 'corruption', and also showed that though 'influence' might still help to secure a majority, ministers were also heavily dependent on the respect and confidence of independent backbenchers, who now numbered about half the Commons. Although Pitt's colleagues were to hold office, in various combinations, for 23 years, they were haunted for much of the time by the shadow of those backbenchers. In fact, they were to lose only two votes of confidence; that of 1812 was soon to be reversed; only that in 1830 was to prove fatal.

Ministers frequently wrote of the precariousness of their position, and their fate really hinged on the following conditions — their ability to retain the confidence of the Crown and the independent backbenchers, and the absence of an acceptable alternative ministry in the eyes of both. Although a majority of the House would normally accept the King's choice of ministers, this was not inevitable. A ministry had to possess a reasonable

[1] Foord, *English Historical Review*, lxii. 484–507.
[2] *Colchester Correspondence*, ii. 169–70, 186. *Life of Wilberforce*, iii. 406–8. Gray, pp. 207–8, 214.

proportion of the politicians of talent of the time, it had to display a reasonable competence and a reasonable respect for the wishes of the 'nation'. The Commons' readiness to accept a particular ministry and the King's range of choice of ministries would clearly be limited if no obvious and satisfactory alternative combination of ministers appeared to exist, and here the Portland ministry was greatly aided by the Catholic prejudices of the King, and by the doubts of many independent members concerning the unity of the Opposition, its attitude to the war, and the influence of the more radical elements that were growing up within it. The condition and principles of the Opposition therefore greatly contributed to the continuance of the Portland government, and were to continue to do so in rather different circumstances after 1809. This state of affairs was of the utmost importance for the survival of this essentially Pittite ministry despite its internal divisions, and actual split in 1809, and despite the fierce controversies that were excited by certain of its policies, especially in the conduct of the war.

The driving force of the ministry was provided by Canning, Hawkesbury, Eldon, Perceval and Castlereagh. Apart from the reliable Bathurst, the rest of the cabinet was composed of mediocrities, or worse. Portland was Prime Minister in name only, and was unable to weld his government into a team. It was, as Perceval remarked, 'a Government of Departments'. Richard Wellesley spoke of 'a want of concert in private and of apparent co-operation in public'. Despite the acquiescence of the majority of Parliament to the King's view that no better combination could be found, the government's reputation with the press and public was low. Confidence in the Greys and Grenvilles was not perhaps much greater, and the educated public was beginning to take an uncomfortable amount of interest in the reduction of political 'corruption', and even in parliamentary reform. The Orders in Council provoked some hostility; there were a few peace petitions, although the distress in the country was never sufficient to provoke a really serious outcry. The overall impact of the ministry, therefore, was not impressive, and all this encouraged talk of ministerial change even within the cabinet itself.

As the two ministers most concerned with the conduct of the

war, Castlereagh and Canning were the most exposed to
criticism. Canning, whose every brilliant virtue seemed to be
balanced by an equivalent vice, was viewed with considerable
suspicion by many; but on the whole it was Castlereagh whose
position in public esteem appeared generally the more vulnerable. As early as October 1807 the *Edinburgh Review* was
accusing him of 'puerility and mismanagement'; his unpopularity
was noted by several observers,[1] and his removal to another
office or to the House of Lords was rumoured in 1808. His solid
successes with recruitment and speedy transport of troops passed
without notice beside the setbacks to British armies, and the
controversies over Copenhagen and the Convention of Cintra.
Castlereagh's blunt and imperturbable defence of unpopular
causes was as yet appreciated and applauded by few witnesses.
Corunna and the corruption charges early in 1809 still further
lowered his prestige, and it was these weaknesses that Canning
now set out to exploit in his endeavour in 1809 to bring the war
in Europe entirely under his control.[2]

In the first year or two of the Portland ministry, Castlereagh
and Canning had co-operated in defence of a strong line in the
implementation of the Orders in Council, and they were at one
in their sympathy for Irish Catholics. This, however, was a dead
issue, and gradually their differences over strategy began to
dominate their relations. There were hints of differences between
them over Sicily and Spain in 1808; they recommended opposing
strategies for the Peninsula early in 1809. Canning felt that
Castlereagh should not have supported Wellington and Moore
the way he did in 1808 and at the beginning of 1809. Finally he
unfairly attributed to Castlereagh part of the blame for the
army's refusal to contemplate offensive operations in northern
Europe until June–July 1809. In March and April 1809, although
Canning was ably assisting in the defence of Castlereagh against
charges of electoral corruption, in private he had begun his
agitation for the removal of Castlereagh from the post of
Secretary of State for War. He was seeking the support of
Richard Wellesley in his bid to increase his influence in the
cabinet, and he finally persuaded Portland that Wellesley should

[1] *Bathurst MSS.*, p. 102. Buckingham, *George III*, iv. 277, 283.
[2] See above, pp. 75 ff.

succeed Castlereagh, though not, as Portland insisted, until
Parliament was prorogued at the end of the session. Procrastination was now almost the sum total of Portland's political
tactics, and Canning's impatience soon revived. In June the
influence of the King was needed to prevent Canning's resignation, and to persuade him to agree to a new arrangement
whereby Canning himself was to assume control of the whole
war in Europe from the end of the session, while Castlereagh
was to retain his colonial responsibilities with the Board of
Control as compensation. To this Canning reluctantly assented,
and it is doubtful if Castlereagh would have acquiesced, had the
offer ever been made to him.

The plan was in fact smashed by Perceval, who, sensing that
Canning's real purpose was to gain control both of the war and
of the cabinet, intervened to postpone any cabinet re-shuffle until
the outcome of the Walcheren expedition was known. The
almost incapacitated Portland could not, however, prevent the
continuance of indecisive and damaging negotiations in July and
August. Many of the cabinet were insisting upon Castlereagh's
retention in some important post, and saw that upon the outcome
of this issue rested the fate of their own place in the cabinet
vis-à-vis Canning. In short, the still unsuspecting Castlereagh
had become a shuttlecock between the rival factions in the
cabinet. Just when a compromise of sorts appeared to be
emerging, with Castlereagh to replace Camden as Lord
President of the Council, Portland was smitten by a paralytic
stroke. Canning, emboldened by news of military disaster from
Walcheren and of retreat from Spain, delivered his ultimatum
on 2 September; Castlereagh must be replaced by Wellesley at
once. It was Perceval, however, as leader of the anti-Canning
faction, who really seized the initiative. He quickly persuaded
Portland to agree tor esign, to drop the Camden–Castlereagh
plan, and to support the retention of Castlereagh in the cabinet.
Portland informed Canning of these developments on 6
September, and it was this which led to his non-attendance at a
cabinet on the following day. Castlereagh's inquiries into the
reasons for his absence gradually elicited part of the truth from a
reluctant Camden over dinner. But he had learned enough to
perceive the invidious position in which he had been placed, and

he at once resigned. This began a spate of resignations, or threats thereof, and by 18 September, only six members of the cabinet were ostensibly prepared to remain in office.

Canning in the interval had made his bid for the Premiership, and failed. He denounced the succession to the Premiership of another aristocratic figurehead, he insisted that there must be an efficient first minister in the Commons for the direction of the war, the government of departments must end. On the one hand he urged Portland to recommend Perceval as his successor, but stated that he could not agree to serve under him. To the King, Canning strove to demonstrate his own suitability for the vacant post, an effort which, however, astounded rather than impressed the old monarch. His conduct, following the paralysis of Portland, confirmed the belief of several ministers that the determination to oust Castlereagh was now no more than part of his strategy to secure the Premiership. Had the future of Castlereagh himself been the real issue, Portland's paralysis and obviously imminent resignation would have afforded an admirable excuse for a total recasting of the ministry, in which Castlereagh might have accepted another post with no loss of face. As it happened, Canning's rash miscalculation of his own influence and strength played into the hands of the more diplomatic Perceval, who, by the beginning of October, was emerging as the obvious successor to Portland. Weak as his ministry undoubtedly would be, it was still stronger and more acceptable to the King and Parliament than any other combination.

Meanwhile, the sensational duel between Canning and Castlereagh had already been fought. The unsavoury story of the intrigues against him had been gradually unfolded to Castlereagh in the fortnight following his resignation. His slow acquaintance with the facts explains why a delay of twelve days occurred before the issue of his challenge to Canning. He did so mainly on the ground that Canning had secretly conspired against him, and he refused to be dissuaded when Perceval produced letters showing that Canning had protested against the continuation of the secret negotiations. The duel was therefore fought on Wimbledon Common on 21 September. When both missed with their first shots, Castlereagh insisted on further satisfaction, and in the second exchange he wounded Canning in the thigh — not seriously — and himself lost a button from his coat. The duel revealed a side of Castlereagh's character which was not often shown in public; several contemporaries remarked on it. Wilberforce, groping for an explanation for the perturbation of the imperturbable, thought it looked like 'a cold-blooded measure of deliberate revenge'. Perceval thought Castlereagh ill-advised, and tried to prevent the duel, and both he and Eldon agreed that Canning alone could not be held responsible for the secrecy. As Charles Ellis remarked, Canning had been called on to fight a duel 'not for his own sake, but for Portland's, Camden's or Hawkesbury's, or almost anybody's but his own'. Romilly went further and declared that even if all Castlereagh's allegations against Canning were accepted at their face value, 'yet there was nothing in all this which any man of the most punctilious sense of honour could think required an appeal to arms'. Thus, although there was widespread agreement that Canning had made some bad mistakes, well-informed contemporaries thought there was much that was illogical and simply emotional in Castlereagh's conduct.

Castlereagh sought to explain his conduct to his family in the following terms. 'I hope my publick and private character will survive the perils to which it has been exposed, but you may imagine what would have been the impression had I submitted to be duped and practised upon, and how small a portion of the world would have believed that I was not *privy* to *my own disgrace* . . .'. He distinguished between the conduct of Canning and the rest of the cabinet by insisting that the latter were moved by 'good intentions', and would never have sought his removal without Canning's prompting. This was true, but many contemporaries did not accept this as adequate justification for his conduct. Castlereagh's insistence on a second shot seemed to underline the emotional motives.[1] In general the episode provides striking evidence of the volcanic forces that struggled for

---

[1] Gray, pp. 242–53. G. Fox-Strangeways, *Further Memoirs of the Whig Party, 1807–21* (1905), p. 35. Rose, *Correspondence*, ii. 349–423. Romilly, *Memoirs*, ii. 293–4n. Lane Poole, *Stratford Canning*, i. 74–76. Marchioness of Londonderry, *Castlereagh* (1904), pp. 38–44.

expression at times beneath what Croker was later to describe
as that 'splendid summit of bright and polished frost', and of
which there exist a few other hints before his suicide in 1822.
Castlereagh, indeed, is reputed to have fought a romantic duel
in his youth in Ireland, while both in Ireland in the 1790s and
later in England he displayed so contemptuous — even reckless
and provocative — a form of bravery in face of the 'mob' as to
suggest an urge to find some form of emotional relief from his
customary impassive behaviour.[1]

Castlereagh left office in September 1809 under the shadow of
military defeat and the duel. Canning's stock had fallen even
lower with most people, although *The Day* in 1810 could see
nothing to choose between them. Canning was worth a song,
and Castlereagh was the equivalent of an Irishman's blessing or
a bad shilling.[2] The political situation, however, promised that
their eclipse might be no more than temporary, and as early as
the spring of 1810 the Perceval ministry began to explore the
possibility of their inclusion. Castlereagh himself had a following
of no more than three or four in the Commons, but his uncle,
Camden, was still in the cabinet, while a second uncle, Lord
George Seymour, was connected with the new Foreign Secretary,
Richard Wellesley. The latter, as ever full of ambition, was
anxious to build up a political following of his own, and both
Castlereagh and Canning seemed likely protégés. Nor was
Castlereagh himself content to wait upon events, but forced
himself back into prominence with his support of an Opposition
motion for an inquiry into the Walcheren expedition. Creevey[3]
noted his evident and intense excitement when the government
was defeated, and the way was open for his three-hour defence of
his conduct on 26 March 1810. One need not take too seriously
the claim of the pro-government *Sun* that this was the best
speech since the death of Pitt, but it undoubtedly benefited both
himself and the government.[4] This speech, with others, stamped
him as one of the most effective spokesmen on the government's
backbenches. Even in economic matters where he was less sure,
and despite one effort on 7 May 1811 against the resumption
of cash payments which a recent historian has described as

[1] Leigh, pp. 25–26, 320–1. See below, p. 260.   [2] Gray, p. 272.
[3] Creevey, i. 122–4.   [4] Buckingham, *George III*, iv. 425–7.

nonsense at the level of economic theory, he was a useful vote-gatherer.[1]

According to Plumer Ward, Perceval's thoughts were turning towards Castlereagh as early as November 1809,[2] though no actual advance proved possible until the following spring. The government was desperately weak in personnel, with only Perceval of the cabinet sitting in the Commons. Fortunately, the Opposition were weakened by divisions, and by ineffective leadership. On the major issue of the war, and upon the current domestic questions, the Perceval ministry spoke the language of the majority of the Commons. Even so, it could not afford to neglect any opportunity to augment its strength. Therefore in the spring of 1810 a general offer was made to Castlereagh, Canning and Sidmouth. Cabinet rivalries prevented a more selective approach, while the divisions between those approached made it quite impossible for them to accept. A more serious offer was made to Canning and Castlereagh in the late summer of 1810, but once again it reflected the cabinet's divisions. The Foreign Secretary, Wellesley, desired to add Canning to the government, but the rest of the ministry would not admit Canning alone. Sidmouth would not serve with Canning at any price, so Castlereagh was again approached. He was offered the Admiralty, a strenuous office much suited to his temperament, and great pressure was brought to bear to secure his acceptance, especially through Lord Camden. But Castlereagh was adamant, insisting that though his quarrel with Canning was at an end, to enter the cabinet again so soon in his company would injure both the government and himself in the public eye.[3]

Before a further permutation of potential recruits could be attempted, politics were thrown into disarray by a recurrence of the King's insanity, which soon necessitated a regency. For the ministry and Opposition it was 1788 over again, with each making the same calculations, and pursuing the same policies. The former endeavoured to impose parliamentary restrictions upon the Regent's powers for at least his first year in office; the Opposition, in full expectation that their hour had at least struck, tried to hasten it by opposing any limits upon the

[1] Gray, p. 383.   [2] *Plumer Ward Memoirs*, i. 290–1.
[3] Buckingham, *George III*, iv. 429–55. Gray, pp. 391–9.

Regent. Castlereagh supported the ministry, but like most people he can have had little expectation that the government would long survive. The Regent, however, proved unexpectedly cautious. His relations with the Opposition were no longer so friendly as they had once been; he was not anxious to see the question of Catholic relief raised at that time; he was eager to see the war against Napoleon prosecuted with full rigour; and he could not trust Grenville and Grey in either of these matters. The Whig grandees, too, seemed unduly arrogant in their claims; they did not show a proper deference to the Prince's position. Nor could George resist the temptation to try his hand at cabinet making on his own account, and seek a broad-bottomed ministry once it was apparent that the King would not recover. Better men than he had chased this will-o'-the-wisp since 1801, and by the beginning of 1812 he was being driven to the conclusion that no ministry was likely to meet his immediate wishes more satisfactorily than the existing one. He did make one approach to the Whigs on 13 February 1812, but it was almost certainly phrased to provoke a refusal. Grenville described it as 'highly offensive', and the offer was proudly declined. Thus the Perceval ministry emerged from more than a year of precarious existence; the removal of the restrictions on the Regent's powers would not mean its replacement by the Whigs, and it is significant that Castlereagh now decided that he could at last make a positive response to the overtures which he was still receiving from Perceval.

The determination of the government to regain his services had become almost desperate at the beginning of 1812 with the resignation of Wellesley from the Foreign Office. The latter had never worked well with his colleagues, and now he repeated Canning's mistake of 1809, believing he could snatch the Premiership by a demonstration of his own indispensability in a period of political uncertainty. Castlereagh was offered the big prize of the Foreign Office, but he refused to be drawn at a time when the Prince Regent's intentions were still unknown, and when, if Wellesley were to become Premier, he might expect advancement from that quarter. He therefore replied that the basis of the ministry must be broadened by the inclusion of Sidmouth and some of the Regent's old friends, and he concluded, according to a correspondent of Buckingham, that 'he would be no stop-gap for any man, that when the restrictions [on the Regent] were at an end, and the Prince chose to make him an offer, he would receive it with humble duty and acknowledgement, and it would be time enough to give an answer'.[1] When the offer was renewed in February, following the end of these restrictions, Castlereagh had no hesitation in accepting, and without qualifications. Interestingly, the offer had nearly been changed to his old post as Secretary of State for War, but Liverpool, the present occupant, had argued against change at so critical a moment when Wellington was commencing his 1812 Peninsular campaign.

Castlereagh was a valuable acquisition for the ministry. Now in his early forties, he was in the prime of life. He was a more comfortable and reliable colleague than Canning or Wellesley. In contrast to the latter he attended cabinets regularly, he answered despatches regularly, and neither ignored nor despised his colleagues. He brought no embarrassing array of associates whose appetite for office, however minor, had to be satisfied. He brought with him few awkward personal prejudices or prickly matters of principle, and even though his sympathy for the Catholics compelled him to insist on the freedom to vote as he pleased on this issue, in one of his earliest speeches he insisted on the injudiciousness of raising that matter in the first half of 1812. Indeed, the cabinet had done better than most of them had at first appreciated. His reserve and aloofness had caused him to be widely under-estimated, whatever credit had been given to his business ability and his imperturbability. It was not long before a cruel stroke of fortune was to push Castlereagh to the very forefront of cabinet discussions, and in the defence of the government in the Commons.

Since the resignation of Castlereagh and Canning in 1809, Perceval had carried the burden of government spokesman in the Commons almost unaided. Castlereagh was a useful reinforcement, but on 11 May 1812 the strengthening prospects of the ministry were shattered by the assassination of the Prime Minister by a lunatic. Perceval had no stamp of greatness, but he had courage, determination and industry in ample measure.

[1] Buckingham, *Regency*, i. 218–19.

Above all he was trusted and respected by a majority of the independents, who distrusted brilliance, and admired and supported his dogged resistance to Napoleon. If many in trade and industry were becoming restless at his refusal to amend the Orders in Council in the face of growing American hostility and declining British exports, if even the House of Commons was becoming sharply critical, there was no reason as yet to doubt his hold on Parliament. His death created a void which no member of the cabinet could at once fill. Castlereagh himself was rumoured as a possible Premier, but he had been with the ministry for so short a time that this was hardly conceivable.[1] There was no other leading figure in the Commons, and Liverpool in the Lords could not at once arouse sufficient confidence. The cabinet certainly entertained no false illusions as to their prospects; Castlereagh thought their survival most unlikely unless 'a proposition' was first made to some other leading politicians. In the eyes of the Regent, Wellesley and Canning were obviously the first to approach. Not all the cabinet were so happy at this prospect; some for fear of their Catholic sympathies, others out of dislike for their personalities and conduct in general; and all feared that their admission would forfeit as much parliamentary support for the ministry as it would gain. Castlereagh's position would also be difficult, and he offered his resignation to facilitate negotiations, and also declined to take part in the cabinet discussions on this matter. But the cabinet were determined to retain him as Leader in the Commons, with Liverpool as Premier, and approached Wellesley and Canning on that basis. The approach failed, as Castlereagh may well have foreseen, but three days later, on 21 May, the Commons intervened and gave a majority of four to Stuart Wortley's motion of no confidence in the present government. Although many members were clearly waiting on events — only about half voted on this important issue — the ministry had no option but to resign.[2]

There followed more than a fortnight of complex negotiations between the Regent, Wellesley, Moira, Grey and Grenville, whose intricacies it is not necessary to follow here. The outcome of these talks was to demonstrate the impracticability of any

[1] Buckingham, *Regency*, i. 293–300.   [2] Yonge, i. 389.

other ministry, given the ill-feeling between the Whigs and the Regent, and the incompatibility of Wellesley with his late colleagues. If he would doubtless have preferred a broader-based ministry, the Regent still returned to Liverpool and his colleagues with considerable relief. They could be trusted to fight the war with the utmost vigour, and to postpone controversial and divisive domestic legislation. Even if Castlereagh and others insisted on the right to vote as they chose on the Catholic issue, this was still the most satisfactory ministry the Regent could hope for in this matter. Furthermore, although the Whigs led the largest group in the Commons, perhaps 150 in all, a sufficient number of unattached members were once again convinced that this was the best ministry obtainable in the current political circumstances. The doubts that were responsible for the success of Wortley's motion were banished, and the ministry gained a majority of 125 when it first faced the House. Such a majority could not, of course, be relied upon in all circumstances, and almost at once parliamentary pressure greatly influenced, if it did not wholly determine, the government's retreat over the Orders in Council. The government's front-bench strength in the Commons was also perilously weak. Apart from Castlereagh as Leader of the House, as well as Foreign Secretary, there were only Vansittart, Chancellor of the Exchequer and no debater, the insignificant Bragge Bathurst, and a number of junior ministers who, like Palmerston, were of little use outside their own specialised fields. Consequently it is not surprising to find the cabinet resuming its search for more support.

The obvious person to strengthen the front bench in the Commons was Canning. Castlereagh was prepared to yield the Foreign Office to him and become Chancellor of the Exchequer. But he, and all his colleagues insisted that he must remain Leader of the House. It was on this point that the negotiations broke down. Canning insisted, and it is possible he may have been over-persuaded by his supporters, that either the Leadership of the House should be shared between Castlereagh and himself, or some third person must be appointed. Canning might easily have been quoted against himself, after his earlier denunciation of figureheads and a government of departments in

1809. Either system would have been unworkable — especially with Canning. The negotiations therefore collapsed, and Canning sacrificed his chance to assist in the direction of the final coalition against Napoleon. Castlereagh was spared the tenure of an office for which he had no obvious talents, where the opportunities to achieve distinction were less, and a situation in which he would have been remembered more as Leader of the House — and therefore the defender of the government's domestic policies — than as one of the main architects of the defeat of Napoleon and the reconstruction of Europe.

The cabinet, having failed to secure the services of Canning in July 1812, decided on a dissolution, the traditional way to improve a government's majority. The general election that autumn was dull and uncontroversial, with only two county contests. Some forty seats were gained by the government, but support by the electorate did not mean support in the country as a whole. Trade was still uncertain, and Britain was now involved in war with the United States as well as Napoleon's empire. Unemployment and low wages bred massive discontent; the Luddites were busy; disturbances, actual and feared, tied down 12,000 troops in the North and Midlands. One of Castlereagh's first acts as Leader of the House was to introduce legislation to strengthen the hand of the government and local authorities against these dangers. Until trade began to pick up, the government was handicapped by the hostility of many of the middle classes towards itself, by the reluctance of juries to convict the disorderly, and by the reluctance of many local authorities to act with vigour lest they should inflame public opinion against themselves.[1] If these circumstances helped to draw the landed gentry and the wealthiest classes closer to the ministry, the general atmosphere of the country was not a happy one.

Yet 1812 was to be the last year of acute domestic and political excitement until the end of the war. The change of mood came swiftly in the winter of 1812–13, with Napoleon's retreat from Moscow, the consequent opening of new markets in Europe, and Wellington's advance into Spain. This sudden improvement in the nation's fortunes reduced parliamentary

[1] E. P. Thompson, *English Working Class*, pp. 552–602.

criticism to a minimum; for the next two years there were to be no domestic politics of real significance. Since 1807 the Pittites had clung uneasily to office; for the rest of the war their hold on office was secure. As for Castlereagh, the chances of politics had placed him at the Foreign Office, an office for which he had shown no particular preference, but which was to assure him a very special place in British nineteenth-century history.

5

Wars and Peace-making
1812–15

The Times remarked on Castlereagh's appointment to the Foreign Office: 'his name, above all others, is noted for mischance; he has been the very darling of misfortune'. Yet within a short time he had made himself so much at home in his new post that none but his most inveterate enemies thought of his removal, save to the Premiership, or as a result of the government's overthrow. Before his appointment, his experience of foreign affairs had been enlarged by the general purview obtainable as a member of the cabinet, and by the specific aspects of foreign affairs that had involved him at the Board of Control and as Secretary of State for War. It is clear that he turned gladly from the affairs of India to those of Europe, even when entrusted with the Board of Control. His memoranda on war and peace with France in 1802–3 revealed an intelligent if sometimes rather academic appreciation of the problems. His next office thrust him into the heart of the struggle in Europe, and entangled him in the intricacies of power politics. In quick succession he grappled with Prussian hesitations, Sicilian ambiguities, Swedish eccentricities, and Spanish pride, all of which profoundly influenced British strategy. Pitt took him into his confidence on many European matters, notably when drafting his design for a grand peace settlement in 1805. European problems remained his prime interest both in and out of office from 1806, and among his latest sources of information was that remarkable Corsican, Pozzo di Borgo, ex-republican deputy of the French National Assembly, one-time Russian diplomatic agent, a future diplomatic rival, and now prudently 'travelling' while that more famous Corsican and the Tsar Alexander I continued their uncertain friendship.[1] Castlereagh was thus well prepared for his new office, even if he had not previously held the seals of the Foreign Office.

Castlereagh inherited a bleak prospect from his predecessor. As yet there were few signs in Europe of the tremendous changes that were impending; relations with the United States were approaching a critical point; the sharp fall in British trade and prosperity since 1810 was leading to popular distress and disturbance; the government was being reduced to desperate expedients to supply Wellington in the Peninsula with specie without any assurance as yet of compensating victories in return.[2] At a lower level, Wellesley had left the Foreign Office, its organisation, and the mechanics of diplomacy in poor shape. Morier declared that 'the confusion that reigns at the Foreign Office is incredible. Everything they can put off they willingly do so, and procrastination and indecision are the order of the day.[3]' Several British diplomats overseas, notably in Constantinople, Rio de Janeiro and Washington, had been left with little or no guidance. Liverpool doubted if Wellesley had attended half the cabinets called while he was Foreign Secretary; his experience as Governor-General of India had eliminated whatever ability he might have once possessed to compromise and work with others. That 'brilliant incapacity', as Croker described him, was 'more capable of doing extraordinary things well than conducting ordinary transactions with safety or propriety'.[4] His successor may not have been brilliant, but he was undoubtedly capable.

This is not to say that Castlereagh did much to improve the efficiency of the Foreign Office itself. The staff remained small, certainly compared with that employed by Metternich, and was not noted for hard work or expertise. It would appear the Office possessed no real expert in the French language, or not one to spare, as Gentz, an Austrian, was often employed by Castlereagh at the Congress of Vienna in work involving a

[1] Buckingham, *Regency*, i. 203–5.
[2] *Bathurst MSS.*, p. xiv. Fortescue, ix. 13. Ward, *Wellington's Headquarters*, pp. 92–96.
[3] Lady Jackson, *The Bath Archives* (1873), i. 145.
[4] Fox-Strangeways, p. 113.

thorough command of French. Edward Cooke served as Under-Secretary of State, and significantly collapsed from over-work at Vienna. William Hamilton, who supervised the southern department, and Castlereagh's private secretary, Joseph Planta, were his main assistants. But he delegated as little as possible, drafting the bulk of the correspondence himself, and escaping with his boxes to his pleasant country retreat at North Cray in Kent. There, amid the delights of its flower gardens, the local walks and rides, he could write his letters and despatches in comfort, entertain ambassadors, and generally find such relaxation that even the hum of conversation in the drawing-room would not necessarily drive him to the seclusion of his study for serious work unless the policy in question was unusually 'metaphysical'.[1]

Anglo-American relations were to impose the first main test on his diplomatic skill, and Castlereagh was to find himself in the unfortunate position of being driven to concede the vital point to the Americans only to discover that the concession had been made too late to save the peace.[2] Admittedly the war was never much more than an expensive side-show from the British point of view, and it was probably never within Castlereagh's power to influence the course of events to any extent. At the same time there is no evidence to suggest that he was the well-meaning victim of circumstances beyond his control. His previous record with respect to the Orders in Council had shown more intransigence than Perceval, the most determined upholder of the Orders in Council immediately before his assassination. In so far as a policy of Castlereagh's own making emerges, it is that of a tactical and reluctant retreat in the face of overwhelming pressure. If he gave more attention to American problems, and showed more tact than his predecessor, he moved too slowly and reluctantly to save the peace.

Anglo-American relations had been deteriorating since 1806. British treatment of American goods and shipping as a result of

[1] Countess Brownlow, *Slight Reminiscences of a Septuagenarian*, (1867), pp. 191–2.

[2] For the origins of the Anglo-American War of 1812 see especially R. H. Brown, *The Republic in Peril, 1812* (1964), and B. Perkins, *Prologue to War* (1961).

the Orders in Council was the greatest single cause of dissension. Britain had also been guilty of impressing seamen from American ships on the ground that the seamen in question were British subjects. The American sense of humiliation as well as material loss was very real, and played into the hands of the small minority who wished for war. Even so, there was a reluctance on the part of the American government to push matters to extremes; this was especially true of President Madison. There had been various incidents, even a brief threat of war in 1807, but for the most part the American government had tried to supplement its diplomacy by economic pressure, which had become increasingly effective with the Non-Importation Act oi February 1811. British exports to the United States crashed during the following year. Sales to South America and Europe also fell sharply, and Britain faced a major economic crisis in the winter of 1811–12. Exports had fallen by over a quarter since 1810, and about half that loss was directly attributable to relations with the United States. But it did not need elaborate statistics to convince the suffering merchants and manufacturers, and for them to convince the still more unfortunate workers, that the Orders in Council were at the root of the trouble. The government indeed tried to confuse the Opposition with statistics, but Brougham retorted that one had only to use one's eyes in the industrial regions, and note the crowded poor-houses and debtors' prisons to perceive the fallacy in these figures. It was pressure from these discontented masses, expressed in thousands of petitions, and with Brougham spearheading the attack in the Commons, that was mainly responsible for the government's retreat.

Doubts concerning the Orders in Council had been expressed in the cabinet as early as 1811, but no change of policy had resulted. Wellesley had turned aside all American complaints and counter-proposals, at first in a manner that was both vague and arrogant, and later with imperious firmness. His conduct did much to harden American opinion, but his successor's greater attention and mildness of tone was no more acceptable. Some time elapsed before Castlereagh made his first gesture of conciliation, an offer to modify the British licensing of neutral trade to the American advantage. At the same time he tried to impress upon Washington that the much-acclaimed French repeal of the Milan and Warsaw decrees — which had done so much to concentrate American hostility against Britain — was nothing short of a fraud. President Madison was not impressed; indeed he later insisted that the 'letter seemed to shut out the prospects of conciliation, and the President considered war as the next necessary step to vindicate the rights and honour of the nation'. Nearly a month was in fact to elapse before the United States declared war, and even then the President and majority in Congress acted with no real enthusiasm. It is difficult to avoid the conclusion that had the British government repealed the Orders in Council more swiftly war would have been averted. The decisive pressure from the British public came too late, and until that time the British government had failed to appreciate American feelings concerning the Orders, impressment and other issues; they had failed to perceive that their policies were leaving the Americans with no option but to fight, and when they began to take the possibility of war seriously, they doubted the American ability to offer serious resistance.

Thus it was not until the end of April 1812 that the British government allowed itself to be persuaded by Parliament to accept a committee of inquiry into the question of the Orders in Council. Brougham's campaign had not borne speedy fruit, and even now the ministry was probably more intent on gaining time than enlightenment. But time bought in Parliament was time squandered in relations with the United States. Perceval's recent biographer believes that to the last he was hoping that no concession would be necessary, so wedded had he become to the Orders as an instrument against Napoleon.[1] His assassination both removed a major obstacle and caused ministerial confusion, so that for nearly a month — that is, until the Liverpool ministry was formed on 8 June — no decisions could be taken. Ironically, it appears that the fate of the Orders was not a matter of dispute in these ministerial negotiations; their repeal had become a matter of time and expediency. Tactical considerations continued to prevail for yet another week, despite ominous news from the United States. War was still not expected, or taken seriously if it came, even by Brougham.

[1] Gray, pp. 450–4.

A graceful retreat, a tactical victory were the respective aims of government and Opposition.

It required keen questioning from Brougham on 16 June to extort from Castlereagh a roundabout admission that the Orders in Council were to be unilaterally suspended, and a further week elapsed before all the details of British policy became clear. As Castlereagh admitted to some manufacturers who objected to such casuistry, 'Aye, but one does not like to own that we are forced to give way to our manufacturers.'[1] The retreat, however, had come too late. Unknown to him, the United States had already declared war, and when the final news of the revocation reached Washington late in July, Madison was more impressed by the qualifications in which the revocation was wrapped than in the revocation itself. In particular, the British reserved the right to reimpose the Orders from May 1813 if they were not satisfied with French and American conduct in the interval. The British were still legislating for the commerce of the whole world; they were still acting as though they expected everyone to understand, support and sympathise with their crusade against Napoleon. Nevertheless, British hopes of an early peace persisted, and were not abandoned until September 1812 when American counter-proposals included a demand for the end of British impressment.[2] Castlereagh's part in the whole background to the War of 1812 was of no great significance; he shared the prejudices and misconceptions of his colleagues, and it was not until 1814 that a distinctive touch begins to emerge in his conduct of Anglo-American relations.[3]

Meanwhile events were taking a new turn in Europe. Wellington's capture of the key fortresses of Ciudad Rodrigo and Badajoz in January and April 1812 had opened up central Spain to carefully controlled offensives. Much would depend

---

[1] *Wilberforce*, iv. 35.   [2] B. Perkins, *Castlereagh and Adams*, pp. 11–15.
[3] A further example of Anglo-American misunderstanding may be seen in the problem of certain Red Indian tribes. The Americans feared that British approaches to these tribes before the war were a sign of offensive intent, but Castlereagh himself remarked concerning the Indians, 'we are to consider not so much their Use as Allies, as their Destructiveness if Enemies', Perkins, *Prologue to War*, p. 285.

upon French distractions elsewhere in Europe, and the degree to which French forces in Spain could be weakened and scattered by Spanish guerrillas, but there was reason for mild optimism as Napoleon and the Tsar appeared to be on the brink of war. Nevertheless Castlereagh had good reason to move cautiously. Anglo-Russian relations in the early nineteenth century had been troubled by various differences even in the periods of co-operation against a common enemy. Although one of the reasons for the split between France and Russia had been the latter's desire for British goods, severe restrictions still hampered British trade, and were not lifted with the outbreak of the new war, and some indeed continued until 1815. All Russians were not enamoured with the idea of a new alliance with Britain; the Chancellor, Rumantzov, was particularly hostile, and strove to preserve the French connexion. The idea was popular in some circles that Russia should strive to maintain a balance between France and Britain, and every increase in British power was jealously watched.[1] Though Castlereagh did not yet know it, he would be able to counter the effect of many of these tendencies by his relationship with the Tsar Alexander I. That able but inconstant figure was to promote as well as obstruct many of the policies of Castlereagh by his transcendence of narrow Russian interests without, at the same time, formulating a consistent and properly elaborated programme for his own guidance. In 1812, however, the decisive fact for the Russians was the knowledge that, if and when war should come, they could rely on British assistance. Castlereagh, with some understanding of the Russian position, perceived the danger of trying to precipitate matters. On the other hand he thoroughly approved of the efforts of young Stratford Canning, the British representative at Constantinople, to hasten the conclusion of a peace between Russia and the Ottoman empire so that Russia would be free to concentrate the bulk of her forces against France. British diplomacy was likewise to assist in the negotiation of a Russo-Persian peace treaty in 1813.

[1] Renier, *Britain and the Netherlands*, pp. 181–90. For the rest of this chapter see especially Sir Charles Webster's, *The Foreign Policy of Castlereagh, 1812–15*, and his *British Diplomacy, 1813–15* (*Select Documents*).

Sweden was a different matter. In 1808, Sweden under her mad King had been an embarrassment as an ally, yet Britain's considerable trading interests in the Baltic could not but suffer when Sweden succumbed to French pressure. Fortunately the Swedes, under their new Regent and ex-Marshal of France, Bernadotte, had made considerable efforts to escape from French influence, and though Wellesley's attempt to renew the alliance in 1811 had been premature, Castlereagh was soon in a position to act. The Swedes made peace with Russia in April 1812, and secured her assent to and promise of support in the conquest of Norway from the Danes. Bernadotte now sought similar support and approval from Britain. Castlereagh was not interested in Bernadotte's local ambitions, but when his own hopes of an alliance with both Sweden and Denmark against France to open the Baltic to British trade collapsed, the temptation to play off one against the other was great. Unfortunately he knew that the conquest of Norway by Sweden would not be popular with the British Parliament, but prolonged haggling failed to secure an alternative agreement. The Swedish position was strong, since she could offer Gothenburg and Stralsund as bases for British commerce, and her military assistance seemed vital in the winter of 1812–13. Napoleon's invasion of Russia in 1812 had resulted in catastrophic retreat, but it was by no means certain whether the Russians would continue their victorious pursuit of Napoleon into central Europe, and whether Britain would be able to enlist other allies in Europe. Castlereagh reluctantly decided that Norway must suffer for the good of Europe, and the bargain was finally sealed on 3 March 1813.[1]

The quest for allies had been pressed in other capitals. In October 1812 Castlereagh had addressed a major appeal to Vienna. Metternich, the Austrian Foreign Minister, was determined to avoid a premature commitment which might prove fatal to the Habsburg domains after the successive disasters which had been suffered at the hands of France. The objectives behind his elaborate diplomacy continue to be a matter of dispute among historians,[2] but he was certainly determined to be

[1] *C.C.* viii. 382–3.
[2] Buckland, *Metternich and the British Government*, pp. 369 ff. Kraehe, *Metternich's German Policy*, i. 166 ff.

involved in war only at the moment of his own choosing, and he was anxious to strengthen the Habsburg position in central Europe, by peace or war, by seeking to maintain a balance between France and Russia. In the winter of 1812–13 he worked incessantly to establish his position as a mediator between the opposing forces, and even tried to enlist British support in February to this end. The British, who had not lost an inch of sovereign territory to the French in this war and whose financial position was that of abundance itself compared with the Austrian, could not comprehend his problems. Liverpool thought that 'nothing could be more abject than the Councils of Vienna at this time'. When Prussia joined the allies early in 1813, and Austria still hesitated, or, rather, put forward peace proposals that were designed to cover and gain time for the reorganisation of her army and finances, British exasperation could scarcely be contained. Austria's intervention, it was believed, would decisively tilt the scales against Napoleon. Castlereagh believed that Metternich exaggerated the strength of Napoleon, and was altogether too submissive to him. On the other hand, of all the British cabinet, he came nearest to understanding the problems of Metternich, and his fear of Russia as well as of France. But it was only after the defeat of Napoleon, and after he had become personally acquainted with Metternich that Castlereagh began to show a full appreciation of Austria's predicament, and to work with her in quest of a new and secure balance of power.[1]

Austrian coyness made the Prussian reaction at the beginning of 1813 of the utmost importance. Napoleon had retreated from Russian territory, but there was no guarantee that the Russians would be able or would wish to pursue him much further. News from the Peninsula was also disappointing, with Wellington once more having retreated to the security of the Portuguese frontier. British offensive success continued to depend heavily on events elsewhere in Europe. Britain herself could provide no significant forces to operate in northern Europe, save for her German Legion. The intervention of another major European power was badly needed, and upon this occasion Prussia not

[1] Buckland, pp. 369–72, 502–11, 526–35. Kissinger, *A World Restored*, pp. 41 ff.

only acted but acted at precisely the right moment. Prussian assistance also opened up more of Europe to British trade, and for a short time the allied armies were in possession of Hamburg, which provided a most valuable inlet for British goods. These boosts to British trade were of vital importance, since the recent lean years had injured Britain's capacity to subsidise her allies. With two millions already committed to Sweden and the German Legion, it was only with some difficulty that Britain was able to promise the Russians and Prussians a similar sum between them, and Castlereagh was obliged to express the hope in April 1813 that his allies would accept a proportion of the subsidies as 'effects' and open their ports to British trade as generously as possible in order to relieve the strain on British supplies of specie.[1]

These preparations came none too soon, for Napoleon resumed the offensive in May. He quickly recovered Hamburg, and soon half Germany was once more under his control. But decisive victories of the Jena–Wagram scale eluded him, partly because of the weakness of his cavalry. His armies were still being reconstructed following the disastrous losses of 1812, and he was as eager as the Prussians and Russians to sign a six-week armistice on 4 June. On the one hand, Napoleon was hoping to use this breathing space to build up a decisive superiority over the allies; on the other, the allies were hoping that by accepting the Austrian offers to mediate, the Austrians would be drawn to their side when Napoleon rejected all compromise. The allies had retreated close to the Bohemian frontier, and would be in a vulnerable position if obliged to resume the war without Austria. Metternich's game was a deep one. Although he strove to persuade the allies that his peace tactics were designed to draw Austria into the war on their side at the right moment, and that it was necessary to convince his sovereign, Francis II, that there could be no compromise with Napoleon, it would probably be unwise to accept this too literally. Metternich had a strong inducement to seek and achieve a compromise peace, rather than to put all to the hazard of war. As was his wont, Metternich was probably making careful provision for either alternative.[2]

[1] *C.C.* viii. 357, 408.

[2] The two main interpretations of Metternich's policy have recently been summarised by Kissinger, pp. 72 ff., and Kraehe, i. 166 ff. The

The armistice and subsequent peace negotiations directed by the suspect Metternich caused considerable dismay among the British cabinet. The armistice had coincided with the completion of the Reichenbach Subsidy Treaties between Britain, Russia and Prussia. The treaties were actually signed on 14–15 June. In return for British subsidies the allies promised to intensify the war against Napoleon and to conclude no peace treaty without consulting Britain. It was not easy to reconcile these promises with the current situation in Europe, and Castlereagh was further handicapped by the slow arrival of the scanty and not always reliable information that was sent to him. Metternich appeared more devious than ever. Nevertheless, Castlereagh wisely if reluctantly suppressed his emotions, and agreed that if the allies insisted on peace talks with Napoleon, Britain must join. 'The risk of treating with France is great,' he wrote, 'but the risk of losing our continental Allies and the confidence of our own nation is greater . . . with respect to the Continent we must sustain and animate those powers through whose exertions we can alone hope to improve it, taking care, in aiming at too much, not to destroy our future means of connexion and resistance.'[1] Britain could not force war upon her allies against their will. The crisis obliged him to consider what peace terms Britain could accept, and also to ponder the problem of binding the alliance into a more effective instrument both for waging war and making peace.

In a moment of optimism, following the news of Prussia's break with Napoleon, Castlereagh had refreshed his memory concerning the memorandum he had helped Pitt to compose in 1805, when alliance negotiations with Alexander had raised the question of the new Europe to follow the defeat of Napoleon. Pitt had been premature then as Castlereagh was now. The latter acknowledged in April 1813, when he sent a copy of the memorandum to the British Ambassador in attendance on the Tsar Alexander I, that many of Pitt's hopes might now be inapplicable or unobtainable, but Castlereagh was to find it useful, especially in British politics, to be able to associate the latter, which favours the peace-if-possible interpretation, is based upon much wider documentation.

[1] *C.C.* ix. 32.

name of Pitt with so many of his peace proposals. As it happened, future developments would make it possible to implement the bulk of Pitt's proposals, and from the summer of 1813 there was to be a steady escalation of the British peace terms. But, in the unfavourable circumstances of July 1813, Castlereagh was obliged to ignore Pitt's desire to create a barrier composed of an enlarged Holland, Prussia, an alliance of small German states, and an extended Piedmont, save in so far as Napoleon might make European concessions to recover French colonies.[1] Britain could insist only on securing the interests of Spain, Sweden, Sicily and Portugal, to which she was pledged by treaty, and on the retention of those colonial conquests vital to her safety. The security of Europe, however, would rest mainly on Austria Prussia, and Russia, whose power and stability must be the prime aim of the settlement. Finally, and most emphatically of all, Britain's maritime rights could never be made a matter of negotiation.

For the moment, however, the question of peace or war in central Europe had passed out of Castlereagh's hands, nor could he look to his representatives at the allied headquarters to exert much influence. The armistice had been extended to 10 August, and the peace negotiations were very much in the hands of Metternich. It was Napoleon's obstinacy that enabled or compelled Metternich to implement his promise to the allies that if and when the armistice expired, Austria would join the coalition. Even after the Austrian entry into the war in the middle of August the success of the coalition was by no means assured. Much turned upon the military, and still more the political discretion of Napoleon. Much disunity and dissension prevailed in the allied camp. Bernadotte appeared to devote most Swedish power to a private war against the Danes in the Baltic. Metternich was soon to resume his search for a settlement with Napoleon, whereby a strong power would be preserved in western Europe — perhaps even in parts of central Europe — to contain Russia. Austria and Prussia continued their rivalry for influence and territory in Germany. Overshadowing all was

[1] Castlereagh had already decided that no French colonies should be restored unless the independence of the Dutch Netherlands was conceded, Renier, p. 78.

the enigma of the Russian Tsar, inspired by a belief that it was his divine mission to overthrow Napoleon, yet easily diverted from it by a series of Napoleonic victories. His faith in God was far from Cromwellian. There were, too, his unconventional ideas for a new European order, and, most serious of all, his ambitions to help the Poles — under his own paternal sovereignty. His was a disconcerting and unpredictable presence at the allied headquarters; Metternich pondered uneasily concerning the 'periodic evolutions of the Tsar's mind'.

From London, Castlereagh surveyed and analysed as best he could the conduct of his allies. The relatively indecisive fighting of August and September helped to increase allied unity, but Castlereagh wisely gave much thought to the problem of concerting policy both for war and peace. He had no wish to see Britain again on the side-lines, but it was not easy to see how a permanent British influence could be exerted. Of his representatives at the allied headquarters, Cathcart was a compound of some shrewdness and more lethargy, too sanguine and easy-going to make the most of his abilities. Castlereagh's half-brother, Sir Charles Stewart, was with the Prussians; he was more of a soldier than a diplomat, too hearty, flamboyant and precipitate to be a good ambassador, and he was not taken very seriously by the allies. The latest envoy to reach the allies was Aberdeen, accredited to the Austrians on his first foreign mission. He was young, inexperienced, and impressionable, matching his credulity only with bursts of over-confidence remarkable in one so basically shy. In unison, the talents of this trio might have been of some service, but their personal rivalries and jealousies completed their inadequacies.

Castlereagh might also hope to influence his allies through the power of the purse, but the British coffers were not inexhaustible, and British subsidies had failed to prevent the armistice of June 1813. Britain could send only a handful of troops to northern Europe; she could also provide arms, though not in profuse abundance. Indeed, British prestige and influence received their main boost from Wellington's successes in Spain, especially his splendid victory at Vittoria. With the French retreating in disorder to the Pyrenees, Britain was at last able to appear as a military power in her own right, and not simply as a paymaster and the wielder of that mysterious — and in continental eyes, perhaps overrated — force, sea-power. Unfortunately, Castlereagh could not be sure that Wellington would produce a trump card whenever necessary. Finally Castlereagh could add his own talent as a diplomat, and test the susceptibility of his allies to argument and reason. Here the difficulty and slowness of communications with the continent created a major obstacle, while Castlereagh's own recognition that Britain would be unwise to stand aside from future peace talks further weakened his position. Nevertheless, whatever could be achieved by reasoned argument he tried to secure.

Allied unity was his central theme. In the late summer and autumn of 1813 he tried to impress upon the allies the necessity for consultation and agreement among themselves before they ventured again to negotiate with Napoleon. No concession by Napoleon to an individual state could provide the same security as allied unity in both peace and war. If Britain were again left to carry on the fight alone, her past survival and success was no guarantee that she could do so in the future. Let Britain once submit, and what would become of Europe? Above all, this was not a time for pessimism; in a phrase that was Churchillian in spirit if not in expression, he begged his allies to remember, 'We have now the bull close pinioned between us, and if either of us lets go our hold till we render him harmless, we shall deserve to suffer for it.'[1] He capped these arguments with his proposal of 18 September that the nine miscellaneous treaties whereby the allies were linked at present should be supplemented by a grand comprehensive Alliance. This Alliance should not only consolidate the allied war effort, and assure their unity in making peace, but should provide permanent mutual security against France in the future. If the advantages of his proposals were not self-evident, he hoped to coerce the allies by making future British subsidies dependent upon the acceptance of his terms. Events on the continent were, however, rapidly out-distancing him as he strove through inadequate representatives and at the end of a slow and perilous channel of communication to make his voice heard at the allied headquarters.

The allies, for their part, had their grievances against Britain.

[1] *C.C.* ix. 41.

They desired more definite promises concerning future subsidies, they resented Britain's veto on the discussion of her
maritime rights, and they resented her evasiveness concerning
the future of conquered colonies. Castlereagh and Metternich,
in particular, remained far apart, with Castlereagh complaining
that the Austrian treated the war, not as a 'contest of nations'
but rather as 'a game of statesmen'; a matter for negotiation
rather than hard fighting.[1] Metternich, on the other hand, was
disturbed by Castlereagh's references to the need to use national
sentiment and the mass of the people against Napoleon. Unlike
Castlereagh, his policy was not solely directed to the defeat of
Napoleon, but was also deeply concerned with the Europe to
emerge from the ruins of that empire. Not surprisingly the
allied draft of a central European peace settlement, concluded at
Toeplitz on 9 September, failed to meet all Castlereagh's hopes.
A diplomatic offensive against Austria, buttered by a subsidy of
£1,000,000, extorted some vague assurances from Metternich
that British interests in Holland would not be ignored, but the
crushing allied victory over Napoleon at Leipzig in the middle
of October 1813 once more firmly placed the diplomatic
initiative in Metternich's hands. The remnants of the French
armies were reeling back to the Rhine; German princelings were
scrambling to make their peace with the allies; Holland itself
was soon to rise in revolt, and all seemed ready for the speedy
and utter overthrow of Napoleon. Castlereagh's optimism was
soon shattered, as he learned that not only had Metternich
persuaded his continental allies to make further peace overtures
to Napoleon, but that he had persuaded the British representative
at his side, Lord Aberdeen, to agree, or at least associate himself
with terms that could never be regarded as satisfactory in Britain.

To speak of the middle-aged Aberdeen's infatuation with
Guizot in the 1840s is not to use too strong a word; now, at
twenty-nine, he succumbed almost as completely to Metternich.
He had recently set out from London, where Metternich's
diplomacy was a byword for 'finesse and trick', and he was soon
assuring Castlereagh from his new post that Metternich, though
vain and delighting too much in 'the appearance of negotiation',
was not clever and was to be trusted. He was later to have the

[1] Webster, *B.D. 1813–15*, pp. 102–6.

effrontery to tell his superior that he had 'so much of the Englishman as not quite to be aware of the real value of foreign modes of acting . . .'. He did not consult with his other colleagues, Cathcart and Stewart, and he allowed Metternich to squeeze an appearance of British assent to phrases in the peace terms to which the British government could never agree. He allowed himself to be misled by Metternich's vague assurances that Castlereagh's September proposals for a grand Alliance would soon be accepted. As Metternich himself said, he was indeed the 'dear simpleton of diplomacy'. It had been a mistake to send him in the first place, and his unsuitability for this onerous post had been increased after the spectacle of the battlefield of Leipzig had so nauseated him that he desired peace at almost any price. Sentiments which did him credit as an individual did not help him as a diplomat.[1]

The Frankfurt peace proposals of 9 November offered Napoleon the natural frontiers of France, but left vague the future frontiers of an independent Holland. The proposals expected Britain to be reasonable concerning her maritime rights, and failed to mention certain British objectives. Castlereagh, as usual, received the news after many delays and in piecemeal fashion, but it was quickly clear to him that Metternich's policy would lead to an early compromise peace which would outrage British public opinion, and injure certain fundamental British interests. Aberdeen was at once ordered to make an official protest against Metternich's inclusion of Britain's maritime rights as a subject for discussion in the proposed peace talks; to eliminate any further possibility of a mistake, Castlereagh drafted the protest himself. He argued in favour of the confinement of France within her ancient limits, and he pointed out that no peace would be popular with the British public which did not include the overthrow of Napoleon. More specifically he was dismayed to find that there was no reference to a 'barrier' to protect Holland, and he now offered to use Britain's colonial gains to improve the frontiers both of Holland and Piedmont. As for Antwerp, he told Aberdeen,

The destruction of that arsenal is essential to our safety. To leave it in the hands of France is little short of imposing upon Great Britain the

[1] Webster, op. cit., pp. 107–20.

charge of a perpetual war establishment. After all we have done for the
Continent in this war, they owe it to us and to themselves to extinguish this fruitful source of danger to both. Press this as a primary
object of their operations.

Nevertheless, as in July, he was forced to admit that if the
allies patched up an imperfect settlement Britain must submit.
He recoiled from the prospect of another lone struggle with
France. But matters were now reaching a point where Castlereagh could no longer hope to protect and promote British
interests from London. On 5 December the allies learned that
Napoleon was prepared to negotiate on the bases of the
'equilibrium of Europe', national integrity and independence,
and they appealed to London to appoint one person with
authority to make decisions on behalf of the British in the
forthcoming talks. The allies were also making counter-
proposals to Castlereagh's grand Alliance project. Great
decisions as to peace and war, and as to the Alliance itself were
thus impending. Even had Castlereagh found his ambassadors
more satisfactory channels of communication, it would still have
been unwise to delegate such immense responsibilities. The
cabinet therefore agreed on 20 December that Castlereagh
should proceed to the continent, and it spent much of Christmas
drawing up his instructions.

The document which resulted from these meetings was only a
résumé of the points discussed, and many points had to be left
vague for Castlereagh's personal decision according to circumstances. This document is part of the testimony to the extent to
which Castlereagh had won the confidence of the cabinet in his
two years at the Foreign Office. Since the allies had already
conceded the British position concerning maritime rights,
Antwerp and the Dutch 'barrier' were the main British demands.
The fate of the southern Netherlands was as yet uncertain; the
French were still in possession, the Austrians might wish to
return to their former territories, while Pitt had favoured their
acquisition by Prussia to present a solid frontier against French
expansion. Outside the continent, the British were determined
that they must retain such strong-points as Malta, Mauritius,
the Cape and Heligoland. The cabinet were, however, prepared
to restore the bulk of the remaining colonial conquests, provided

'the Maritime Power of France shall be restricted within due bounds by the effectual establishment of Holland, the Peninsula, and Italy in security and independence'. Above all, Holland and Antwerp must be independent of France. As Lord Harrowby later remarked, 'Antwerp and Flushing out of the hands of France are worth twenty Martiniques in our own hands.'[1]

It was also hoped to make as a condition of colonial restoration the establishment of a post-war Alliance to guarantee Europe against Napoleon, it being generally expected that Napoleon would still be Emperor of France even if peace were concluded. Castlereagh, in particular, had been impressed by Napoleon's powers of recovery after the heaviest of defeats, and, as a member of Addington's ministry, he could not forget how great had been Napoleon's capacity for mischief even in time of peace. There was consequently the utmost need for permanent unity and watchfulness in peace as well as in war. Grenville in 1797–9, and Pitt in 1805 had been groping towards something of this nature in their negotiations with European powers, so that the new territorial settlement of Europe might be guaranteed.[2] These earlier projects contributed to Castlereagh's new quest. Interest in this policy was increased by the feeling that it would be unwise to meddle with the internal affairs of France to try to secure Napoleon's overthrow. Austria had already opposed a suggestion on these lines in September 1813; the attitude of the other allies was unknown, and there was little or no sign of an impending French revolt against Napoleon's rule. Wellington was now entering southern France, but his popularity was to be explained mainly by the absence of taxes and requisitions, or so Castlereagh believed. There were certainly no grounds for permitting the Bourbons to attempt any mad escapades in France; counter-revolution might recoil on the initiators, and Castlereagh was prepared to contemplate its possible use only if Napoleon refused to make peace. He therefore ignored the strong feeling in the country against negotiations with Napoleon — a feeling particularly to the fore, so Stratford Canning maliciously claimed, among women and Methodists. He informed the allies

[1] Webster, op. cit., pp. 123–8. *Bathurst MSS.*, p. 261.

[2] J. M. Sherwig, 'Lord Grenville's Plan for a Concert of Europe, 1797–9', *Journal of Modern History* (1962), pp. 284–93.

on 29 January 1814 that Britain would treat with Napoleon as *de facto* ruler of France as long as the French themselves accepted him as such.[1]

Castlereagh spent three uncomfortable weeks on the journey to the allied headquarters at Basle; he was delayed first by a Channel fog and calm, and then by poor continental roads, very different from those he knew so well to Shrewsbury and Holyhead. Nor was he welcomed by reassuring news along the way. Dissension in the allied camp was rapidly increasing. As Metternich had foreseen and feared, the Russian and Prussian appetite for territory in central Europe was mounting, but at the same time they were anxious to continue the war against Napoleon. The Tsar was believed to be toying with the idea of Bernadotte as the new Emperor, and presumably aiming at some sort of Russo-French alignment.[2] Metternich, on the other hand, was anxious that Napoleon should grasp his final chance of peace, and, as Emperor of a reduced but still considerable empire, play his part in maintaining the balance of power in Europe. Britain's idiosyncrasies of policy were no longer matters of moment; instead, her approaching Foreign Secretary was awaited with great impatience, each side hoping to enlist him in its cause. When Castlereagh at last reached Basle, on 18 January, Metternich alone was still there to greet him; the Tsar had lost patience, and moved nearer the front. This did not mean that Metternich was able to win Castlereagh to his side without interruption so much as it enabled two politicians, who had hitherto disliked and distrusted much of each other's policies, to discover through personal contact that they had much in common. Within three days of the other's arrival Metternich was writing, 'Lord Castlereagh est ici et j'en suis fort content. Il a tout; aménité, sagesse, modération. Il me convient de toute manière et j'ai la conviction de lui convenir également.' Or again, 'I find that in no single instance does he differ from us, I can assure you that he is most peacefully inclined — peacefully in our sense.'

Castlereagh's subsequent summing-up of Metternich was not

[1] *C.C.* ix. 123–5, 130–3. Yonge, i. 500.

[2] F. D. Scott, 'Bernadotte and the throne of France, 1814', *Journal of Modern History* (1933), pp. 465–78.

quite so flattering. He found the latter 'constitutionally temporising', and though charged with more faults than were properly his, 'he has his full share, mixed, however, with considerable means for carrying forward the machine — more than any other person I have met with at headquarters'. He still found him timid, and perhaps never fully recognised the weakness of Metternich's position as Chancellor of a ramshackle empire. But these early meetings were so successful that past suspicions and misconceptions were soon dispelled, and the foundations laid of an important personal relationship and understanding that was to survive until Castlereagh's suicide, and which was frequently to exert profound influence upon European diplomacy. Their first important essay in partnership was indeed near at hand, for Castlereagh agreed with Metternich that the experiment of further peace negotiations had to be tried with Napoleon, even if his own expectations and hopes of success were less lively than those of Metternich. The latter was relieved to find that Castlereagh was firmly opposed to Bernadotte as a possible successor to Napoleon, and it was not difficult for them to agree that the choice between Napoleon and the Bourbons should be left to the French themselves. Any other possibility would create political instability in France, and with it the risk of further wars, or it might lead to an upset in the balance of power by linking France too intimately with another power. Metternich, for his part, now moved closer to Castlereagh's desires concerning France's eastern frontiers, an important departure from his Frankfurt proposals. Both Castlereagh and Metternich were therefore in a rather stronger position when they joined the other allied representatives at Langres.

These preliminary talks with Metternich in no way handicapped Castlereagh in his effort to play the mediator and conciliator in the allied camp; rather he had been strengthened by drawing Metternich closer to his point of view. With Britain's major interests no longer matters of dispute, he could concentrate upon winning the trust of all by his moderation, sincerity and impartiality. As he informed his subordinates in February 1814, 'The interests of Great Britain neither require to be asserted with chicane nor with dexterity — a steady and temperate application of honest principles is her best source of authority.' Lest Castlereagh should appear too naïve or Gladstonian for this world of cut-throat rivalry, it should be noted that he was prepared, if necessary, to use Britain's power of the purse and her colonial conquests as more material inducements. Even so, he continued to put his main faith in his powers of persuasion in private meetings with the allied leaders singly, or in formal conference. Careful and conscientious as he was in the preparation of letters and documents, he often added personal explanations to avoid any confusion. He also favoured regular formal meetings of all the representatives of the great powers to encourage frankness and trust, and to expedite business. The future Lord Ripon, who attended Castlereagh on his continental mission in 1814, later recalled,

In the course of our journey from Frankfort to Bâle, he stated to me that one of the great difficulties which he expected to encounter in the approaching negotiations would arise from the want of an habitual confidential and free intercourse between the Ministers of the Great Powers, *as a body*; and that many pretensions might be modified, asperities removed, and the causes of irritation anticipated and met, by bringing the respective parties into unrestricted communications common to them all, and embracing in confidential and united discussions all the great points in which they were severally interested.[1]

The creation of such an atmosphere took time, and the system was not infallible, but Castlereagh himself found it sufficiently rewarding for him to favour its use on several occasions over the next eight years. This was to be the heart of his version of the future Concert of Europe. But he could make no progress without some support from the Tsar, Alexander I. His instant success with Metternich was not repeated, and more than a month passed before he began to make an impression. Alexander, at this time, saw himself entrusted by providence with the task of destroying Napoleon, and then, with magnificent magnanimity, restoring France to her true position in Europe, with an enlightened new government largely fashioned by himself. The prosaic Castlereagh found all this too 'chevalresque'; unless the Tsar's ambitions were curbed he feared that he would wreck the Alliance, and create instability both in

[1] *C.C.* i. 125–9.

France and Europe as a whole with his wild schemes. There were no signs of movement within France to overthrow Napoleon; if he fell, Castlereagh was convinced that only the Bourbons could prevent further revolutions and the revival of Jacobinism or Bonapartism. Meanwhile, the Tsar's irresponsibility would have driven Austria and perhaps others from the Alliance, and wrecked the one instrument which promised long-term security for Europe. Yet it was not easy to see how Metternich's insistence on negotiations with Napoleon could be reconciled with the Tsar's dreams of a victory march into Paris.

A common-sense compromise, which was close to Castlereagh's own wishes, was adopted. The war should continue, but the possibility of peace should be explored now that Napoleon's power had been sufficiently reduced to give Europe some security even if he retained his throne. Napoleon was to be offered the ancient frontiers of France — that is, roughly those before the Revolutionary Wars began. Castlereagh delayed his specification of the colonies that Britain would restore for as long as possible in the vain hope that this would somehow induce his allies to reach a satisfactory agreement on the fate of the rest of Europe. In practice this merely added to the confusion caused by the rivalry of Russia, Prussia and Austria over central Europe, no agreed redistribution of which was even remotely in sight. Castlereagh would have to plunge much more deeply into the mire of central European territorial disputes before any agreement could emerge that gave the slightest promise of continuing European unity after the defeat of Napoleon. All he was able to achieve in February 1814 was an agreement to talk with the French, but apart from the terms that could be offered to France herself, there was no consensus on what to say. The ensuing negotiations at Châtillon were, as an Austrian remarked, an unworthy comedy.

Fortunately for the allied sense of honour and dignity, the French were no better. The powers of Napoleon's representative, Caulaincourt, varied according to his master's measure of success on the battlefield. The allied armies were as unco-ordinated in their advance as allied diplomacy at Châtillon, and against even the exiguous forces of Napoleon this was fatal. By rapid marches, Napoleon won several tactical victories between

10 and 14 February, and threw the allies' right flank under
Blücher into confusion. Napoleon now swung south in search
of the more cautious Schwarzenburg. It was these victories
which eventually brought the allied leaders to their senses, and
forced upon them a measure of harmony. Above all, they played
into the hands of Castlereagh in his struggle to persuade the Tsar
to see reason. Alexander had withdrawn his delegate from the
peace talks on 9 February, and so exasperated the Austrians that
they were threatening to make a separate peace. The Tsar as
forcefully threatened total war against Napoleon; his desire to
play the kingmaker was as strong as ever. On 13–14 February
Castlereagh used all his skill to try to persuade the Tsar of the
dangers of the course he was pursuing, and in particular to
divert him from his desire to meddle in the internal affairs of
France. One interview came near to boiling point when the Tsar
asserted that Castlereagh did not represent the true wishes of
the British cabinet and the Prince Regent. There was some truth
in the remark, though not enough to be of real consequence.
Castlereagh's reply that he possessed full powers, and would not
be swayed by 'any supposed wishes formed in England in
ignorance of the real circumstances' was more accurate than he
perhaps dared hope at the time. The Tsar was not to be moved,
but it is not improbable that Castlereagh's manner and firmness
so impressed him as to contribute to the friendly relationship
that was soon to grow up between them.

Meanwhile Napoleon's successes had intimidated the Prussians, and soon began to shake even the Tsar's self confidence.
Their military dependence upon the Austrians had been brought
home to them, and on 15 February Alexander agreed that the
original compromise which had led up to the conference at
Châtillon should be respected. In particular he agreed that the
fate of Napoleon was an internal matter to be left to the French
to decide. Indeed, at one point, Napoleon's successes threatened
to create too great a reaction among the allies. Alexander joined
those who argued that an armistice was essential to prevent
military disaster; there was a brief epidemic of defeatism, even
moments of panic. This mood soon passed; Napoleon's victories
began to be viewed in their proper perspective, while his failure
to exploit the brief psychological advantage he had gained from

his victories by offering moderate peace terms hardened the allied resolve. By 25 February the allies were again seriously discussing the resumption of the campaign, and had regained sufficient confidence for Austro-Russian differences to re-appear. Nevertheless, Napoleon's brilliant campaign in the middle of February had chastened the Tsar, while his combined military and political moves had taught the Austrians that a compromise peace with him would be neither so easy to arrange, nor so agreeable afterwards as they had once imagined. Castlereagh himself observed with much satisfaction to Liverpool on 26 February,

I could not but perceive the altered tone of my colleagues — their impressions being strongly tinctured with the demoralising influence of a rapid transition from an advance under very lofty pretensions, to a retreat of some embarrassment and of much disappointment and recrimination.

There is strong temptation to see Castlereagh in this crisis as the epitome of the cool-headed Englishman keeping his head when all around were losing theirs. There may be much truth in this picture, but it is one that emerges mainly from British sources.[1] Castlereagh's assistant, Ripon, claimed that his energy and nerve 'decided the fate of the campaign', and there can be no doubt that he contributed heavily to the outcome. His role in securing reinforcements from Bernadotte at the end of February to enable Blücher to resume his advance on the right flank was certainly of great importance, if only because no other allied minister was willing to incur the displeasure of the wayward Swedish Regent.[2] The 50,000 Prussian and Russian troops thus secured enabled Blücher to win the important battles of Craonne and Laon on 7–10 March, battles which largely ended the military effectiveness of Napoleon's remaining forces, and swung the fortunes of war irrevocably in favour of the allies. After this, Napoleon's military and political moves were mere pretence, and the way to Paris was open at last.

[1] e.g. Kraehe, who draws heavily on Austrian sources, largely ignores the crisis, pp. 296–303. Thiers, xvii. 214 ff., draws attention to the mixture of motives in the allied camp.

[2] Thiers, xvii. 414–15.

Castlereagh's influence in Europe was now reaching one of its highest points. This is reflected particularly in his changed relations with the Tsar. As Castlereagh noted on 5 March, 'His Imperial Majesty now encourages me to come to him without form. I see him almost every day, and he receives me with great kindness and converses with me freely on all subjects.' Castlereagh had thus achieved the second of the personal relationships that provided the main foundation for his diplomacy by conference of the future. Significantly, this important future development was heralded by the conclusion of the Treaty of Chaumont on 9 March. This gave concrete expression to the grand Alliance which Castlereagh had sought since September 1813. It was brought about at this time by Castlereagh's own unrelenting pursuit of his objective, reinforced by the alarm occasioned by Napoleon's February victories, and by his subsequent refusal to compromise. Increased British subsidies were also an inducement.

In many ways the Treaty of Chaumont merely drew together into a single document many of the provisions already contained in previous treaties. It was again impossible to be precise concerning the future of central Europe, but an enlarged Netherlands was secured, together with further promises of no separate peace treaties with Napoleon. Each ally agreed to contribute 150,000 troops at least for the duration of the war; Britain was committed in addition to annual subsidies of five millions sterling, with further payments if her military contingent fell below 150,000. Thiers thought that, with the British navy, the British contribution roughly equalled that of all the other powers combined. Certainly the British contribution was both large and onerous, and rather beyond what Castlereagh had been authorised to promise. But, as he had warned Parliament in November 1813, the time had arrived for 'one great effort' to free Europe; the time had passed for husbanding one's resources. Parliament had supported him almost unanimously then, and the cabinet did so now. Castlereagh even welcomed the British commitment, declaring that as the allies 'chose to make us a military power I was determined not to play second fiddle. The fact is that . . . our engagement is equal to theirs united. . . . What an extraordinary display of power! This, I trust, will put an end to any doubts as to the claim we have to an opinion on Continental matters.'[1]

The greatest novelty of the Treaty, however, remains to be noticed. This lay in its clauses relating to the post-war situation, for the allies agreed not only to fight until Napoleon had been defeated, but to continue the Alliance for twenty years to provide assistance and security against any French attempt to upset the peace settlement. Castlereagh also viewed the Alliance as 'a refuge' for the minor powers, especially those of Germany, but his hopes that the Treaty would settle all the frontiers of Europe and would guarantee peace against all the powers, and not merely against France, were disappointed. He had to content himself with Articles V and XVI which promised that the Alliance would strive to secure 'the equilibrium of Europe', and that the allies reserved 'to themselves to concert together on the conclusion of a peace with France as to the means best adapted to guarantee to Europe and themselves reciprocally, the continuance of the peace'. Castlereagh had thereby managed to preserve a little of his master's hope in 1805 that a general territorial guarantee by all the powers would prove possible.

Meanwhile the final effort to conclude a peace with Napoleon was drawing to a close. The French reply of 10 March was dismissed by Castlereagh as largely a political pamphlet, containing few concessions. Napoleon subsequently tried to blame Castlereagh for the continuation of the war, but both Metternich and Caulaincourt praised his earlier efforts for peace. In any case, the allied military position had so much improved that the allies felt free to demand that Napoleon should stop procrastinating, and give straight answers to straight demands. News was arriving from Paris of a hostile movement against Napoleon, and at long last it appeared that Napoleon had exhausted both his military and political resources. Even the ultra-cautious Schwarzenburg believed that an advance on Paris might be possible, and though Metternich still hoped for a compromise peace, the talks were doomed and ended on 18 March. From Castlereagh's point of view, all had worked out very well in the long run. The circumstances of the Alliance and

[1] C.C. xviii. 419. Webster, *B.D. 1813-15*, p. 166. On the crucial importance of Britain's financial power, see Thiers, xvii. 53-55.

the non-existence of a French movement to overthrow Napoleon
had driven him to negotiate. He had proved, even to the satisfaction of such critics of the government in Parliament as
Whitbread, that there was no negotiating with Napoleon. If the
allies had contributed to the failure at Châtillon by their own
disunity and confusion, Castlereagh had worked to reduce these
to a minimum. Only in March, when he felt circumstances were
changing, and opinion in Britain was agitating for an end to the
parleying, did he become impatient and take a more warlike
line. Napoleon had had his chance in February; March was too
late. In this Castlereagh was at one with the bulk of allied and
British feeling. But more significant had been his efforts
throughout to preserve allied unity, and to sustain their resolve
that Napoleon must be crushed if he would not come to
terms.

The allied armies, encouraged by reports of Napoleon's
weakening position in Paris, began to march directly on the
capital. The Tsar was in the forefront, and when Paris sur-
rendered on 30 March he was able to fulfil his cherished
ambition. He led the victorious armies into Paris the following
day. Castlereagh and Metternich, meanwhile, remained at a
discreet distance from Paris, torn between their fear of what the
Tsar might do in their absence and their desire to escape personal
involvement in the establishment of the regime to succeed
Napoleon. It is true that the prospects of the Bourbons were
improving daily; that arch-political manipulator, Talleyrand,
was in Paris, and was believed to be favourable. Castlereagh had
already advised Royalist agents to consult with him.[1] This faith
in Talleyrand was not misplaced; he not only removed the
Tsar's remaining sympathies for Bernadotte, or any other
solution, he also organised the appearance of a national appeal to
Louis XVIII to resume the throne of his ancestors. Admittedly
Castlereagh found some of the clauses in the new constitution,
the *Charte*, a little too liberal for his taste, nor was he entirely
happy when the Tsar, largely on his own initiative, agreed by
the Treaty of Fontainebleau of 11 April that Napoleon should
receive the island of Elba. This Mediterranean retreat was all

[1] E. J. Knapton, 'Some Aspects of the Bourbon Restoration of 1814',
Journal of Modern History (1934), pp. 411–15.

too close to the French mainland. These, however, were small losses beside the all-important point that the allies had not imposed the Bourbons on France, an appearance of which might well have caused more dissatisfaction in France, and provoked unfavourable comment in Britain.

Some six or seven weeks were spent on the conclusion of a peace treaty with France.[1] Castlereagh found Paris 'a bad place for business', with far too much time being devoted to entertainment. All the while he was anxious to return to Westminster, where his deputy, Vansittart, was said to be 'so overpowered in the House of Commons'. Nevertheless, when the first Peace of Paris was signed on 30 May, it meant that most of Britain's main interests had been secured. Thus Castlereagh could now attempt to mediate in the complex central European disputes, free from the embarrassment of seeking the assistance of other powers to secure outstanding British demands. In the actual negotiation of the Treaty of Paris, the French had made a half-hearted attempt to retain part of Belgium, but Castlereagh, with Austrian support, had little difficulty in cutting short this sort of nonsense. The French were permitted to retain two-thirds of the vast fleet they had been constructing at Antwerp, but as most of the timber used in these new ships was unseasoned, and as the French finances were in no state to continue expensive naval programmes, the ships were as much a liability as an asset. Nor had Castlereagh any objection to some slight additions to the ancient frontiers of France, those of 1792 being broadly restored. With the Austrians and Russians, he opposed a Prussian demand for an indemnity, and only certain private claims against the French government were admitted. This magnanimity occasioned some protest in Britain, but Castlereagh was probably more worried by the Tsar's generosity towards France, which seemed to be inspired more by a desire to win France as an ally

---

[1] On the peace negotiations, 1814–15, see Webster's *Castlereagh, 1812–15*, *B.D. 1813–15*, and *Congress of Vienna*; likewise the previously cited works of Kissinger and Kraehe, and in addition E. V. Gulick's *Europe's Classical Balance of Power*. For the eighteenth-century character of much of Castlereagh's policy see S. R. Graubard, 'Castlereagh and the Peace of Europe', *The Journal of British Studies* (Nov. 1963), pp. 79–87.

than by his own principle of conciliation to make France both stable and peaceful.

In continuation of this policy, Castlereagh reopened the Newfoundland fisheries to the French on the same terms as in 1792, the French commercial posts in India were restored, and of the captured French colonies, only Mauritius, Tobago and St. Lucia were retained. Tobago was retained out of deference to British commercial interests, who pointed to their heavy capital outlay in the island; St. Lucia was withheld at the request of the Admiralty for strategic reasons. This generosity provoked a few critics in Britain, but the biggest outcry arose over Castlereagh's failure to secure immediate French abolition of the slave trade. He had agreed to a delay of five years, and for most members of Parliament, from Whitbread to Grenville, this represented the only serious blot on the Peace of Paris. The French at the time, and some historians since, have viewed this outcry as mainly inspired by a commercial desire to ruin the French colonies — and certainly Baring argued that the continuation of the French slave trade would be a disaster for the British West Indies. Nevertheless, it would seem that British commercial interests were never more influential than when they were allied with the philanthropic drive against the slave trade. At one point, the possibility of restoring another French colony for immediate abolition was considered at the suggestion of Wilberforce. The cabinet itself was very impressed by the pressure from the humanitarians, while Castlereagh complained that the degree of public excitement impeded his efforts to abolish the slave trade by increasing French suspicion and national pride.[1] By 1815 he had convinced most of the ardent abolitionists that he had done all that could be done for their cause.

By the beginning of June 1814 it appeared that one of the bases of the peace settlement envisaged by Castlereagh had been laid. A peaceful, conciliated France, under a stable Bourbon regime seemed possible. But Castlereagh looked to a second safeguard, for France was still powerful and perhaps unpredictable. This second safeguard was the continuance of the unity and friendship of the other great powers of Europe, but to achieve this the many differences between Austria, Prussia and

[1] *C.C.* x. 73. Yonge, ii. 119–22. *Hansard*, xxviii. 364 ff., 432 ff.

Russia over the fate of central Europe had to be resolved. Although Castlereagh took up the role of mediator and conciliator with tremendous eagerness and self-assurance, he was soon to discover the shallowness and inadequacy of his approach and understanding. His earlier difficulties with his allies when Napoleon was still in the field against them might have been a warning, yet even now in his mid-forties Castlereagh retained a little of that youthful enthusiasm and precipitation that had so attracted the Rev. Dickson in 1783. A more worldly-wise and world-weary politician might never have plunged with such zest into the muddy politics of central Europe. Certainly Castlereagh's zeal dismayed his more insular and less energetic political colleagues.

Castlereagh had already done his best to encourage a central European settlement on several occasions; he hoped that the visit of allied monarchs and ministers to London in June would break the deadlock, but no amount of festivity or persuasion could induce a mellower mood. He did, however, make one important gain. As yet his new-found sympathy for Metternich was not shared by his colleagues or the Prince Regent, who still enthused over Alexander as the hero of the hour. The Tsar had already disenchanted Louis XVIII, and by his conduct he now proceeded to antagonise the Prince Regent and the rest of the cabinet. Alexander reserved all his charm for the Opposition; he even visited Bentham, and in his cloudy way, postured as an enlightened despot. The Whigs, however, were nearly as annoyed as the ministers; to insult the Prince Regent was an Englishman's prerogative; a Russian had no place in this private quarrel. Metternich, on the other hand, did not put a foot wrong, and was soon described by the Regent as 'the wisest of Ministers'. Castlereagh was therefore able to move towards Austria in the near future without provoking so much hostility from his colleagues as he otherwise might have done. The indigestible feast of entertainment, climaxed by a Guildhall banquet for 700 guests at £30 per head, was not all loss, even though the critical discussions had again been postponed, this time to the autumn when sovereigns and ministers would meet in Vienna to prepare for the great congress which was to ratify the peace settlement.

K

If Castlereagh was of a sanguine disposition, he reinforced it with immense industry. Once freed of his parliamentary responsibilities, he prepared for the negotiations in Vienna with great care. He possessed no advantage in intellectual ability — perhaps the reverse — over the personalities with whom he would be negotiating at Vienna, but he could surpass them all in industry, application and self-control. He had the strongest nerves, and could expect to prevail in many matters through sheer perseverance and mastery of all aspects of the question. References to his charm in private conversation abound, though to some — whether by intent or not is not always clear — he appeared too suave, too cold, or disconcertingly impassive. But whatever the guise, the majority were impressed. The French Royalist de Vitrolles once found himself exhausting his arguments without the slightest inkling of their effect upon Castlereagh. But unlike that more notorious exponent of this art, Calvin Coolidge, Castlereagh normally utilised it more constructively.[1] Castlereagh hoped to reinforce his own diplomatic talents with a reputation for moderation, fair-dealing and impartiality. He hoped to impress his allies and win their trust by reducing British demands to a minimum. Napoleon and Gentz were certainly baffled by this restraint, but in general Castlereagh failed to make the impact he had hoped. In any case, his conception of British moderation was broadly in accordance with British interests. Merchants might grumble, but Liverpool was already appalled by the expected rise in garrison costs for the new strategic bases, and further acquisitions for commercial reasons, such as Tobago, Demerara, Essequibo and Berbice, were granted with some reluctance. The Dutch East Indies were restored to strengthen the Dutch in Europe, and this concession was facilitated by the absence of any important British commercial interest in these islands as yet. British generosity over the acquisition of the Cape was more apparent than real, since the compensation of £2,000,000 was to be expended upon the barrier fortresses, a basic British strategic objective.

One of the strongest elements in Castlereagh's position was his considerable freedom to pursue an intensely personal policy. Parliament was ill-informed and not greatly interested in the

[1] Renier, p. 213.

affairs of Europe. Castlereagh did nothing to facilitate or encourage this interest. Only the slave trade evoked consistent and strong attention; otherwise domestic issues predominated, with pride of place going to the passion for government economy and tax reductions. This passion, coupled with intense insularity, had an indirect restraining effect upon his policy, as Liverpool more than once pointed out. There were occasional bursts of interest over the fate of Saxony and Poland, and more especially over Norway and the Genoese republic.[1] With reference to the Poles, Castlereagh paid lip-service to the principles of nationality and constitutionalism, but no more. He personally was uneasy over the transfer of the reluctant Norwegians to the Swedes, especially when an outbreak of fighting in the summer of 1814 necessitated some British naval intervention. He argued, however, that Britain was bound by treaty to Sweden, and that decisive British action would leave the Norwegians under no false expectations of British assistance. Probably, too, Britain desired a quick solution lest Russia should be afforded further opportunities for mischief.[2] Ultimately British diplomacy was able to contribute to the establishment of a union which was little more than personal under the Swedish Crown. Whig protests against British policy were defeated by majorities of 3 to 1 in both Houses, while in the Commons Canning strongly, and Wilberforce reluctantly pointed out that Britain had no alternative.

In normal circumstances, therefore, Castlereagh had little to fear from Parliament, especially as he could rely on the hostility of a considerable majority to Whig and Radical policies which did not aim at tax reductions. Nor did the cabinet create many problems. He was apparently given no formal instructions, and the few letters sent to him at Vienna rarely influenced his policy. Of the cabinet, only Liverpool and Bathurst followed events closely, though Vansittart, as became the Chancellor of the Exchequer, raised some difficulties on financial grounds. Liverpool himself was almost paralysed at times by the fear of a new war, which might unleash another flood of revolution, and

[1] *Hansard*, xxvii. 768 ff., 834 ff., xxx. 265 ff., 891 ff. See also R. J. White, *From Waterloo to Peterloo*, pp. 4–5, 7.

[2] *C.C.* x, 77.

was disposed to sacrifice almost everything for a few years of peace. In time he came to recognise that Castlereagh, though moved by similar fears, was in fact helping to avert these dangers by more positive and constructive policies. Distance and rapidly changing circumstances also made it difficult for the cabinet to influence affairs at Vienna to any extent, and Castlereagh had little difficulty in interpreting such instructions as were sent to suit his purposes.

Castlereagh, as usual, had few experts to assist him. Of these the best were Clancarty, Planta (his private secretary), and Cooke, who broke down through overwork. Contemporaries were puzzled and amused by the presence of his half-brother, Charles, whose flamboyance, indiscretions and scrapes made an odd contrast to the cool-headed Castlereagh. Lord Apsley tried to save British face at Vienna by explaining that Charles was, after all, Irish. But the British delegation was at least proof against the Austrian secret police; waste-paper baskets were carefully cleaned out, feminine seduction avoided, and the biggest scoop of the secret agents was apparently a glimpse of Castlereagh himself practising a new Viennese dance with the aid of a chair. Even the endless festivities, which Castlereagh found a terrible waste of time, had their dangers, for when diplomats were not listening to indiscretions, they were trying to gauge the political significance of the dancing partners chosen by the leading personalities. The Tsar dancing a polonaise with Lady Castlereagh was indeed a matter of moment, while Metternich seems to have drawn political advantage as well as personal satisfaction from the social round which often delayed more serious business. The politicians had also to be constantly on their guard against the camaraderie of the monarchs, especially under the inspiration of the Tsar, and it must have been a constant source of relief to Castlereagh that the Prince Regent was not present in this intoxicating atmosphere. As for himself, he was somewhat out of place amid this tinsel finery, but his 'glacial good manners', his perfect dress sense (in sharp contrast to that of Lady Castlereagh), and his general distinction carried him through the social ordeal without much apparent difficulty.

His prime aims at Vienna were to bring the world back to 'peaceful habits' and to establish 'a just equilibrium' between the powers. The objectives were complementary, and both were menaced by the ambitions of Prussia and Russia. Alexander's bid to secure most of Poland was the greatest danger, but Austro-Prussian differences over the future of Germany both aided the Tsar and threatened to extend the area of contention into the heart of Europe. Already France, under the skilful direction of Talleyrand, was showing signs of trying to exploit the dissension. In the late summer of 1814 Talleyrand demonstrated his anxiety to co-operate with Britain. There might be dangers in acceptance or rejection; the latter might precipitate France into the arms of Russia, whereas the former might offend Britain's old allies. Castlereagh correctly calculated that Talleyrand's objectives were limited, and that a policy of restraint would not forfeit his friendship. Here was a reserve force that could be brought forward later if necessary, and he worked through Wellington in Paris to modulate French policy according to his wishes.

Castlereagh reached Vienna in September, and passed the autumn endeavouring to eliminate the Austro-Prussian differences over the German settlement, so that their friendship could be used to strengthen his own appeals to the Tsar to relinquish part of his Polish ambitions for the good of Europe. His negotiations with the Tsar, many of them in private interviews, ranged over a wide variety of arguments. Nevertheless, no amount of dialectical skill on the part of Castlereagh could alter the fact that Alexander was the man in possession, with a vast army at his back; in these circumstances, as the Russians were fond of remarking, 'on ne négocie beaucoup'. Even when Castlereagh asked whether the Tsar would 'be satisfied to rest his pretensions on a title of conquest in opposition to the general sentiments of Europe', his argument had little force. He had yet to iron out Austro-Prussian differences to secure such 'general sentiments', while from his own cabinet he was receiving no support. Liverpool was dismayed by the parliamentary pressure for economy, by the continuance of the war with the United States, and by a dread of an early recurrence of war in Europe. Already there were disturbing reports of unrest in France, and he could perceive no British interest in Poland that could justify a further risk of war. Vansittart strongly supported him.

Castlereagh was not to be shaken from his purpose by this insularity. He retorted that unless the Tsar were resisted, he might turn into another Bonaparte; 'acquiescence will not keep him back, nor will opposition accelerate his march'. Unless Russia were resisted, it might be impossible to avert a quarrel between Prussia and Austria — since compensation for disappointed Prussian or Austrian expectations in Germany could only be found in Poland. Unless Prussia and Austria were united, the opportunities for Russian mischief in the heart of Europe would be immense; there would be no 'just equilibrium'. Even if Poland could not be saved, a policy of firmness might deter Russia from undue meddling elsewhere. The cabinet, however, were not impressed, and Liverpool hoped to protect what he felt to be Britain's only vital interest in Europe, the Netherlands, by reciprocating the evident French desire for close relations. But Castlereagh refused to retreat from his general policy until the last possible moment, confident that the French partnership would be available when and if he needed it. Until the first week in November, his main energies were directed against Russia and towards the reconciliation of Austro-Prussian differences. His great misfortune here was that neither Metternich nor Hardenburg, who represented Prussia, were free agents. Both were impeded by rival politicians and by their generals; neither could depend upon their respective sovereigns. By the end of October an impressive paper edifice had been painfully erected, by which Hardenburg temporarily waived the Prussian claim to Mainz as a too immediate threat to Austria in south Germany, while Metternich ambiguously promised Saxony to Prussia if the Polish negotiations with Russia should succeed. Both ministers promised Castlereagh that they would support his stand against the Tsar's claims in Poland. The German alliance which would stabilise central Europe, and exclude both French and Russian influence, seemed on the point of achievement.

The first public test of this Austro-Prussian solidarity was fatal. It occurred in the first week of November, and the Tsar's outburst in defence of his Polish policy reduced the King of Prussia to abject submission. On 11 November Castlereagh himself admitted that his policy had failed, and that the bulk of

Poland must now fall to Russia. But this was not the end of the matter, because, as he had foreseen, failure in Poland reopened the Austro-Prussian dispute over the future of Germany, and especially of the Kingdom of Saxony, whose ruler's loyalty to Napoleon had been a little too long-lived to earn much respect for his opinions. The Austro-Prussian compromise of October was at an end; on the one side Prussia and Russia were drawing together, and on the other Austria was attracting the support of most of the small German states and, more impressively, that of France as well. Even now Castlereagh refused to be hurried. Desperately he tried to prevent an open split in the old alliance, although he was forced to warn Liverpool on 5 December of the danger of 'a total stagnation and that it may suddenly end in war'. It would be difficult for Britain long to remain aloof from such a conflict, and of the various possibilities open to Britain, Castlereagh felt that armed mediation in association with France would perhaps be the best policy to attempt first, before going to the assistance of Austria. His prestige at Vienna and in London was now at its lowest; Talleyrand likened him to a man 'who had lost his way', and expected him soon to return to London. Yet Castlereagh's reluctance to change his course is understandable; to do so might jeopardise his whole policy. He refused to commit himself to Austria and France until he was convinced there was no alternative.

Castlereagh hesitated until 31 December. At a dramatic meeting of the four powers — France had yet to be admitted to the inner councils at Vienna — Hardenburg threatened to treat as tantamount to a declaration of war a refusal to recognise a Prussian annexation of Saxony should it be considered necessary. Castlereagh at once retorted that if 'such a temper really prevailed . . . it were better to break up the Congress'. He followed this by submitting a draft treaty of alliance to Metternich and Talleyrand, having declined a similar proposal from them on 23 December. The secret alliance was completed on 3 January 1815. His latest information from London gave him no reason to suppose that the cabinet's aversion to his policy had changed in any particular, but the news of the end of the war with the United States, which reached him on New Year's Day, came at a most opportune time. As Castlereagh informed

Liverpool on 15 January, 'It is difficult to describe . . . the impression produced here by our pacification with America.'[1] Britain would again be a continental military power by the spring. Castlereagh's position in the eyes of his colleagues at home was also strengthened by the fact that France, the Netherlands, Piedmont, and most German states were drawing behind Austria. This was a European crisis, and the states whose friendship Britain desired favoured his policy. In fact, the secret alliance provoked less comment in Britain than might have been expected. Liverpool regretted that the proposal for the alliance had come from Castlereagh, but agreed that Britain had no choice but to ratify and that as quickly as possible. He thought the alliance would give *éclat* to Castlereagh's presence at Vienna, 'which was certainly wanting'. Such personal grumbles apart, Liverpool now showed an increasing readiness to leave everything to Castlereagh. He welcomed the close association with France, whom he regarded as a graver threat than Russia; there was no longer any immediate danger of a Russo-French alliance. Bathurst, the only other member of the cabinet to follow foreign affairs closely, agreed with these verdicts.[2] Nevertheless, although Castlereagh had calculated the cabinet's reaction correctly, his had been the decision. Similarly, although Metternich and Talleyrand had done most of the preparatory work of the alliance, British support was desirable if it were to deter and impress the Prussians. Again, Castlereagh's readiness to act without referring home was of great importance.

Although military preparations had been noted in both camps at the end of 1814, there were indications at the same time that the Tsar wished to be conciliatory, while the Prussian resolve appeared to weaken even during the dramatic meeting of the 31st. None of the European powers was in a financial condition to contemplate another war with equanimity; on the other hand, no one was under any illusion as to Britain's potential in such matters by this time.[3] Castlereagh would not therefore

[1] Glover, pp. 10–12.
[2] *Bathurst MSS.*, p. xv and note; also pp. 314–15, 321–9.
[3] Castlereagh warned Bathurst, 30 Jan. 1815, to stop paying subsidies to the allies for the moment; poverty would be a great force for peace, Leigh, p. 305.

appear to have run a very considerable risk on 3 January, even if it were still a sufficient risk for a lesser man to have hesitated. In the event, the tension speedily evaporated, though the task of negotiating a compromise settlement was still a very laborious one. Castlereagh's services as a mediator were consequently much in demand, and for the next four weeks, until 6 February, he was deeply involved, carving and re-carving the map of Germany in an endeavour to satisfy Hardenburg and Metternich. He was working under additional pressure, since Liverpool, alarmed by the growing independence of the House of Commons, was anxious that Castlereagh should abandon the obscurities of continental politics, and reassert the government's authority over recalcitrant country gentlemen. Castlereagh found the problems of Europe more to his taste.

Prussia had agreed to waive her claims to all of Saxony, but she demanded compensation for the parts she had sacrificed. Nor did she accept the role of protectress of the Rhine so eagerly as Castlereagh had hoped. The Austrians were adding to his difficulties, as they hoped to capitalise on the Prussian retreat by demanding still more concessions. Castlereagh, however, was determined that Prussia should be both a great power and a power on the Rhine. To overcome the obstinacy of Hardenburg and Metternich and their advisers he made personal though vain appeals to their respective sovereigns. Even when Metternich began to weaken, the situation was really saved by the Tsar's belated agreement to Castlereagh's suggestion that the district of Thorn should be ceded to Prussia to improve the latter's security on the Vistula. The Tsar had become increasingly co-operative since December, and had already promised the Tarnopol district of Poland to Austria. Castlereagh was also assisted by Talleyrand's decision not to oppose his west German policy. Liverpool and Vansittart, however, were not so pleased when they discovered that Castlereagh had won the Tsar's co-operation by giving his assent to British acceptance of responsibility for nearly half of the Russian debt to the Dutch; they had other occasions to bemoan their colleague's lordly extravagance in the conduct of his foreign policy.

Castlereagh, for his part, had considerable cause for satisfaction, as by his settlement of the Saxon question he had firmly established Prussia on the Rhine. Pitt had hoped to place Prussia on part of the eastern frontier of France, and his disciple, through many changes of policy, had never lost sight of this desideratum. Under his pen, the frontiers of Hanover, the Netherlands and other states in this north-eastern corner of western Europe had bulged and contracted with the shapelessness of amoebae. At one time, it seemed that the Netherlands might reach the Middle Rhine, but Castlereagh had gladly interposed the greater military power of Prussia, having no high regard for the martial calibre of the Dutch, and perhaps fearing also that if the Netherlands became too large, their independence of Britain would be that much increased. Russian intrigues at The Hague demonstrated the dangers of this.[1] Early in 1815 he felt free to boast that Germany now possessed the best frontier of her history against France, with the Netherlands, Hanover, Prussia and Bavaria as its sentinels.

The Polish-Saxon crises demonstrated Castlereagh's aims and methods at Vienna to perfection. In method, there was the determination to retain the confidence of all for as long as possible; the refusal to be driven into separate alliances and arrangements until the last possible moment. The utmost reliance was placed on personal contacts, and few important letters were sent to other ministers or sovereigns without Castlereagh providing personal explanations. He was never afraid to speak his mind, or take a strong stand when the situation demanded, and in consequence Metternich in particular left the most unpopular tasks to him. But a mark of his success in personal diplomacy was his continuing good relations with Alexander. On the other hand, in his quest for a 'just equilibrium' he perhaps allowed his policy to become too inflexible, too mathematical, even unrealistic at times.[2] There were times when he perhaps made insufficient allowance for the power of emotion and unreason in international relations, and underestimated the difficulty of the problems that lay ahead of him. Yet his basic calculation was correct; he alone could mediate,

[1] Renier, pp. 218, 285–92.

[2] It was no accident that Castlereagh was the creator of the Statistical Committee of December 1814, which did much to provide accurate information to facilitate the redistribution of populations.

and could exercise considerable influence wherever circumstances denied to another power a position of overwhelming strength. His policy had more point and purpose than the cabinet could perceive, and he had achieved a more stable central European settlement than would have been the case had he bowed to Liverpool's isolationist leanings. On the other hand, Gentz's complaint that he might have done so much more had he exerted British power to the full is totally misleading. Castlereagh's great problem was to mobilise British support for his more limited objectives against the fears of his cabinet colleagues, the insularity of most members of Parliament, and the criticism of an Opposition whose sources of information were far from reliable.

Contemporary criticism of Castlereagh's policies in 1814–15 arose from Whig and Radical sympathy for Finns, Poles, Norwegians, Venetians and Genoese in their forced unions with Russians, Swedes, Austrians and Piedmontese. The French ruler of Naples, Murat, also enjoyed some Whig support, but most of the criticism was provoked by Castlereagh's neglect of historic states and historic liberties, rather than by any defiance of emergent nationalism or liberalism on his part. Grenville insisted that the restoration of as many ancient frontiers as possible would most contribute to European stability, whereas Whitbread defended ancient states on moral grounds.[1] Such sentiments were praiseworthy, but they were quite impracticable. To have sought their implementation would have caused the separation of Britain from her war-time allies; such a policy might even have precipitated revolts in some parts of Europe, and presented Britain with the painful dilemma of armed intervention or humiliating retreat. In a sense Castlereagh was kinder to the Norwegians when he sought to demonstrate that they could expect only hostility from Britain as long as they opposed union with Sweden. The only sensible alternative to Castlereagh's policy of participating in every major aspect of the resettlement of Europe would have been one of quiet aloofness. Liverpool's doubts concerning Castlereagh's conduct were more realistic than the comments from the Opposition.

Liberal critics of later generations have been even more

[1] Renier, p. 153. *Hansard*, xxviii. 364–9; xxx. 265 ff.

sweeping, and have complained that Castlereagh tried to freeze Europe into a state system that was becoming obsolete with the rise of nationalism, and that he was allying himself with the forces of reaction in an age of dawning liberalism.[1] It is abundantly clear that Castlereagh was endeavouring to create a world safe for aristocracy, yet this is not to say that his policy in the conditions of 1814–15 was wholly unrealistic, or, indeed, that he sought to petrify Europe. It will be seen later that he was prepared to use moderate constitutional change in some countries as a step to greater overall European peace and stability. But more important is the fact that later generations of historians have often exaggerated the strength of liberal and national movements in the early nineteenth century. Liberals and nationalists certainly existed in Europe, but their weakness is nowhere better demonstrated than in the criticisms directed against the Carbonari of the 1820s by the young Mazzini.[2] Even as late as 1848–9, the weaknesses of such movements were all too often apparent, and the champions of change outside France were normally strong only in the weakness of their opponents. Their strength had been exaggerated by the opportunity provided to them by the advancing armies of the French Revolution and Napoleon, and after 1815 their dependence upon and exploitation by military adventurers was very marked.[3] Illiberal Castlereagh's policy may have been, but it was eminently practical.

But Castlereagh, in 1814–15, gave no blind obeisance to the principles of reaction. His main purpose was European peace, and the preservation of a monarchical-aristocratic order, but not necessarily one which was a carbon-copy of that of the eighteenth century. Indeed, in the struggle against Napoleon, Castlereagh had not been averse to the enlistment and utilisation of the popular passions that Napoleon had provoked against himself.

[1] H. Nicolson (*The Congress of Vienna*, pp. 259 ff.) is one of the more recent critics, but see also Webster, *The Foreign Policy of Castlereagh, 1815–22*, ii. 504.

[2] E. E. Y. Hales, *Mazzini and the Secret Societies* (1956).

[3] See especially H. G. Schenk, *Aftermath of the Napoleonic Wars* (1947); also *Journal of Modern History* (1955), pp. 27 ff., and Kraehe, i. 79.

The struggle had become a war of peoples as well as of kings and armies. He remarked in October 1813, 'The people are now the only barrier. They are against France and this is the shield above all others that a State should determine to interpose for its protection, which is so wholly destitute as Austria of a defensible frontier.'[1] The real European conservative, Metternich, found such sentiments decidedly disturbing. Castlereagh's pragmatism, his respect for — and perhaps even more his need to respect — the principles of 1688 and British parliamentary traditions often created a yawning gap between himself and the average aristocratic politician of the continent.

Castlereagh's enthusiasm for popular movements varied sharply according to circumstances, diminishing to a very moderate constitutionalism as Napoleon's fortunes waned. In September 1812 Castlereagh agreed with the Whig Lord William Bentinck, his representative at the Sicilian court, that revolt on behalf of the Bourbons of Sicily should be encouraged in Naples, and that the people should be inspired to rise by promises of political reform under the restored dynasty. The Sicilian constitution would help to rally support, but he remained insistent that there could be no question of an elective Neapolitan monarchy. Other letters showed an awareness that the political character of many European states was beginning to change, and that not only could these forces be used against Napoleon, but that they must be reckoned with in the governance of those states after his defeat.[2] He believed this to be particularly true of France. Before, and especially after the Hundred Days, Castlereagh insisted that every effort should be made to include in the restored Bourbon regime moderate representatives from the Napoleonic government. On the other hand, Castlereagh had very firm ideas as to how far these constitutional experiments should be allowed to proceed, and how far they were applicable to various countries. For instance, he feared that the liberalising process might be going too far in Prussia in December 1815.[3]

With reference to Spain, for example, Castlereagh informed Sir Henry Wellesley on 10 May 1814[4] of his hopes that

[1] Webster, *B.D. 1813–15*, p. 105.

[2] Ibid., pp. 287–8. *C.C.* viii. 275–6. Renier, p. 73.   [3] *C.C.* xi. 106.

[4] *C.C.* x. 25–26.

Ferdinand VII would, without trying to restore the old despotic order, moderate the existing constitution which Castlereagh described as 'amongst the worst modern productions of that nature'. He criticised its exclusion of ministers from the legislature, and he wished to increase the share of political authority to be enjoyed by the landed proprietors and the clergy. He was convinced that 'the temper of the times' would no longer permit the exercise of military autocracy, but he wished to root the emerging political order in property, that great foundation of the British constitution. Nevertheless, he tended to judge the pros and cons of constitutional innovations on practical grounds; he did not favour the spread of British constitutional ideas in principle; only when their adoption promised to add to the political stability of the country in question, and provided this did not excite international complications. Thus he favoured the modest constitutional experiments that were conducted in France, the Netherlands and Sweden–Norway as measures calculated to increase the loyalty of their subjects. In Italy, on the other hand, he dropped his previous interest in constitutional concessions now that it was no longer necessary to rouse Italian feeling against France. He saw that further agitation in this direction would antagonise the Austrians, and might add to the confusion and instability in that region. As he informed Bentinck after the defeat of Napoleon, British policy in Italy should aim at the restoration of 'disciplined force under sovereigns we can trust'. He complained to Liverpool that Bentinck 'seems bent on throwing all Italy loose : this might be well against France, but against Austria and the King of Sardinia, with all the new constitutions which now menace the world with fresh convulsions, it is most absurd'. To restrain Bentinck in his 'Whiggish and revolutionary politics', which were threatening to alarm Britain's allies, and which were no longer authorised by London, Castlereagh wrote one of those discreet and tactful appeals at which he was now a past-master, but which might appear to the unwary reader as an expression of cautious sympathy for constitutional regimes which he did not really feel.

It is impossible not to believe a great moral change coming on in Europe, and that the transition may be too sudden to ripen into anything likely to make the world better or happier. We have new constitutions launched in France, Spain, Holland, and Sicily. Let us see the result before we encourage further attempts. The attempts may be made and we must abide the consequences; but I am sure it is better to retard than accelerate the operation of this most hazardous principle that is abroad.[1]

It was not surprising, therefore, that Castlereagh made no serious effort to save the Sicilian constitution of 1812. Its institution in the first place had owed much to British diplomacy. It had been seen as a means to improve the effectiveness of the Sicilian government in the war against France, and to ensure that British subsidies and action generally in the area did not run into the sands. The constitution was never a success, and Bentinck himself believed that it would survive only under a British protectorate. His successor, A'Court, had no faith in it at all, but British influence at the Bourbon court was fast disappearing in any case, with the end of the wars, and the belated Bourbon return to Naples. Castlereagh, in September 1814, favoured the modification of the constitution to the advantage of the Crown, and in the main his efforts to preserve the vestige of a constitution seem to have been inspired by his fear of British parliamentary criticism. Ferdinand, however, was intent on absolute power, and by 1816 all but the name of the Sicilian Parliament had been erased. Castlereagh not merely acquiesced; he had already gone further by secretly approving an Austro-Neapolitan treaty of June 1815 whereby the King of Naples promised that he would make no change in the political order of his kingdom without the approval of Vienna.[2] In Castlereagh's vision of the new Europe, Italy was to fall squarely under the influence and protection of Austria; a power with no maritime or territorial interests which threatened Britain; a power to whom the task of excluding the French from Italy could safely be entrusted. Castlereagh was determined that nothing should be permitted to disturb Austria in the fulfilment of this role. He confined himself to a little neighbourly advice,

[1] Webster, *B.D. 1813–15*, pp. 180–3. *C.C.* ix. 433–4, x. 10, 18.
[2] *Cambridge Historical Journal* (1923–5), pp. 158 ff. See also H. M. Lackland, 'The Failure of the Constitutional Experiment in Sicily, 1813–14', *English Historical Review*, xli. 210–35, and E. W. Crawley, 'England and the Sicilian Constitution of 1812', ibid. lv. 251–74.

designed as always to promote peace and stability. In January 1816 he expressed the hope that Austrian influence in Italy would be 'liberalised, . . . in some of its views and better adapted to the prejudices of the country'. He also pointed out that undue Austrian interference in Piedmont might cause that kingdom to look towards France. Thus not all his references to constitutionalism were designed merely to pacify and hoodwink the British Parliament — at times he really meant what he said.

Castlereagh's subservience to wider international considerations was still more strikingly demonstrated by his conduct towards Murat, ruler of Naples, who at one time seemed likely to survive the fall of his creator, Napoleon, and prevent the restoration of the Sicilian Bourbons which Britain desired. In the winter of 1813–14, Castlereagh had bowed to the Austrian desire to conciliate Murat, lest his forces in Italy should embarrass them during the closing stages of the struggle with Napoleon. After the overthrow of Napoleon, French, Spanish and Sicilian Bourbons were all soon pressing for the expulsion of Murat. The French, in particular, feared lest he should become a source of strength to Napoleon on Elba. The Austrians, too, began to take alarm lest this energetic, if not very pleasant, soldier should form a focus for revolutionary and anti-Austrian feeling in Italy. Castlereagh was delighted to adjust his policy once again, though caution was required as some of the British Opposition sympathised with Murat, while Liverpool raised his usual warnings that the policy in question did not seem to justify the complications that might ensue. His Foreign Minister, however, was more impressed by the great-power purposes to be served by support of this policy. It was true, as Wellington later admitted, that there was insufficient evidence of Murat's hostility or treachery towards the allies to justify the preparations that were being made against him in the winter of 1814–15. Although Britain had made no pledges to Murat, she was still conniving at aggression against him. Castlereagh himself admitted that 'there will be some nicety in giving to our line on this question a form most likely to prove satisfactory to Parliament'. Webster bluntly describes the episode as 'one of the greatest blots' in his career,[1] from which he was perhaps

[1] Webster, *Congress of Vienna*, p. 127.

saved from some embarrassment by Napoleon's brief return to power, and Murat's decision to throw in his lot with the latter before the allied plans against him were complete. Interestingly, Castlereagh has left a hint that he might have changed his policy once again had he been sure of Murat's sincere support against Napoleon, so completely was the fate of Naples in his mind subordinated to the overall problem of the future peace and stability of Europe.[1]

To the same end the Venetian and Genoese republics were gladly sacrificed to Austria and Piedmont respectively to strengthen northern Italy against France. Apart from a handful of Italian nationalists, the sentiment that was outraged was not national, but local; the alternative to the Italian settlement of 1814–15 was not a united Italy, but more small states, with the increased possibility of a return of French influence.[2] Some of the criticisms of these arrangements are as unhistorical as would be the claim that Castlereagh was far-sighted in adding Genoa to Piedmont, the main creator of a United Italy. In Germany, Castlereagh was similarly preoccupied with a territorial settlement that would provide most security for central Europe from French and Russian pressure. Parcels of territory were consequently shunted around rather like trucks in a railway goods yard until security could be reconciled with the local ambitions of Prussia, Austria, and, to a lesser extent, Bavaria. An alliance or confederation of the German states appealed to Castlereagh for similar reasons, as did the reconstruction of Switzerland with good frontiers and properly regulated inter-cantonal relations. For the Norwegians he may have felt some sympathy; his proposals on the future of Poland varied, but his references to an independent Poland or a Polish constitution were probably made with an eye to parliamentary approval, and he would have preferred to carve up that people between the three eastern powers in the interest of his European equilibrium.

At first sight it would appear that Castlereagh's appreciation of what was stable and enduring was sadly at fault when he insisted upon the union of the Dutch and Austrian Netherlands.

[1] Webster, *B.D. 1813–15*, p. 315.
[2] R. Weigall, *The Correspondence of Lord Burghersh, 1808–40* (1912), pp. 92–94.

L

Where most of the Vienna settlement survived for more than forty years — admittedly under considerable strain at times — the union of the Netherlands collapsed after only fifteen. In 1814 Belgian delegates warned Castlereagh that they would prefer to continue their link with Austria rather than join with the Dutch. They claimed that most of their countrymen disliked the idea of union. Liverpool foresaw that it would not be easy to reconcile the two peoples, but Castlereagh was not to be put off by such objections. The historian has no means of knowing whether he would have hesitated had Belgian opinions been more united and decisive than they were. As it was, with some Belgians favouring union with France, with others favouring Austria, and with many disposed to flow with the strongest current, Castlereagh was convinced that a firm lead on his part, coupled with a wise moderation on the part of the Dutch, would soon overcome all difficulties. He had considerable justification for this belief. Economically and strategically the union had much to commend it, and though by a successful revolution the Belgians were able to secure their independence in 1830, even then in its inception it was far from being the spontaneous revolt of an outraged nation. The international scene favoured them in 1830, and a clear-sighted statesman of Palmerston's calibre was able to perceive that an independent Belgium need not necessarily succumb to French influence. Castlereagh, in 1814–15, would have had less reason to be so optimistic. Once again, although the spirit in which he handled the fate of the Belgians was that of an eighteenth-century diplomat, his policy is both understandable and realistic in the circumstances of the time.[1]

From the above it should be clear that Castlereagh's basic aim was so to arrange the map of Europe that no great power would feel a sufficient sense of grievance to resort to war. The gravest threat came, first, from France, and secondly from Russia, and he hoped that the territorial settlement from the North Sea to northern Italy would deter, or at least impede aggression, and provide a breathing-space for the organisation of a European coalition, particularly against France. The removal of Austro-Russo-Prussian differences would facilitate the for-

[1] Renier, pp. 153, 225 ff. H. R. C. Wright, *Free Trade and Protection in the Netherlands, 1816–30* (1955).

mation of this coalition, and Castlereagh quite ruthlessly subordinated other considerations to his grand purpose wherever possible. In the process the principle of legitimacy might be ignored as freely as that of nationalism or liberalism. The prime British interest in Europe was peace; any great power war might unleash revolutionary or Napoleonic forces once again, and Castlereagh sought the most effective synthesis of monarchical, aristocratic, and even constitutional forces to prevent this catastrophe. To posterity he may appear to have been working against a phantom threat; the legions of France were never again to threaten to revolutionise Europe. But, in the short run, his precautions seemed all too necessary, as, shortly after his departure from Vienna, Napoleon escaped from Elba and toppled Louis XVIII from his throne with contemptuous ease. On 20 March 1815 Napoleon was again in Paris, and six days later Castlereagh anxiously wrote to Wellington, 'If Bonaparte could turn the tide, there is no calculating upon his plan; and we must always recollect that Poland, Saxony, and much Jacobinism are in our rear.'[1] Fortunately for the allies they were able to concentrate upon the threat of Napoleon without serious distractions in their rear, and for Castlereagh the main problem lay in Parliament where a vociferous minority favoured peace with Napoleon, and where decisive majorities were required to vote vast subsidies to the allies once again, and finally to commit Britain to war with Napoleon. At the same time he had also to prepare for the day when, with the second overthrow of Napoleon, he would be able to resume the task of bringing repose and stability to Europe. The miserable collapse of the Bourbon monarchy boded ill for the future, and though his preference lay with another restoration, he was ready to act according to circumstances. Certainly there was no enthusiasm for the Bourbons in Britain; worse, the cabinet threatened to complicate his task by demanding a punitive peace as the best way to reduce France to quiescence. There was little indication of French sympathy for the Bourbons; Talleyrand and Metternich were unco-operative, while the Tsar brooded over schemes of his own. It was therefore of immense value to Castlereagh that Napoleon should have been defeated by Wellington and the

[1] Webster, *B.D. 1813–15*, p. 317.

politically obtuse Prussians, before the main forces of the other allies could enter the fray. Wellington was thus able to reach Paris first, and seize the initiative in the negotiations with the French emissaries, and so secure the restoration of Louis XVIII in accordance with the wishes of Castlereagh.

It was not long before Castlereagh was also in Paris, with a three-point plan to promote peace. He looked to the continuance of the four-power Alliance as the main safeguard, reinforced by a new provision whereby 'an European invasion [would be] the inevitable and immediate consequence of Bonaparte's succession or that of any of his race to power in France'. But his immediate objective was to consolidate the Bourbons on the throne of France as the best guarantee of France's good behaviour in the future. This could be done by a lenient peace, but also by impressing upon Louis XVIII the arts of a constitutional monarch. He had the techniques of Charles II much in mind, and he pointed out the degree to which the responsibilities of office tamed opponents of the Crown, and reduced their popularity in public. Able men and powerful parties should not be permanently excluded from office, but office should be allowed to divide them and exhaust their energies. Powerful figures such as Fouché and Talleyrand should be employed. The Crown should withdraw as far as possible from controversy and responsibility, and avoid a headlong clash with its opponents. If not a great deal of this sound advice penetrated the dull Bourbon mind, it illustrates the gulf that existed between Castlereagh and many European conservatives. In his second line of action to consolidate the Bourbons, and thereby the peace of Europe, Castlereagh was more successful. But first he had to overcome the desire of his cabinet colleagues to impose a punitive peace on France, a desire shared by many on the continent. As Liverpool informed him in July, 'The prevailing idea in this country is that we are fairly entitled to avail ourselves of the present moment to take back from France the principal conquests of Louis XIV.'[1]

Several other letters in the same spirit followed, with the government being particularly impressed by the strength of popular feeling. As Bathurst told Castlereagh on 25 August,

[1] Yonge, ii. 193–6.

'The public could never be made to understand why we should be severely taxed, in order to preserve the integrity of France.'[1] Liverpool put forward various proposals as to how France might be more effectively controlled in the future; he feared that generosity a second time would be treated by the French as allied weakness, and was convinced that the Bourbons would not long survive the withdrawal of allied troops. At the very least the numerous French fortresses in the north-east and east should be held until the allies' frontiers had been made secure at French expense, and they should only be returned to Louis XVIII or a legitimate descendant of him, and only then if Napoleon were dead or a prisoner. Mulgrave and Sidmouth shared his concern, and were to complain of Castlereagh's leniency even after Liverpool had changed his mind. The Prussians were still more exorbitant in their demands, while the Austrians wavered uneasily between retribution and moderation. Fortunately for Castlereagh he had two powerful allies. Wellington was at one with him concerning a lenient peace, so much so that it is not always possible to separate their ideas. The Duke's reputation, especially on questions of military security, was now such that the cabinet could not withstand his arguments, while his general prestige in Europe after Waterloo could be employed against the more vindictive allies. A second resource was the Tsar, who, despite his past intrigues against the Bourbons, now came out strongly and effectively for moderation. The Russians and British co-operated closely in the drafting of the peace terms, and the Tsar personally presented them to the assembled allies.

Earlier, in the middle of August, Castlereagh and Wellington had decided that the time had come for a show-down with the cabinet. The British press were encouraging the Prussians in their extreme demands; there was danger that the Tsar would gain influence in Paris as the sole advocate of generosity. The cabinet was therefore bluntly informed that the best security against revolution and war would be the preservation of the Bourbons, that to insist on large cessions of French territory would weaken Louis XVIII's position in the eyes of his people, and that the cession of territory — especially to petty states — would be a cause of further war. If the cabinet were convinced

[1] *C.C.* x. 500–1.

that France was not to be trusted, their recent demands did not go far enough. They must strive to cripple the real power of France, and not indulge in a policy of provocative pin-pricks. Castlereagh insisted that 'it is not our business to collect trophies, but to try to bring the world back to peaceful habits'. He believed, with his eye on Russia, that France might yet prove 'a useful rather than a dangerous member of the European system'. Ample security to the allies would be provided by the temporary occupation of some French fortresses, and these could be returned as soon as France had given *'protracted proofs* of having ceased to be a revolutionary state'. With this statement of their case, Castlereagh and Wellington demanded the express approval of the cabinet, or a firm directive for an alternative policy.[1] Liverpool gave way with some reluctance, and plainly with some anxious glances towards the Francophobe British public. It is striking how his own doubts faded as the latter lost interest in the question, and he was soon to be found reminding Mulgrave and Sidmouth that 'the real reduction of the power of old France is a chimera, unless it were produced by a moral and internal schism in the country'.[2] By the beginning of September the Austrian hesitations were being overcome, and the isolated Prussians were soon compelled to give way. By 20 September the allies had reached agreement.

Castlereagh's own faith in the Bourbons was briefly shaken at this time by the King's acceptance of Talleyrand's resignation, but the succeeding Richelieu ministry soon proved itself a moderate representative of the Right. Nevertheless, Castlereagh agreed with many other observers at this time that the early withdrawal of allied troops would probably be followed by the overthrow of the regime, and the stationing of an allied army of occupation in northern France for three or five years was designed as much to prevent this as to protect Europe against France. By the other terms of the second Treaty of Paris the French frontiers were reduced broadly to those of 1790, France was to pay an indemnity, and meet the claims of certain private creditors. The policy of Castlereagh, Wellington and the Tsar had prevailed; precautions were taken 'not against France as a nation, but against France as the concentration of military

[1] Gurwood, xii. 596–601. *C.C.* x. 484–91.   [2] Sidmouth, iii. 131–7.

Jacobinism'. As Henry Kissinger remarks, 'At no other time in his career did Castlereagh show to greater advantage than in his battle for the equilibrium of Paris.'[1] Machiavelli would also have approved; 'men ought either to be well treated or crushed, because they can avenge themselves of lighter injuries, of more serious ones they cannot; therefore the injury that is to be done to a man ought to be of such a kind that one does not stand in fear of revenge'.[2]

Critical as were these negotiations for a peace settlement with France, one suspects that more to Castlereagh's taste were the discussions which led to the conclusion of the Quadruple Alliance in November 1815. He noted, 'In deciding upon any arrangement, the first object to attend to is that it shall preserve unimpaired the Alliance to which Europe already owes its deliverance, and on the permanence of which union it ought in wisdom to rely above every other measure for its future peace and preservation.' But his ideas on the form which the Alliance should now take had undergone some modification since the beginning of 1815; in particular, its objectives and composition became more limited. During the last few weeks of his residence at Vienna early in 1815 he had enthusiastically taken up the problem of a general guarantee of all Europe against aggression, an idea mooted by Pitt in 1805, and one which Castlereagh himself had vainly tried to include in the Treaty of Chaumont in 1814. At this time he wished to include France in the great-power declaration to this end. He defined his aim as 'a *general accord and guarantee* between the Great Powers of Europe, with a determination to support the arrangement agreed upon, and to turn the general influence, and, if necessary, the general arms, against the Power that shall first attempt to disturb the Continental peace'.

Castlereagh was greatly assisted in the preparation of draft proposals by Gentz, a student of Kant, and a great enthusiast for the development of the public law of Europe and international co-operation. Gentz was responsible for many of the details. For a time it appeared that the guarantee might receive general approval, but difficulties arose when an attempt was made to extend its operations to the Ottoman empire. It also speedily

[1] Kissinger, p. 180.   [2] *The Prince* (London, 1908), p. 19.

became apparent that the idea was viewed with the utmost suspicion by the British Parliament, and possibly also by the cabinet. Castlereagh was obliged to assert before the Commons that Gentz's draft declaration of guarantee was not an official document, and though most of the details are obscure, the momentum in favour of the proposal was soon lost. It was quietly forgotten until the autumn of 1815 when Castlereagh firmly opposed the inclusion of such a clause in the Quadruple Alliance. He knew that the British Parliament was averse, and consequently he was seeking more limited means whereby the peace of Europe might be assured.

The miserable collapse of the Bourbons in March 1815 in the face of Napoleon had also helped to bring Castlereagh down to earth, and drove him to the conclusion that the Alliance should not merely protect Europe from French aggression, but from Napoleon himself. The French must be made to see that their acceptance of Napoleon or his family would inevitably precipitate a European invasion of France, now, and in the future. Only by such a threat could French opinion be mobilised against the Bonapartes. This was an important innovation in his policy, but in other matters respecting the Alliance he was obliged to proceed with caution lest opinion in Britain should be aroused. He therefore insisted that the remaining provisions of the Quadruple Alliance must be confined to assurances of mutual aid in the event of French aggression. Britain could not pledge herself to maintain the Bourbons on the French throne, and in the event of revolution in France he could agree to no more than that the allies should 'concert among themselves . . . the measures which they may judge necessary' against revolutionary aggression alone. To provide for the more general problems of Europe and to try to preserve the Alliance in their solution, Castlereagh turned from his ambitious proposals for a general guarantee to the more limited, yet excitingly novel commitment described by Article VI of the treaty of Alliance. The four allies agreed to renew their meetings 'at fixed periods, . . . for the purpose of consulting upon their common interests, and for the consideration of the measures which at each of these periods shall be considered the most salutary for the repose and prosperity of nations and for the maintenance of the peace of Europe'.

The cabinet was later to remind Castlereagh that only the exceptional international conditions which Britain had experienced since 1789 enabled the government to accept such commitments in November 1815. The Commons had accepted the treaties by 240 votes to 77 on 20 February 1816, but not before several critics had spoken in alarmist terms of the threat from the Quadruple Alliance to the liberties of Europe, and perhaps of Britain also. Horner thought one military despot had been overthrown only to be replaced by three new ones. Romilly believed this to have been the most important debate in which he had ever participated.[1] Even the British government approved the Alliance with no great enthusiasm, so that from the outset Castlereagh was endeavouring to pursue a policy for which only Wellington among his leading colleagues showed any enthusiasm. Not that this was a new development. A year earlier the negotiations at Vienna over Poland and Saxony had demonstrated how far he was parting company with the rest of the cabinet. Castlereagh was intent on something more than a few years of peace, after which the world might have returned to the eighteenth-century version of international politics. Then, Britain had relied upon her economic power, upon her navy, and, in time of crisis, upon *ad hoc* alliances. Now, Castlereagh, without propounding schemes for 'perpetual peace', was more ambitious. He relied upon the traditional bases of British power, but he had had too much personal experience of the difficulty of conducting a war against so formidable an antagonist as Napoleon for him to rely on such supports alone. Hence his desire for a long-term Alliance of the other great powers, and, to preserve the unity of that Alliance as well as to facilitate its management of the French problem, occasional meetings of the ministers of each of these powers.

Yet the above conclusion begs at least one important conclusion. Others, besides Castlereagh, had had personal experience of the difficulty of conducting a war against the Napoleonic empire, but this had not made them enthusiasts for the emerging 'Congress System'. It may be more than a coincidence that only Castlereagh and Wellington, of all leading

[1] *Hansard*, xxxii. 350 ff., 673 ff., 748 ff. Romilly, iii. 220–9. See also White, *From Waterloo to Peterloo*, pp. 4–7.

British personalities, had actually been on the continent of Europe in the thick of many of the great events of the last few years. They thus had personal knowledge and personal acquaintanceships which their countrymen could not share; they had seen how easily the Alliance could disintegrate, how deep the rivalries ran, how narrowly disaster had been averted. This may be so, and at the same time they may have been drawn by their close personal contacts with all the leading political figures on the continent to seek a perpetuation of the old relationships into the peace. The old Whig story that Castlereagh's head had been turned by association with kings and emperors may not wholly be without foundation, but if so, the attraction lay in the political and not the social contacts, which he found so tedious. Indeed, if one can be sure of anything in a problem where the evidence is so tenuous, what seems to emerge above all is Castlereagh's conviction that these occasional meetings of international statesmen were an excellent way of doing business. Never in his life was Castlereagh given to building elaborate, theoretical structures. Not surprisingly, therefore, most of his comment on the Congress System was confined to the fact that it worked, and generally worked well.

His policy with respect to the Congress System was therefore an intensely personal thing. Not surprisingly it was misunderstood and misrepresented. Castlereagh saw it as the most effective means of preserving the Alliance, and therefore the peace of Europe, which he held to be Britain's greatest interest.

But in the eyes of many contemporaries and of subsequent generations, the association with the reactionary powers of Europe appeared to be the main feature of his policy.[1] The great spokesman of repression in Britain appeared equally intent on blackening the name of Britain internationally by conniving at the suppression of liberal and national sentiments throughout Europe. Substance appeared to be lent to this charge by the

[1] As lately as 1946 Sir Harold Nicolson claimed (*Congress of Vienna*, pp. 259–65) that Castlereagh withdrew from the Holy Alliance in 1818. There is a treble confusion here, as Britain never belonged to this Alliance, never subscribed to the principles which Nicolson attributes to it, nor was the Holy Alliance as signed in 1815 the instrument which Nicolson assumes it to have been.

efforts of Metternich and other European statesmen to turn the Quadruple Alliance and the Congress System into an instrument for the suppression of revolution throughout Europe. Such a policy was far removed from the intentions of Castlereagh, and he strove to prevent this distortion of his concept of the Alliance. How far he succeeded and how far this led him into deepening difficulties will be the subject of a later chapter. What must be noticed here is the continuous theme running throughout Castlereagh's policy during the whole period of peace-making, from the territorial redistribution to the provisions of the Quadruple Alliance. Peace founded upon a satisfactory and equitable balance of power was his prime aim; if, in the process, he appeared to favour despotic states and conservative principles, this tendency arose out of more than his own admittedly strong political prejudices; it arose out of a belief that these would best subserve his basic policy.

6

Leader of the House of Commons 1812–22

The Leadership of the House of Commons is the least explored aspect of Castlereagh's career; it is also one of the most criticised. It coincided with one of the greatest eras of popular distress and discontent in British history. Yet even this phase of his career has its admirers. Sir Charles Webster has described him as the best manager of the Commons since Walpole,[1] and indeed once one has cut through party prejudice, a remarkable degree of unanimity is to be found among contemporary opinion. Creevey, one of his arch-critics, thought party management his only talent. '[He] managed a corrupt House of Commons pretty well, with some address. This is the whole of his intellectual merit.' Greville, who confessed to little personal knowledge of Castlereagh, made a determined effort to sum up his career from the opinions of others. He concluded, 'I believe he was considered one of the best managers of the House of Commons who ever sat in it, and he was eminently possessed of the good taste, good humour, and agreeable manners which are more requisite to make a good leader than eloquence, however brilliant.' Lord John Russell, looking back over his vast experience of parliamentary life, remarked, 'yet I never knew two men who had more influence in the House of Commons than Lord Castlereagh and Lord Althorp'. Even Brougham, his greatest opponent in debate, was generous in his praise. He thought Castlereagh more important than the rest of the cabinet put together; he had good judgement and good manners; he was the only gentleman in the cabinet.[2]

[1] Webster, *Castlereagh, 1815–22*, p. 31.
[2] *Greville Memoirs*, i. 127–8. Lord John Russell, *Recollections and Suggestions, 1813–73* (1875), p. 262. Creevey, ii. 44, 49.

At the time of Spencer Perceval's assassination in May 1812, there was little in Castlereagh's past career in the British House of Commons to suggest that he would ultimately be able to command so much respect and attention. If some had been impressed by his talent as 'a man of business', by his courage and imperturbability, he was not regarded as an obvious choice for the first or second place in a government. There is perhaps a hint of surprise in Liverpool's commendation of his parliamentary success as early as December 1812. He thought Castlereagh had very considerably raised his reputation in the Commons in the last few months.[1] In the past his failings as an orator had helped to conceal his potential as a parliamentarian, and indeed they continued to prove something of a handicap after 1812. Brougham concluded that Castlereagh's 'capacity was greatly underrated from the poverty of his discourse; and his ideas passed for much less than they were worth, from the habitual obscurity of his expressions'. Castlereagh's delivery was often halting, punctuated by quaint Irishisms, and lacked 'the charm of poetic fancy . . . the force of condensed expression'. He once spoke of 'a company making new strides, and taking fresh dimensions of prosperity', and added 'there was no distress in this country that could not be removed by a due application of the principles of resurrection'. It is not surprising that his speeches were awaited with some interest. Young Stratford Canning a little pompously but none the less truly remarked, 'A habit of using the first word that came to hand without much regard to its signification, and an involved method of composition . . . had exposed him to criticism and even to ridicule, nor was he in private conversation altogether free from the same defects'. But he went on to reveal Castlereagh's strong points, for, as he said, 'a strong natural capacity and a clear judgement cropped out from under the rubbish, and further intercourse with him served to confirm my new conception of his better qualities'.[2]

Even as an orator Castlereagh had some strong points. Henry Hobhouse commented, 'It has been often remarked that he

[1] Yonge, i. 448.

[2] *Annual Register* (1822), pp. 208 ff. Lane Poole, *Stratford Canning*, i. 213.

always spoke best when most severely attacked. He has been likened to a top, which spins best when it is most whipped.'[1] He made much use of irony and sarcasm, and the overall impact — once his idiosyncrasies are set on one side — was impressive. Greville concluded, 'he never spoke ill: his speeches were continually replete with good sense and strong arguments, and though they seldom offered much to admire, they generally contained a great deal to be answered'. Much as the sharper intellects and connoisseurs of debate might lament the passing of Pitt and Fox, and bemoan an age of mediocrity,[2] it is clear that many of the less intellectual members were happier under the leadership of second raters such as Addington, Perceval and Castlereagh. Sturdy country gentlemen delighted in uncomplicated politics, they disliked brilliance and Classical allusions, which were meaningful only to the erudite few, nor were they worried when Castlereagh stumbled in his discourses in his weakest subject — finance — for they were no better at figures themselves. Lord John Russell summed up the position admirably with both Castlereagh and Althorp in mind,

There are qualities which govern men, such as sincerity, and a conviction on the part of the hearers that the Minister is a man to be trusted, which has more to do with influence over the House of Commons than the most brilliant flights of fancy and the keenest wit.[3]

At times, inevitably, Castlereagh misunderstood the temper of the House, as, for instance, in 1816 when he spoke of 'the ignorant impatience of taxation', or when, in 1805, he had shocked City interests by welcoming the news that Villeneuve had sailed for the West Indies. What is perhaps more surprising is his success despite his frequent efforts to remove the conduct of foreign policy from the purview of Parliament. Although in his early days in the Irish Parliament he had fiercely attacked Irish ministers for their secrecy, his own experience of office had encouraged a similar uncommunicativeness. Possibly the nature of Irish politics at the end of the eighteenth century was peculiarly responsible for this trait, but it is also in accordance

[1] Aspinall, *Hobhouse Diary*, p. 92.

[2] Holland, ii. 213. Fox-Strangeways, pp. 157–9.

[3] Russell, *Recollections*, pp. 26–27, 262.

with his character as a whole. As it was, the insularity of the average British member of the Commons saved him from persistent interrogation on foreign affairs. More serious in its effects would appear to have been his reluctance to delegate parliamentary business, in part a product of the poorness of the government front-bench material at his disposal for much of this period, but also a result of his own character. At the Foreign Office, his inability to delegate has already been noted, and he was charged with the same fault as Leader of the House. There are also hints of personal jealousies being at work which prevented him from making full use of the services of Canning and Peel.[1] Lord Melbourne recalled,

Partly from the easiness of his nature, which let everybody do as they liked, partly from a knack which he had of shuffling over important questions nobody knew how, and partly from jealousy of Canning, Castlereagh had either taken or suffered to be cast upon him the whole business of the House and management of every question. When Canning succeeded to him he . . . at once determined to make each Minister transact his own business . . . and only himself to exercise a general superintendence. . . .[2]

Lord Colchester, for one, expected Canning to keep the House in better order, but according to Creevey some government supporters were soon deploring Canning's irritability, and regretting the passing of the urbane Castlereagh. Hobhouse certainly preferred Castlereagh as Leader, despite his 'disposition to compromise'. Finally, for what it is worth, Charles Arbuthnot had assured Castlereagh in 1819 that he stood with the Commons 'as well as man can do, that there is the greatest confidence in you, & that when you are present & are from good health able to make exertions, *all does well*'.[3]

A major problem facing the Leader of the House at this time was the fact that about half the Commons prided themselves on their attachment to no party. This mass of independents was a frequent cause of political uncertainty. It was over taxes in time

[1] Gash, *Peel*, i. 290–2.
[2] L. C. Sanders, *Lord Melbourne's Papers* (1889), pp. 98–99.
[3] Colchester, iii. 240, 256. Creevey, ii. 63. Aspinall, *Hobhouse Diary*, pp. 91–92, 102–3. Aspinall, *Arbuthnot*, pp. 13–18.

of peace that cabinet and Parliament most sharply divided, and
here the independents would halloo with Brougham and Joseph
Hume in pursuit of the government fox who had made off with
their rents as keenly as any Whig or Radical.[1] Over the Corn
Laws and other measures deemed necessary for the protection
of their interests they could be as obdurate as any fixed opponent of the government. It was problems of this nature that
made the task of government so difficult in the early nineteenth
century. It meant that basically there were two oppositions; the
formal one of true Whigs and Radicals, normally 170 or so in
strength, and the informal one of unknown potential which,
when some matter of interest to it arose, might destroy the
government's majority, and continue on its wayward course
unless or until the cabinet confronted it with an issue of confidence — a precarious proceeding, but normally safe in view of
the majority of the independents' dislike of the Whig-Radical
alternative. Castlereagh himself at times appreciated this fact,
and remarked to Mrs. Arbuthnot in 1822 that certain members
liked to cut a figure in the Opposition press and please their
constituents, but 'they trust to good luck that their votes will
only lessen, not overturn our majority'. It was not always easy
to take so detached a view of the matter.

This dislike of the Opposition by a majority of the unattached
members sprang from a variety of causes. During the last years
of the war some of the Opposition had been suspect as advocates
of a negotiated peace, while the readiness of the remainder to
pursue the war with sufficient vigour was doubted. Grenville, in
particular, seemed anxious to reduce the expense of the war, and
to withdraw from the Peninsula. The growing number of allied
victories from the end of 1812 greatly strengthened the government, and discredited the defeatists, and the sessions of 1813–14

[1] It will be noted in this chapter that I continue to exclude the word
'Tory' to describe the government. As late as 1812 the ministry
rejected Opposition claims to the exclusive use of the title 'Whig', and
it was not until about 1818 that the Grey–Grenville claims were
widely accepted. Even then, the description 'Tory' was mainly used by
writers and some backbenchers, and only very slowly by members of
the government. A. S. Foord, *His Majesty's Opposition, 1714–1830*
(1964), pp. 443 ff.

were unusually quiet for this reason. Similarly, although the
cabinet contained some who desired to remove the disabilities of
the Catholics — and these included Castlereagh[1] — the ardent
Protestants could view the Liverpool cabinet with more confidence than the Opposition, who had made Catholic relief into a
major principle in their relations with King and Regent. Many
country gentlemen and rich business men were also drawn to the
government when the hard times following the conclusion of
peace gave rise to popular discontent and disturbance. The
government appeared a more unqualified champion of law and
order than the divided Opposition. The latter were further
weakened by the many shades of opinion within their ranks,
ranging from the conservative Grenvilles, through the cautious
Greys and progressive Whigs to the increasingly vociferous
Radicals. These divisions often prevented the emergence of a
united strategy, and they caused the leadership in the Commons
to fall to so innocuous a figure as Tierney.

Consequently spirited efforts by Whitbread, Brougham and
Hume did not always secure the support they deserved, even
from the formal Opposition. But more serious for the future of
the Opposition was the fear that, if a ministry were to be formed
from among its ranks, the Radicals would exercise dispro-
portionate influence. W. H. Fremantle observed on 24 January
1821, 'Never was anything, however, so low and wretched as
the Treasury Bench', but he was forced to add that so great was
the parliamentary aversion to the Radicals, and consequently to
the Whigs, that the ministry was certain to survive.[2] The
Radicals were also contributing to the slow drift of the Grenvilles
towards the government, which was to result in an actual
junction in 1821. Nor could the Opposition draw hope and
strength from the existence of a 'reversionary interest', that is,
of an heir to the throne around whom a potential ministry might
gather. The Regent had changed sides before 1812, and the
death of his daughter in 1817 had removed all immediate
prospect of the creation of such an interest. If the absence
of a 'reversionary interest' added to public discontent by
diminishing still further the possibility of a change of government by parliamentary means, the ensuing discontent added

---

[1] See above, p. 35.   [2] Buckingham, *George IV*, i. 112–13, 118.

M

to the government's supporters among the upper classes.[1]
Consequently, much of the government's strength in the
Commons was based upon the weakness and nature of the
Opposition.

This did not mean that the government could ignore the
wishes of independent members; important concessions,
especially in matters affecting taxation and agriculture, had
often to be made to them. The government was also expected to
make the best possible use of political talent that was not far
removed from it in ideas and policy; hence the continuing
negotiations with Canning after June 1812, and the expensive
concessions made by the government to win the Grenvilles in
1821. In short, the majority of independents may have disliked
the Opposition, or may have been prepared to acquiesce in the
Regent's choice of ministry, but the latter could not ride rough-
shod over their vital interests, and it had to embrace a reasonable
proportion of the political talent of the country in order to
retain confidence. Therefore, although the choice of ministry
still lay with the Crown, and although Parliament would have
accepted the Whigs in 1812 had the Regent been so minded, the
wishes and prejudices of the Commons could not be ignored. As
for the Regent himself, his choice of ministers had been effectively
limited in 1812 by his own quarrel with the Whigs, and by the
impossibility of forming an effective alternative combination
of ministers from the remaining leading politicians in 1812. So
long as the Prince was determined to have nothing to do with
the Whigs he was left with no alternative to the Liverpool
ministry. When the latter failed to procure him a divorce in
1820, shortly after he became King, his grumblings and threats
were of no avail. Admittedly the cabinet often took a black view
of their own prospects, but the King could find no suitable
alternative, and he was reduced to personal slights at the
expense of his ministers, and innocent flirtations with the
Opposition as the only means whereby to salve his injured ego.
Indeed, the Grenvilles believed in June 1820 that a political
position had been reached wherein no third party could control
a majority in the Commons, and that it was barely within the

[1] F. O. Darvall, *Popular Disturbances and Public Order in Regency
England* (1934), pp. 309–10.

competence of the government or present Opposition combinations to do so.[1]

Although the personality of Castlereagh, the likes and dislikes of the Crown and the independents, and the character of the Opposition afford many important clues to the political history of this period, it is necessary also to glance at the powers at the disposal of the government to facilitate the creation and control of a parliamentary majority. It has, for instance, been asserted that the government could have lost the election of 1818 had the electorate been so minded; as it was, the new House was so independently minded that the government survived mainly because sufficient unattached members feared a Whig–Radical government. Certainly the power of the Liverpool ministry to influence the composition and voting of the Commons had dropped sharply compared with the eighteenth century. Legislation between 1780 and 1809 had made vast inroads on government influence, and an investigation in 1821 revealed fewer than fifty placemen in the Commons who held offices 'in a sense to which influence could be fairly attached'. The number of Treasury boroughs now barely reached double figures. The government had little money for electoral purposes, and, according to Liverpool, dared not use it as a result of Curwen's bill of 1809 against electoral corruption.

Admittedly, more use had been made of honours to win supporters from the days of the younger Pitt, but Liverpool shared the reluctance of George III to create new peers too indiscriminately. Likewise the war had created considerable opportunities for the purchase of support — through contracts and new offices — but the war had ended in 1815, and there had followed a vast run-down in government expenditure and establishments. Castlereagh claimed in 1822 that no less than 2,000 civil offices had been abolished since the war. There were still many small favours that could be dispensed, including occasional use of tax remittances to government supporters after 1815. M.P.s had also to approach the government to secure control for themselves of some forms of local patronage, and some complained that there was not more to be shared among them. On the other hand, Lords Lieutenant were no

[1] Buckingham, *George IV*, i. 32–33.

longer removed with a change of ministry; revenue appointments had lost their political value in the last century. Francis
Horner in 1811 thought that judges were now appointed
impartially, while Castlereagh claimed in 1822 that seven-
eighths of colonial appointments were now in the hands of local
officers. His argument that the Admiralty and Horse Guards
were no longer taking political opinions into account in their
appointments and promotions does not appear wholly accurate,
at least so far as the navy was concerned, while there was talk of
disfranchising dockyard employees more than a generation later
as these appointments appeared to be so much at the mercy of
political opinions. The government was also reluctant to part
with certain offices, which were basically superfluous to
efficient and economic government. They were by now too few
to be of significant political importance, but it is interesting to
note that political considerations continued to influence the
appointment of, for instance, junior Lords of the Admiralty
until the 1850s.[1]

In these circumstances Castlereagh and his colleagues had
often to tread warily in trying to ensure a majority for a
particular issue. Indeed, on one occasion in 1819 Charles Wynn
noted two government Whips, Holmes and Lushington, vainly
trying to prevent the departure of many members who were
considered to be steady government supporters. Placemen could,
of course, be easily dealt with, but more delicate methods were
needed for most supporters. It was important to arrange the
dates of the parliamentary sessions so that they did not clash
with the shooting season; it was desirable to end the session
before the summer was far advanced, and it was inadvisable to
open a session in the autumn if it could be avoided. Even when
the country gentlemen were in town, and were not fidgeting to
escape to the freedom of their broad acres, and to return to the
local politics which they dominated, they had to be handled with
care. Peel remarked in 1828 that they were 'most excellent men,
who will attend one night, but who will not leave their favourite
pursuits to sit up till 2 or 3 o'clock fighting questions of detail

[1] N. Gash, *Politics in the Age of Peel* (1953), *passim.* A. S. Foord,
English Historical Review, lxii. 484–507. C. J. Bartlett, *Great Britain
and Sea Power, 1815–53* (1963), pp. 7–8, 45–46, 297.

on which, however, a Government must have a majority'.[1] Late
in the session of 1822 Castlereagh penned a personal appeal to
a supporter, declaring that his assistance was much needed, and
adding that he had 'every reason to hope that the division will
take place in time to go away to dinner'.[2] In the case of the most
distinguished of the country gentlemen such pains were well
worth taking, as their standing in Parliament often swayed other
votes. Castlereagh was also careful to maintain a close and
friendly relationship with the very influential Wilberforce,
whose opinions he sometimes made considerable efforts to try to
influence.[3]

Castlereagh did much of the letterwriting himself, either brief
notes to a large number of supporters, or a longer letter to a
person of some influence, who could explain the policy to others,
or who directly controlled votes in the Commons, such as great
borough-mongers like Lord Lonsdale or the Earl of Rutland.
Often the task could be accomplished verbally, and here Charles
Arbuthnot — Joint-Secretary of the Treasury and a controller
of government patronage — was very active. Sometimes more
forceful measures were required, as on 20 June 1820 when
Castlereagh summoned all the office-holders under the Crown
to the Foreign Office, and there impressed upon them the critical
nature of the impending debates. Party meetings as such were
few and far between, and were not called to hear the opinions of
backbenchers, but to inform them of government policy. Lord
Colchester records occasions in 1817 and 1818, when Liverpool
summoned up to seventy M.P.s to Fife House to explain
controversial points of government policy. The second of these
meetings, however, failed to prevent a government defeat on the
question of grants to the royal dukes on their forthcoming
marriages. The government's machinery for controlling its
supporters was completed by the appointment of five or six
Whips, who nominally served as Lords of the Treasury.[4]

[1] Gash, *Mr. Secretary Peel*, i. 454.
[2] Aspinall, *English Historical Review*, xli. 399. Asa Briggs, *The Age
of Improvement* (1959), p. 188 n.
[3] *Wilberforce*, v. 96.
[4] Colchester, ii. 604, iii. 43. Aspinall, *English Historical Review*,
xli. 396–7.

Among the most important of the government's regular supporters were the Irish members, of whom only about one-fifth normally supported the Opposition, but whose discipline, according to Castlereagh, was 'very relaxed'. Castlereagh himself continued to follow Irish politics closely,[1] but he was doubtless happy to delegate the management of the temperamental Irish members to the Chief Secretary of Ireland. It was particularly difficult to secure Irish attendance in London before Christmas, and if this were achieved they were unlikely to be present in the New Year. In any case, many were anxious to return to Ireland for the March assizes. The government's task was eased by the proportionately greater residue of patronage in Ireland, but it was not always easy to find the time and patience to manage the applicants. About half of the correspondence of the Chief Secretary was devoted to Irish patronage. Irish support of the government perhaps reached its peak after the election of 1818, when the ministry counted on the support of 71 of the 100 Irish members, but an interesting analysis of voting patterns on 36 major questions in 1821–2 shows only 45 voting regularly with the government, 21 against, with 2 splitting their votes, and 32 not voting at all.[2]

The same analysis, when applied to English constituencies, reveals that nearly half of the government's support came from close boroughs. Welsh, Scottish and Irish constituencies provided another quarter between them. The counties, open boroughs and cities provided the rest, but twice as many of their representatives normally voted with the Opposition, who drew only about one-third of their remaining support from other sources. But it would appear that in the critical divisions of 1821–2, of the seventy-two county members who voted during these sessions, nearly half voted with the government, and several abstained rather than turn the government out. Ten county members voted both for and against the ministry in this period.[3]

[1] See above, pp. 35 ff.

[2] McDowell, *Public Opinion and Government Policy in Ireland*, ii. 46–49. Gash, *Peel*, i. 118–19. Yonge, ii. 249. *English Historical Documents, 1783–1832*, p. 254.

[3] *English Historical Documents, 1783–1832*, p. 254.

Such, then, were the strengths and weaknesses of the Liverpool ministry in the Commons, with its survival resting on the twin support afforded by royal and 'independent' favour and prejudice. These were the considerations which Castlereagh had to weigh as Leader of the House, and a brief survey of the period when he held this office may help to illumine the operation of this system. Once the initial difficulties of the new ministry had been overcome in 1812, the rising tide of allied victories, and especially those of Wellington in Spain, gave the cabinet both prestige and popularity. The sessions of 1813 and 1814 were among the quietest in the history of Parliament, with little of note taking place. This undoubtedly facilitated Castlereagh's lengthy absence on the continent in the early months of 1814. As Thomas Grenville remarked in April 1814, 'In the meantime, the general success of the moment carries on the business of the House of Commons, without Lord Castlereagh', and despite the fact that his subordinate, Vansittart, was 'so overpowered'.[1] But peace brought depression; trade, prices and rents all declined, and the demand was all for reduced taxes. The Commons in November 1814 was once again a noisy place. Liverpool begged Castlereagh to return from Vienna as soon as possible; no other member of the government could command such respect in the Commons. Napoleon's Hundred Days merely interrupted the outcry, and Castlereagh approached the parliamentary session of 1816 with many apprehensions.[2] With his customary optimism, however, he hoped with '*firmness*' to prevail.

The ranks of the Opposition had now been reinforced by the return of Brougham to the Commons after an absence of four years. He was up on the first day of the new session, and, according to one observer, he 'shook Castlereagh and frightened the other side more than they had been for years'. A widespread hostility to the government's desire to retain the income tax to ease its complex post-war financial problems gave Brougham his first great opening. He organised this discontent into an effective public outcry, and turned a government majority of over 50 into a minority of 37. 'By Heaven!' wrote Squire Western, 'you never saw men so chopfallen as the Ministers —

---

[1] Buckingham, *Regency*, ii. 63, 66.
[2] Aspinall, *Letters of George IV*, ii. 150.

Castlereagh beyond belief, I see it in every line of his face.' The malt tax had likewise to be abandoned, and the Treasury was reduced to the shameful expedient of borrowing in time of peace in order to meet current expenditure. For once the Commons' boasted sense of responsibility had been sadly absent, though the government may have been driven to some useful economies in the process. Certainly the somewhat over-ambitious plans of the Admiralty were pruned.[1] But it was perhaps fortunate for the government that Brougham, for all his brilliance and energy, lacked the nicety of judgement so necessary if his parliamentary victories were to gain any quality of permanence. Intoxicated by his success, he turned his guns on the Regent, and forfeited much of his support in consequence. Castlereagh noted that Brougham's violence was a major government asset, and ministerial confidence revived.[2]

Nevertheless, it is doubtful, even had Brougham shown more discrimination, whether he could have overthrown the government — that is, unless they panicked as Liverpool seemed near to doing on 23 March 1816. Fremantle subsequently noted in February 1819,

As to the idea of the Government breaking up, or there being the least intention of a change, be assured it is no such thing . . . whenever a question comes of vital importance to them, you will see the country gentlemen come forward to prevent the Opposition coming in.

Or as one intimate of Holland House put it, one violent speech could disrupt the Opposition, and give Liverpool the power of Pitt after 1792.[3] As it was, the sessions of 1817 and 1818 were less perilous for the government in Parliament, the popular disturbances acting as a restraint on many members, while the Opposition was plagued with its customary divisions. The situation changed again in 1819, partly as a result of the election of 1818, which returned a large number of new and uncommitted members to the Commons, and the government speedily ran into difficulties in the new session.

[1] Bartlett, *Great Britain and Sea Power*, pp. 13–26.
[2] Aspinall, *Letters of George IV*, ii. 154–60. Fox-Strangeways, p. 234. Creevey, i. 250–1. New, *Brougham*, p. 164.
[3] Buckingham, *Regency*, ii. 308. Creevey, i. 260.

There was the usual pressure for government economy, the additional provision for the royal princes in 1818–19 was unpopular, and the ministry suffered major defeats on criminal law reform, and the reform of the royal burghs of Scotland. These defeats owed much to bad management. Castlereagh was ill for part of the session, and while his own standing in Parliament was unshaken, he gave signs of tiredness and lack of confidence. There was no one on the ministerial benches who could take his place, and worse, several junior ministers were failing to attend as regularly as they should. Eldon bluntly complained of a 'supineness in the official attendance which disquieted the independent members, and a general want of energy in the H. of C. by which the Opposition has been allowed to originate every motion and to have got possession of the Committees upon the main questions now under consideration'. Independent members told Arbuthnot that they did not see why they should support a government which did not support itself, and both Arbuthnot and Huskisson finally warned Liverpool that the ministry would be broken unless official attendance improved. They found the Prime Minister verbose, but weak and disinclined to act without Castlereagh.[1] The crisis was finally surmounted on 18 May when the Opposition pressed a division on a motion for the appointment of a committee to inquire into the state of the nation. The government was able to rally its forces, and secured a vote of 357 against 178 in an unusually full House. Some three weeks later an Opposition attack on the government's financial policy was even more convincingly defeated, with Castlereagh winning great applause for his spirited defence.[2]

The sessions of 1817 and 1819 were much concerned with popular disorder, but since parliamentary opinion mainly favoured the government, these problems can more conveniently be dealt with later. The next issue to test the ministry's parliamentary strength occurred in 1820, when the government vainly endeavoured by the Bill of Pains and Penalties to procure a divorce for George IV. Since 1806 his relations with his wife,

[1] Aspinall, *Arbuthnot*, pp. 13–18. Colchester, ii. 71–73. Aspinall, *Letters of George IV*, ii. 288.

[2] *Hansard*, xl. 912–74.

Caroline of Brunswick, had been like a grumbling appendix in
the body politic. After their breach with George, as Prince
Regent in 1811–12, some of the Whigs, and many Radicals, had
begun to explore the political advantages of association with the
Princess. Castlereagh, as Leader of the Commons, had endeavoured to quieten the occasional splutters of political interest
which the Prince's relations with his wife provoked. The Prince
had several times spoken of divorce, but his government had
expressed themselves dissatisfied with the evidence of Caroline's
reputed infidelity, or perhaps they perceived that George's own
reputation and popularity were not such as to permit an easy
passage for divorce proceedings.

George III died on 29 January 1820, and one of the new
King's first acts was to press for his release from his wife. The
government were again averse, and proposed 'a liberal provision' for Caroline provided she remained abroad, and tried to
salve the King's pride by agreeing that her name should be
omitted from the Liturgy. George, however, threatened to part
with his ministers, and on 13 February 1820 Castlereagh thought
the government was 'virtually dissolved' and himself about to
become a 'Kentish farmer'. At this time he was the main cabinet
negotiator with the King as the latter had fallen out with
Liverpool. The King was persuaded to submit, but the careful
plans of the cabinet were upset by the arrival of Caroline in
London to a tumultuous reception from the masses. Castlereagh
and Wellington continued the quest for a compromise solution,
but Caroline insisted on her inclusion in the Liturgy. To this
Castlereagh replied, 'You might as easily move Carlton House'.
Opinion in the Commons was at first with the government, and
391 voted against 124 in favour of Wilberforce's resolution
urging Caroline to accept the government's offer. When she
still refused, Castlereagh believed that a Bill of Pains and
Penalties could easily be carried through Parliament. He later
admitted that the government would have striven to avoid the
scandal had the character of the trial been foreseen. The trial
opened in the Lords in August, and from the outset it was clear
that the government's laboriously collected evidence and
witnesses could not stand up to the withering attacks of
Brougham. More and more peers felt with Grey that no case

was being made against Caroline; Harrowby and Canning in the cabinet secretly opposed the bill, while other ministers showed little vigour. Castlereagh maintained a public air of optimistic nonchalance to the last, though Wilberforce at one point privately found him very impressed by the dangers of the situation.[1] In the public mind Castlereagh and Sidmouth were regarded as the chief persecutors of Caroline, and the former was hooted out of Covent Garden early in November.[2] Faced by a falling majority in the Lords, Liverpool withdrew the bill.

The popular excitement soon died down, and not even Caroline's effort to secure entry to Westminster Abbey for the Coronation in the following year could revive it. But the political situation was far from clear. George IV was outraged against his ministers, and would have changed them had a satisfactory alternative existed. Failing the pleasure of dismissal, he wallowed in self-pity, and revenged himself with rudeness and intrigues, directed particularly against Liverpool, though his relations with Castlereagh also remained cool until October 1821. The Queen's Affair was followed by the resignation of Canning, and it remained to be seen whether the Commons still had confidence in the ministry. The latter took no chances, and made unusually careful preparations for the forthcoming session. Castlereagh sent a well-considered circular to all government supporters on 5 December 1820, explaining ministerial policy concerning Caroline, and inviting comments. Liverpool himself wrote to some independent members.[3] This concern for individual backbenchers was in sharp contrast to the usual perfunctory treatment. The government was learning from its past defeats.

The crucial debates took place in the Commons in January and February 1821. Castlereagh spoke well; in general the government made considerable efforts to restore its reputation, and as in the past it was able to rely on the belief of a majority of the independent members that the existing ministry was preferable to a Whig–Radical combination. Indeed, Wilberforce commented concerning the strong support for the government's motion to exclude the Queen's name from the Liturgy that most

[1] *Wilberforce*, v. 77. Twiss, *Eldon*, ii. 395.   [2] Creevey, i. 338.
[3] Aspinall, *Arbuthnot*, p. 22.

members regretted the measure, but still voted for it.[1] For Castlereagh the 1821 session was to be one of his most successful as Leader of the Commons. Arbuthnot and Wellington were both particularly impressed, the latter noting, 'It is true that Lord Londonderry[2] has in this last session done wonders. He has achieved more than could have been expected from any single man. . . .' Nevertheless, the government had suffered some setbacks, and Castlereagh and others were persuaded that it badly needed additional strength. Great sacrifices were made to secure the support of the handful of Grenvilles. This, it was also hoped, would increase Whig dependence on the Radicals, and so increase their unpopularity. Castlereagh and Wellington were mainly responsible for concluding this alliance.

The Grenvilles, however, could not save the cabinet from the ire of the country gentlemen in 1822 when falling corn prices provoked the customary protests and threats to the government's majority. The government vainly offered the repeal of the malt tax, a revision of the Corn Laws, a renewal of the committee on agricultural distress, and even loans to farmers. But the gentry had their eyes on more thorough-going remedies; they were attracted by Attwood's theories on paper currency, with his promises of higher prices; they objected to the government's insistence that the Sinking Fund must be treated as sacrosanct so that confidence in public credit should be unshaken. In practice, however, they were content to assault the government on lesser matters, and in particular they allowed the ministry to be defeated on relatively small matters such as Opposition motions for the elimination of two Lords of the Admiralty, and one of the joint Postmasters-General. In March Wellington complained that the gentry were 'acting in concert, and as a party independent of, and without consultation with, the government they profess to support, but really oppose'. The government lost patience with these sniping tactics, and when on 15 May a committee was proposed to inquire into the expenses of a portion of the Civil List, especially affecting British embassies, Castlereagh threw himself powerfully into the fray and threatened his

[1] *Wilberforce*, v. 84–85.

[2] Castlereagh succeeded his father as the 2nd Marquis of Londonderry in 1821.

resignation if it were carried. Eldon noted, 'This seems to have brought the country gentlemen to their senses and the Government succeeded by a majority of 127.'[1]

The government's position in the Commons was thus often an uncomfortable one. Although the threat of resignation would bring the rebels to heel, it was not a threat that could be used too often, and several government measures had to be given up in consequence. For Castlereagh, therefore, the post of Leader of the House was no sinecure. In 1817 it has been estimated that he spoke on some 85 occasions; only the irrepressible Brougham was on his feet more often. Save when Canning was a member of the cabinet from 1816 to 1820, and until Peel became Home Secretary at the end of 1821, Castlereagh was poorly supported by such cabinet colleagues as sat in the Commons. Palmerston, Peel and Croker as junior ministers gave valuable support in defence of their own departments, but Liverpool more than once lamented the poverty of government spokesmen in the Commons apart from Castlereagh. It is not surprising, therefore, that Castlereagh at times despaired of the government's survival, and exaggerated the seriousness of the threat from the Opposition. Each session undoubtedly took its toll on his nervous energy, and the particularly strenuous nature of that of 1822 cannot be ignored as a contributory factor leading to his suicide in that year.

These, then, were the circumstances and considerations that Castlereagh had to take into account as Leader of the House of Commons. But his role in the ministry from June 1812 was speedily transcending that of being the chief government spokesman and manager in the Commons. In addition to his almost unchallenged control of foreign policy, he was exercising considerable influence over government policy as a whole. To some extent, this grew out of his position as Leader, since many in the Commons resented the fact that so many of the cabinet sat in the Lords, and that in consequence many government measures were originated 'in another place'. Arbuthnot heard complaints of the Commons being 'dragged in the mire'. Consequently many turned to Castlereagh to champion the claims of the Lower

[1] *Wellington Supplementary Despatches*, i. 219–20. Hansard, new series, vii. 604–53. Twiss, *Eldon*, ii. 451.

House, quite apart from the obvious fact that he was the member of the cabinet it was easiest to consult. This role of chief spokesman of the Commons in the cabinet increased his authority, and by a combination of responsibilities and personality Castlereagh was able to wield tremendous influence. Although the reputation of Liverpool has been rescued in the twentieth century from the jibes of Disraeli, it is impossible to ignore contemporary evidence of instances of indecision and inactivity on his part, and it is clear that some politicians found Castlereagh more to their taste as a vigorous minister. Huskisson complained in January 1819 that Liverpool 'is in one of his grand fidgetts', thereby implying it was not an infrequent occurrence.[1] The question of a successor to — or even replacement for — Liverpool was discussed several times. George IV reviewed the claims of Sidmouth and Wellington, but finally concluded that Castlereagh was the best substitute, while Eldon conceded that most of the government's supporters in the Commons would opt for him. He added, however, that many powerful peers would oppose Castlereagh because of his Catholic sympathies,[2] and it is clear that Charles Wynn's enthusiasm for Castlereagh as Premier owed much to his expectation that a 'Catholic' ministry would ensue. Liverpool therefore possessed a strength to which Castlereagh could not lay claim; he could bridge 'Protestant' and 'Catholic' factions in Parliament. Not surprisingly, then, although Castlereagh on many counts was the main driving force of the administration, Liverpool survived quarrels with George IV and momentary waves of dissatisfaction. He did so because of his indispensability to the government, and because of the wide esteem in which he was held by many people of consequence in the country.[3]

Castlereagh's pre-eminence in the cabinet, and his role in the

[1] C. R. Fay, *Huskisson and his Age* (1951), p. 196. Aspinall, *Arbuthnot*, pp. 13–18.

[2] Twiss, *Eldon*, ii. 434–5.

[3] Useful pieces of information on the above problems are to be found in Gash, *Peel*, i. 290–1, Webster, *Castlereagh, 1815–22*, pp. 13–15, Buckingham, *Regency*, ii. 11, and Aspinall, *Letters of George IV*, i. 164–5, 179. Note also *The Morning Chronicle* of 3 Feb. 1815 with its description of Castlereagh as 'the prop of the administration'.

Commons explain why he figured so prominently in the minds and writings of those who opposed and hated the government. In 1811–12, Perceval had personified 'that Damn'd set of Rogues . . . to whom we attribute all the Miseries of our Country'; after his assassination it was the turn of Castlereagh and Sidmouth. Shelley wrote in their honour,

> As from an ancestral oak
> Two empty ravens sound their clarion,
> Yell by yell, and croak by croak,
> When they scent the noonday smoke
> Of fresh human carrion : . . .[1]

But many difficulties arise once the attempt is made to assess Castlereagh's individual contribution to the formulation of policy other than that of foreign affairs, and especially with reference to the repressive policies of 1812 and 1817–19. Undoubtedly he was at the centre of all the critical discussions and inquiries, and, unlike his colleagues, he had his massive experience of disorder in Ireland in the 1790s to draw upon. Indeed, part of his notoriety in the public mind may have been derived from the influx of Irish migrants into Lancashire with memories and myths of the rebellion. Nevertheless, his popular association with the suspension of Habeas Corpus in 1817, the Six Acts of 1819, and other acts of oppression would appear to spring essentially from the fact that he was chief spokesman for the government in the Commons, and consequently the measures became as much associated with his name as with that of Sidmouth — if not more so. Basically, however, it would appear that the legislation of 1812 and 1817–19 was the work of the Home Office, with some assistance from Perceval in 1812, and from the Lord Chancellor and the Law Officers of the Crown later.[2] Castlereagh was concerned only with the political aspects of the legislation as a member of the cabinet, and there is no

---

[1] *To Sidmouth and Castlereagh.* I am indebted to Professor D. F. Macdonald for drawing my attention to these verses.

[2] Both the *Annual Register* (1822, pp. 208 ff.) and *The Morning Chronicle* of 13 Aug. 1822 thought that the main reason for Castlereagh's unpopularity sprang from his supposed conduct in Ireland during the rebellion.

evidence to distinguish his responsibility from that of his leading colleagues.

Within the last generation or so, there has been a tendency among historians to present the conduct of the Liverpool ministry in the face of popular unrest in rather more favourable terms than hitherto. It is also noticeable how verdicts upon this period have come to vary not only with the sympathies of the writer, but also according to the nature of his approach, whether it be legal, administrative, political or social. Thus the student of legal history may well be most impressed by the desire of the government to stay within the law of the land, and may see the 'infamous' Six Acts of 1819 as mainly inspired by an awareness of the inadequacies of the existing law. The administrative approach underlines the inadequacies of the police, information system, and local authorities at the disposal of the Home Office; the political historian may emphasise the influence upon contemporaries of the French Revolutionary and Napoleonic era, or eulogise the superiority of the Whig or Radical approaches to the problem. The social historian may be more impressed by the suffering of the masses, and may sympathise with their efforts to escape from hopeless drudgery or poverty. Indeed, a recent social study has condemned the government's policy as 'sheer counter-revolutionary opportunism', though the author has also very frankly admitted the difficulty of substantiating some of his conclusions with sufficient evidence.[1]

The year 1816 was one of declining trade prospects. Wages shrank and unemployment grew. In the closing months of the year, and in the first half of 1817, multitudes of work-people began to seek remedies of their own for the destitution with which they were afflicted. For most of them their efforts did not go beyond idle talk and threats, attendance at public meetings where — when all else was emptiness — they could take their fill of rhetoric

[1] See especially E. P. Thompson, *English Working Class* (and the extensive review of this book in the *Historical Journal*, 1965, pp. 271–81), D. Read, *Peterloo* (1958), White, *From Waterloo to Peterloo*, Gash, *Peel*, and H. P. Bridges, *Bulletin of the Institute of Historical Research*, v. 49–51. The case for Sidmouth and the Home Office has recently been restated very effectively by Ziegler, especially pp. 312 ff.

THE DOCTOR.

" At his last gasp—as if with opium drugg'd."

DERRY-DOWN TRIANGLE.

" He that sold his country."

THE SPOUTER OF FROTH.

" With merry descants on a nation's woes—
There is a public mischief in his mirth."

THE GUILTY TRIO.

" Great skill have they in *palmistry*, and more
To conjure clean away the gold they **touch**,
Conveying worthless dross into its place;
Loud when they beg, dumb only when they steal.

     *   *   *   *

————————— Dream after dream ensues ;
And still they dream, that they shall still succeed,
And still are disappointed."

This is **THE DOCTOR**
         of *Circular* fame,
A Driv'ller, a Bigot, a Knave
         without shame:

A cartoon of Sidmouth, Castlereagh and Canning
by George Cruickshank

and invective, or the perusal of the critical literature of which Cobbett's *Political Register* was the supreme example. This, in itself, was disturbing enough for government and magistrates, but some went further, and exploded briefly into history through their part in the Spa Field riots, the march of the Blanketeers, the 'Ardwick Bridge Conspiracy', or the Pentridge Rising, all notable for their lack of organisation and co-ordination, and for their tragic futility. The full explanation of some of these episodes continues to elude the historian, nor is it clear how much of the iceberg of revolutionary or merely violent feeling remained submerged. It is not therefore surprising that the government treated them with deadly seriousness, not least because all its leading members had lived through the bloodiest years of the French Revolution. As Sir Alexander Cockburn remarked concerning the post-war frame of mind of the ruling classes, 'everything was connected with the Revolution in France, which for twenty years was, or was made, all in all, everything'.[1] Sidmouth himself commented that no one should be a politician who was not prepared to die a violent death. Castlereagh made provision in his will so that his wife might sell her diamonds in case of need in the event of revolution.

Most members of Parliament supported the government's view that it was outside its power and duty to try to ease the economic crisis. Grey, for the Whigs, could only suggest in 1819 that distress might be lessened by public economy and lower taxes. In 1821, when the Commons were considering proposals of Robert Owen that a commission should be appointed to examine his model mills at New Lanark, and also examine his other ideas for poor relief, there was overwhelming support for Castlereagh's view that Parliament should not be made the automatic vehicle for such inquiries. The Radical, Joseph Hume, for once enthusiastically agreed with him.[2] In December 1819 Castlereagh forcefully replied to an exponent of greater government action against distress,

[1] Briggs, *Age of Improvement*, p. 129. For the government's failure to distinguish between the various popular movements see A. T. Patterson, 'Luddism, Hampden Clubs, and Trade Unions in Leicestershire, 1816–17', *English Historical Review*, lxiii. 170–88.

[2] *Hansard*, new series, v. 1321–2.

N

When the hon. member said, 'give the people food and employment', did he think that it was possible for the legislature to do that? Was it possible for any fund to be established that would secure employment, amidst all the fluctuations of commerce and manufactures? Upon what principles could government act, if in seasons of difficulty they were to recognise the policy of taking from one class merely for the purpose of giving to another? Such a practice was equally inconsistent with all the rules of sound policy, and with the very nature of property in general.[1]

On various other occasions Castlereagh defended the government's inaction by referring to current economic theories of *laisser faire*. In 1819, for instance, he insisted that 'no sober-minded rational man could for a moment believe that they [the current distress and unemployment] were to be removed by any parliamentary interference . . . time alone would bring an effectual remedy'. With Liverpool, Peel and Sidmouth, he insisted again and again that wages must be allowed to find their natural level, that the laws of supply and demand must be allowed to operate without restriction. The Corn Laws were of course the greatest exception, and critics noted the government's dependence upon the votes of country gentlemen, and the absence of working-class representation in Parliament. In vain, workers protested at the removal of the remnants of Tudor paternalist legislation during this period, though its survival would probably have profited them little, as it was both obsolete and largely unenforceable in the circumstances of the early nineteenth century.[2] Nor did many contemporary social reformers look to the state for aid, other than through the necessary permissive legislation. The parish, or some similar local organisation, was viewed as 'the great creative, ameliorative unit' by Godwin, Spence and Owen; Attwood was in a small minority with his advocacy of government spending and lending to stimulate demand. In general Castlereagh could be sure of a sympathetic hearing in Parliament and among most of the educated public for his arguments against state action. Not that the government was wholly inactive, as money was provided for public works and church-building in 1817–18 to relieve some of the worst unemployment, and also, in the case of the churches,

[1] *Hansard*, xli. 901.
[2] Sir J. Clapham, *Economic History of Modern Britain*, (1926) i. 336.

to try to increase the social restraints against violence.[1] Castlereagh himself expressed interest in measures to ensure the independence and self-respect of the poor, but at the same time he warned against high wages lest they should corrupt the lower classes, injuring morals, health and happiness.[2] Castlereagh's attitude to the working class was therefore that of a moderately enlightened member of the possessing class; a ready exponent of the ideas of *laisser faire*, yet tempered by a family background of model landlordism, and more generally by eighteenth-century conceptions of aristocratic paternalism and responsibility.

The same mental attitudes are revealed in his explanation of the disorders of 1816–17, which he attributed mainly to the poisonous propaganda disseminated by men of culture and ability among the ignorant and suffering — the successors in his mind to the 'deluded masses' of 1798 in Ireland. In fact, the majority of literate reformers such as 'Orator' Hunt and William Cobbett, or Burdett, Cochrane and Cartwright, for all the violence of their language, had no thought of revolution, and in so far as they encouraged wild and violent schemes they did so by accident and misunderstanding. But if Castlereagh's comprehension of mass discontent and disturbance was blinkered by his social background and political position, he was thoroughly representative of many in his station of life.[3] If, for the unemployed and impoverished he seemed the most malignant oppressor of them all, to the historian he seems rather to personify one of the strongest sections of the upper class, and that not the most reactionary, since there were critics of the inadequacy of the government's counter-measures as well as of their extremism from men of property.

---

[1] M. W. Flinn, 'The Poor Employment Act of 1817', *Economic History Review* (1961–2), pp. 82–92. This Act was the ancestor of nineteenth-century public works' developments.

[2] *Hansard*, xxxv. 1069, new series, vi. 354. See also E. P. Thompson, pp. 356 ff., and S. G. Checkland, *The Rise of Industrial Society in England, 1815–85* (1964), pp. 232–3. For the long continuance of this attitude, see S. Nowell-Smith, *Edwardian England* (1964), pp. 57–58.

[3] E. P. Thompson, pp. 421, 599–600.

Cobbett accused the government in December 1816 of sighing for a revolutionary plot; 'they are absolutely pining and dying for a plot!' Whigs and Radicals and many subsequent historians have made great play with the supposed use of 'agents provocateurs' by the government, and in particular of the notorious 'Oliver'. Whatever these spies may have achieved on their own initiative, no real evidence exists of government connivance; at most one can establish government foreknowledge of intended disturbances, such as the Pentridge rising near Nottingham in June 1817, which they allowed to proceed so that they might have concrete evidence of revolutionary intent which otherwise was so difficult to procure, and on which it was so difficult to secure convictions.[1] But on the whole in the winter of 1816–17 the impression from the official records is rather one of a stream of alarmist information from all parts of the country, much Home Office concern, but little in the way of decisive action until the second half of January, when the cabinet accepted Sidmouth's conclusions, and endorsed his proposed counter-measures. The matter was then referred to Parliament and to secret committees with a view to the suspension of the Habeas Corpus Act. Castlereagh was the main government spokesman in the Commons, and drew alarmist pictures of the situation, especially on 24 February. But these were hardly necessary, and the government easily won convincing majorities of 160 and upwards for its chief measures. The Radicals and some Whigs championed the liberties of the individual, but Canning was more representative of parliamentary feeling when he spoke of the danger not only of rebellion but of treason, not only of treason but of confiscation.[2] Upper-class ranks closed impressively in the face of what was believed to be both a political and social threat.

The implementation of the measures against disorder rested with Sidmouth at the Home Office. Castlereagh did, however, participate in the examination of some of the offenders before

[1] Thompson (ibid., pp. 649–69) attacks the defenders of Sidmouth, but gives no evidence to prove that Oliver did not exceed Sidmouth's instructions. One can only agree that such evidence is unlikely to have existed if such instructions were given.

[2] *Hansard*, xxxv. 590–639 etc.

the Privy Council. It was then that Samuel Bamford, the Radical weaver from Middleton, penned his interesting portrait of some of his interlocutors. 'Quite a merry set of gentlemen', he found them, especially Sidmouth. Castlereagh he described as 'a good-looking person in a plum-coloured coat, with a gold ring on the small finger of his left hand, on which he sometimes leaned his hand as he eyed me over. . . .' Improved economic conditions, with some assistance from the government's measures, restored a measure of calm from the summer of 1817 until the second great upsurge of Radical and reform agitation in 1819. Pamphlets and newspapers streamed from the Radical press, parliamentary reform societies mushroomed, and monster popular meetings began to be held. The Midlands and the northern and Scottish industrial districts were the great centres of this new and essentially constitutional agitation. These meetings reached their climax in August when an enormous crowd assembled in St. Peter's Fields, Manchester, to listen to 'Orator' Hunt, only to be forcibly dispersed at the cost of eleven dead and many injured. There followed an explosion of national emotion and soul-searching over what came to be known as the Peterloo Massacre.

The casualties at Peterloo on 16 August were caused primarily by the unsuitability of the force, the local yeomanry, with which the magistrates at first tried to arrest Hunt. For the government Sidmouth may have hoped that it would be possible to arrest Hunt at the meeting, but he was unprepared for the violence which resulted. Liverpool, Castlereagh, Sidmouth, Wellington, Vansittart and Eldon were all in London when news of Peterloo arrived. Eldon commented, 'Without all doubt, the Manchester magistrates must be supported; but they are very generally blamed here.' The first consideration undoubtedly outweighed any doubts felt by the cabinet; above all it was feared that unless the magistrates were backed to the full in this matter, other magistrates on future occasion might fail to act.[1] As it was, magistrates often appeared reluctant to act after Peterloo, and their task was further complicated by new government efforts to supervise their conduct more closely. Just as the Pentridge rising had underlined the inadequacy of the government's means of

[1] Feiling, *Second Tory Party*, p. 299.

collecting information, so Peterloo underlined the inadequacy of
local government and police forces in the dawning era of
industrial towns. Castlereagh's role in the cabinet discussions
remains unknown, but he had no hesitation in coming forward as
one of the most active champions of the Manchester magistrates.[1]

Sidmouth and Eldon, however, wished to do more, and
pressed their colleagues hard for an early recall of Parliament in
order to introduce new legislation. Eldon, in particular, had been
pointing to the inadequacy of the existing laws to protect the
realm from popular disturbance; he feared that the government
would soon be driven to a choice between anarchy and military
rule. Sidmouth was anxious for new laws against drilling and
political meetings which could be called at any time and by any
one. After some hesitation the government gave way, and
agreed to introduce the famous Six Acts when Parliament was
recalled at the end of November.[2] The Six Acts dealt with the
procedure of bringing cases to trial, they prohibited meetings
for military training, and were concerned with the issue of
warrants for the search of arms. More controversially they
imposed additional restraints upon the existing freedom of
public meeting, while the remainder were directed against
'blasphemous and seditious' literature, and, by extending the
Stamp Act, were designed to reduce public access to Radical
pamphlets and newspapers. To a more regimented posterity in
the twentieth century, the Six Acts have lost some of their
original infamy,[3] and at the time there existed critics of their
inadequacy and timidity as well as of their tyranny.

In general, men of property of most shades of opinion were
disturbed by the popular agitation of 1819, and by the demands
for annual parliaments, universal suffrage, tax and currency
reform. Grey feared that the aim was 'not Reform but Revolution'; Brougham agreed that the Radical conduct was 'bad

[1] E. P. Thompson, pp. 669 ff., especially p. 683 n. White, pp.
106–13. Read, *Peterloo*, passim. Twiss, *Eldon*, ii. 338. Yonge, ii.
419–34, contains some interesting evidence of Liverpool's eighteenth-
century view of local government.

[2] Twiss, *Eldon*, ii. 336–52. Sidmouth, iii. 281–3.

[3] Gash, *Peel*, i. 248.

enough to make reflecting men consider that the time was come for taking some steps in support of order'. Wilberforce thought of 1646; Grenville of 1789; Canning thought the condition of Britain worse than in the 1790s; Wellington in October thought a general rising could not be far off.[1] Not surprisingly, although Castlereagh was called upon to fight several keen parliamentary duels in support of the Six Acts against the Radicals and many Whigs, the new legislation passed the Commons by majorities of at least two to one, while the verdict of the Lords was still more overwhelming. Indeed, the Grenvilles and some of the country gentlemen felt that the government had not gone far enough,[2] while a Whig effort to force an inquiry into Peterloo was defeated by 231 votes in the Commons. The Whigs, magnificent as was their air of Olympian detachment, and important as their arguments were on behalf of the rights of the individual, offered little in the way of constructive alternatives, and were themselves to deal almost as heavy-handedly with disturbances when they were in office in the early 1830s.[3] A sympathetic defence of their conduct at that time by the Hammonds might, without much difficulty, be transcribed and applied to their *bêtes noires*, Castlereagh and his colleagues.[4] Whatever criticism may be levelled at the unconstructiveness of government policy between 1817 and 1819, in the task of maintaining law and order more evidence has appeared to substantiate the constitutional and conventional nature of its

[1] In 1820 Wellington had serious doubts concerning the loyalty of the Guards, Schenk, *Aftermath of the Napoleonic Wars*, pp. 123–4.

[2] Buckingham, *Regency*, ii. 382–3.

[3] D. Southgate, *The Passing of the Whigs* (1962), p. 41. The government's efforts to control the press separated them most sharply from the Whigs' later conduct, see W. H. Wickwar, 'The Struggle for the Freedom of the Press, 1819–32', *Bulletin of the Institute of Historical Research*, v. 51–53. See also A. Aspinall, *Politics and the Press* (1949), p. 60. Brougham, after Peterloo, expected many on his side of the House to welcome measures against the Radicals, especially 'their vile press' (see his *Life and Times* (1871), ii. 348). For Grey's hostility to the Radicals, see G. M. Trevelyan, *Lord Grey of the Reform Bill* (1920), pp. 182–8.

[4] J. L. and B. Hammond, *The Village Labourer* (Guild Books, 1948), ii. 114–17.

conduct than to the contrary. Eldon, for all his faults, was
intensely loyal to the constitution and law of the land.[1]

In view of Castlereagh's overall reputation as one of the most
decisive personalities in the cabinet, and since he was mainly
responsible for the presentation of the government's case to the
Commons, his part in the formulation of the repressive policies
was almost certainly an active one, but it should also be apparent
that there are no grounds for accepting the widespread contemporary belief that he was in some way peculiarly responsible
for these measures. Nevertheless, this belief has contributed to
the idea that his death in 1822 and the beginning of the so-called
Liberal Toryism around that date were more than a coincidence.[2]
Undoubtedly there was a change in the character of legislation
in the 1820s, certainly by comparison with the previous decade,
though measures for the relief of Catholic and Protestant
dissenters and for the partial recognition of trade unions were
wrung from the government in exceptional circumstances, and
the spontaneous ministerial reforms were mostly concerned
with penal and fiscal matters. It is also important to recall the
musings of Peel in March 1820 when, observing that the temper
of the country might have become more liberal, he asked, 'Will
the Government act on the principles on which without being very
certain, I suppose they have hitherto professed to act? Or will
they carry into execution moderate Whig measures of reform?'[3]
It is therefore important to establish whether Castlereagh was
an obstacle to the reforms envisaged by Huskisson and Peel, and
how far his removal from politics was necessary in order to
liberalise the government.

[1] Briggs, *Age of Improvement*, pp. 91–92, gives a brief account of the
paramount influence of law in eighteenth century British political
thought.

[2] H. Martineau, *History of the Thirty Years' Peace* (1849), i. 286–7.
W. Harris, *History of the Radical Party in Parliament* (1885), pp.
163–5. Spencer Walpole (*History of England from 1815* (1890), ii.
53) thought the effects of Castlereagh's death 'revolutionary'; he
believed this 'gave the deathblow to a system'. See also Sir E. L.
Woodward, *The Age of Reform* (1946), p. 67. Ziegler, p. 404, makes
the more valid point that Castlereagh's death made the infusion of new
blood into the cabinet necessary, and by this indirect means the liberal
element was strengthened.   [3] *Croker Papers*, i. 170.

Peel had very shrewdly noted the government's lack of clarity as to the principles on which it professed to act. The Revolutionary and Napoleonic wars had distracted Pitt and his followers from their financial, fiscal and political reforms of the 1780s. It has been said that Pitt's nineteenth-century followers inherited only his war policies and principles, and then grappled blindly and ineffectually with post-war problems that were beyond their comprehension and ability. This is too sweeping, and makes no allowance for the magnitude of the problems which they faced. Not only was the industrial revolution proceeding apace, and creating economic and social problems of enormous complexity and disturbing novelty, but the economy of Britain and of other countries had been distorted by the recent wars. To mention but three of the problems, there was the vast apparatus of war to be dismantled and reduced to peace establishments, there was a colossal public debt to be serviced which would devour perhaps one-twelfth of the national income, or more than half of the government's income, and there was the aggrieved landed interest which saw falling agricultural prices jeopardising its income and also its ability to pay off the heavy debts incurred to finance the great expansion of British agriculture during the war. The government's freedom for manœuvre was limited; economy was vital, but rapid demobilisation swelled the ranks of the unemployed; financial confidence would be undermined if the fundholders were not paid their interest, but this necessitated heavy impositions on the rest of the community; to afford relief to agriculture would injure the prospects of British exporters and deny to the masses the chance of cheap food imported from abroad. The concerted attack on the income tax in 1816 seriously limited the government's freedom to think in terms of fiscal reform — only of enforced improvisation in the face of powerful and competing interests.[1]

Tierney might declare, and with much justice, that the ministry was 'governed by no principle, and attached to no system', but it is difficult to see what principle or system would have availed it in such circumstances. Although the Pittites had

[1] The government's financial policy at this time is a highly controversial subject; see Checkland, pp. 327–8, and H. C. Acworth, *Financial Reconstruction in England, 1815–22* (1925).

been described as the party of trade, the reluctance to abandon the Orders in Council had alienated many merchants and businessmen, while the ranks of the latter were continually inflated by new men, often self-made, whose taste in politics was far removed from the great men of the East India Company. In any case, the landed interest continued to dominate Parliament, returning at least three-quarters of the members of the Commons, and a government would ignore their wishes at its peril. Lord Redesdale might complain that 'Trade, manufactures, and money are everything . . . The landed proprietors are mere ciphers, they are of no consequence, either with ministers or with Opposition.' Squire Western might lament the government's attention to the fundholders, but the cabinet feared the landed representatives, even when they sat behind the Treasury bench, more than the formal Opposition itself.[1] At most, the government could do no more than prevent the almost prohibitive price, at which point foreign corn would be admitted, from rising above 80 shillings per quarter. The ability of the landed interest to extort other concessions in periods of agricultural depression has already been noted. If the government shared many of the prejudices of the landed interest, it is quite clear that upon several occasions the latter was able to secure far more than the former was eager to concede.

In commercial matters, however, the ministry was able to anticipate some of the main trends of the nineteenth century, and to demonstrate a little continuity from Pitt the reformer.[2] In 1813 Castlereagh was one of those who contributed to the ending of the East India Company's monopoly of British trade with India, and when, in 1817, Brougham introduced resolutions condemning the government's trade policies, he was told by Castlereagh that he would have accepted an inquiry into the matter had Brougham proposed one.[3] Robinson,[4] the President

[1] *English Historical Documents, 1783–1832*, p. 19. Feiling, p. 279. W. R. Brock, *Liverpool and Liberal Toryism* (1941), p. 104.

[2] On continuing business support, see Feiling, p. 281. On the reforming trends, see also Brock, *passim*.

[3] *Hansard*, xxxvi. 1399.

[4] F. J. Robinson had served briefly under Castlereagh in 1809 as Under-Secretary for the Colonies, and had accompanied him to the

of the Board of Trade, agreed that there was much to be regretted in the prohibitory aspects of British trade, but insisted that there were immense difficulties in the way of their removal. Three years later Thomas Tooke, after experiencing some difficulty in mobilising mercantile support for a petition to Parliament in favour of freer trade, declared that he had found more sympathy and understanding for his case in some sections of the government, and especially the Board of Trade. The wheels of government were grinding slowly, partially at least because the state of the revenue, and the pressure for tax reductions in other directions, were deterring it from fiscal reform. Some preparation at least had been made for the changes to be made by Huskisson in the less straitened financial circumstances of the 1820s.

Admittedly not all was enlightenment worthy of Cobden and Gladstone. United States diplomats would have read with relish Castlereagh's lectures on the advantages of commercial freedom to the Spaniards at the height of the struggle with their American colonists, and contrasted them with his obduracy in the face of United States demands for the unrestricted opening of West Indian ports to their shipping. Rush indeed received a long lecture on British eighteenth-century mercantilism from Castlereagh, and was told that his demands would 'effect an entire subversion of the British colonial system'. Liverpool was equally sensitive in this matter, and gave way with the utmost reluctance in 1821 to the insistence of Robinson and others that the ports must be opened, as the British West Indian islands were on the brink of ruin through American retaliatory measures. His great fear was that British shipping would suffer, as indeed it did, catastrophically, from 1822. The first revision of the British Navigation Acts arose therefore essentially from the success of foreign counter-measures.

There were other indications between 1819 and 1822 that the government was beginning to attune its policies to the changing economic needs of the nation. After much hesitation the resumption of cash payments was decided upon in 1819, with Castlereagh as one of the dissentients, and if its early con-

continent in 1814. See Feiling, pp. 316–17, for a brief reference to their relationship.

sequences were not wholly satisfactory, the measure has normally
been praised by posterity as one of the foundations of the British
economy of the later nineteenth century. In 1822 other forward
looking measures included the first attempts to devise a
satisfactory sliding scale of duties to eliminate some of the worst
effects of the Corn Laws, and in the same year the government
began negotiations with the Bank of England which resulted in
1826 in the Act of Parliament which permitted the establishment
of Joint Stock Banks in England at a radius of more than 65 miles
from London.[1] The government's attitude to social problems
was less positive, but this was true also of the period after 1822
save in the matter of Peel's penal legislation. Nevertheless, the
ministry inaugurated or permitted some social reform, notably
in Poor Law administration, the treatment of insolvent debtors,
and in the extension of juries to civil cases in Scotland. The only
factory legislation of the period was the work of a private
member, Sir Robert Peel senior, but Brougham's massive inquiry
from 1816 into the education of the London poor and into the
general management of Charitable Foundations was rewarded
with a government bill in 1819 which incorporated most of his
recommendations, and which was carried through against the
criticism of some of the government supporters who sat in the
Lords, notably Lord Eldon.[2] Castlereagh personally expressed
his approval of Brougham's efforts, and promised government
assistance where possible.

There is no evidence, save in the instance of the resumption
of cash payments, to suggest Castlereagh was in any way an
obstacle to the implementation of these modest reforms, an
indication that the emergence of Liberal Toryism was less
sudden than has often been suggested. Equally there is nothing
to show that Castlereagh would have been an obstacle to the
type of reform introduced after 1822. Indeed, in the question of
Catholic Emancipation he was, in his unobtrusive way, one of
the most forward-looking of the cabinet; so much so, in fact,

[1] *Hansard*, new series, vii. 161.

[2] Feiling, pp. 278–9. New, *Brougham*, pp. 209–20. The government
tended to leave the initiative in reform to Parliament and select
committees; a more positive approach emerged in the 1820s. See
Briggs, *Age of Improvement*, pp. 205–6.

that he was viewed with some suspicion by the most ardent 'Protestants' among the government's supporters.[1] More convincing is the argument that in his foreign policy he would have projected a less liberal image,[2] and he may be compared unfavourably with Canning — both as Foreign Secretary and Leader of the Commons — as a speaker and publicist. Canning was more disposed to take Parliament into his confidence; he had a gift for the ringing phrase; he could make policy sound more dramatic and liberal than it sometimes was, and in this sense Canning was undoubtedly an asset. He gave the ministry a 'new look' which Castlereagh, with his aloof manner and undramatic style, would not even have attempted. After all, Castlereagh once made a wry and ambiguous joke to the effect that he believed unpopularity to be the more gentlemanly fate for a politician.

Castlereagh was also a temporary obstacle to the admission of Peel to the cabinet. Peel was to be one of the main reforming personalities of the 1820s, but it would appear that Castlereagh's objections to him arose from personal rather than political considerations. In the spring of 1821 he opposed the admission of Peel to the cabinet as Chancellor of the Exchequer on the ground that this would make 'an opposition' to the government in the Commons. It seems unlikely that Castlereagh was seriously worried by Peel's position as leader of the 'Protestant' party, or that he felt that a strengthened 'Protestant' group in the cabinet would be able to delay Emancipation. He was assuring the Grenvilles that Emancipation would be decided in Parliament — not in the cabinet. Professor Gash hazards the interesting suggestion that Castlereagh was already beginning to suffer from the psychopathic distrust and persecution-mania which led or contributed to his suicide a year later. That Peel was subsequently admitted to the cabinet as Home Secretary possibly indicates that Castlereagh feared that Peel, as Chancellor of the Exchequer, might be able to secure a general influence over policy which would not be open to him at the

[1] E. Halévy (*History of the English People, 1815–30* (1926), pp. 149–51) describes Castlereagh as the leader of the 'liberal faction' in the cabinet following the resignation of Canning.

[2] See Chapter 7, and Harris, pp. 163–5.

Home Office. Certainly he told the Princess Lieven about this time that the Chancellor ought to be the strongest member of the government in time of peace.[1]

He displayed no similar jealousy towards Canning,[2] who had resigned from the cabinet over the royal divorce, but whose services were once again being sought in 1821. George IV was determined to exclude Canning; Liverpool was disposed to resign if the King persisted, while Wellington furiously opposed so drastic a step as it would open the door to a Whig–Radical coalition, which would drag the country into 'irretrievable ruin'. Castlereagh adopted a middle position,[3] and finally in November 1821 George IV agreed that Canning should become Governor-General of India. The one firm conclusion that emerges from the cabinet reshuffling that took place in 1820–1 is the absence of any fundamental differences in matters of principle. It was essentially a struggle for place and power, with personal dislikes and prejudices, especially those of George IV, mainly determining the outcome. The one principle that showed any real life was that of Catholic Emancipation, but the continuance of Liverpool as Prime Minister, reinforced by Castlereagh's argument that this was not a cabinet matter, painlessly killed it. As for Castlereagh himself, many eyes were beginning to turn towards him, some hopefully, some a little apprehensively, as possibly the next Prime Minister.

In 1821 Liverpool was badly out of favour with George IV, partly through the failure of the divorce bill, partly through differences of opinion over household and government appointments, and partly through the spoiled child streak in George, who liked to flaunt his power in petty insults and intrigues. Castlereagh himself had lost ground with the King when his aunt, Lady Hertford, had been displaced in the royal favour by Lady Conyngham. A family loss was made worse by a family

[1] Gash, *Peel*, i. 290–2, 309–10, 313–15. Peel was able to begin his measures for police, prison and penal reform before Castlereagh's suicide. See also Aspinall, *Hobhouse*, pp. ix–x, 61, 93.

[2] Wellington and Mrs. Arbuthnot agreed that Castlereagh would have welcomed Canning as his successor, F. Bamford and the Duke of Wellington, *Journal of Mrs. Arbuthnot* (1950), i. 191.

[3] Rolo, *Canning*, pp. 104, 114. Aspinall, *Hobhouse*, pp. 61, 66–67, 79.

quarrel, since Lady Castlereagh and Lady Conyngham were bitter enemies. Nor could Castlereagh himself escape some of the King's displeasure over the failure of the divorce bill. The King was talking of a change of ministry, and his ministers took the threat seriously. It is doubtful whether George could have brought himself to the point of actually summoning Lord Grey, but it pleased his vanity to threaten, and he may have hoped to show his power by snubbing Liverpool into handing in his resignation, and then creating a new ministry around one of his colleagues. Liverpool was in danger of playing into his hands, as the illness and death of his wife in 1821 left him with no desire to carry on. He became irritable and obstinate, and seemed to court his own downfall. The Grenvilles hoped that Castlereagh would be appointed, and a Catholic ministry established. Many in the Commons favoured Castlereagh, not least because he promised more decisive leadership than Liverpool. Eldon reluctantly conceded that there seemed no obvious alternative.[1] The session of 1821 was a personal triumph for Castlereagh, and despite Opposition protests against his foreign policy, which seemed to associate Britain too closely with the European autocrats, his position in Parliament was never stronger. Croker's famous pen portrait will perhaps bear quotation once again.

Londonderry goes on as usual, and, to continue my similes, like Mont Blanc continues to gather all the sunshine upon his icy head. He is *better* than ever: that is, colder, steadier, more *pococurante*, and withal more amiable and respected. It is a splendid summit of bright and polished frost which, like the travellers in Switzerland, we all admire; but no one can hope and few would wish to reach.[2]

George IV was slow to renew his friendship with Castlereagh, though Croker heard the King speak well of him in July. Castlereagh accompanied George IV on his Irish trip shortly afterwards, but the King was not yet ready to end the coolness. For once Castlereagh found himself well received in his homeland; the previous year he had been returned for County Down without difficulty, and at no cost to himself save 'a good dinner to friends'. But George remained unbending, and it was not until his trip to Hanover with Castlereagh in October that he

[1] Twiss, *Eldon*, ii. 434–5.   [2] *Croker Papers*, i. 219.

relented. At the same time he informed Metternich that he was seriously considering Castlereagh as his next Prime Minister. Castlereagh, however, out of loyalty to Liverpool, and perhaps also out of political wisdom, was determined not to accept office without Liverpool's approval. The latter's favour would have been vital to form a strong cabinet. Back in England he found that Wellington had persuaded Liverpool not to insist on Canning's inclusion in the cabinet on pain of his own resignation, and the way was now clear for him to negotiate a reconciliation between King and Prime Minister. After some further difficulty it was arranged that Canning should go to India, that there should be a compromise over the household appointments, and the ministry should be strengthened by the inclusion of the Grenvilles and Peel. A delighted monarch informed the Austrian Ambassador that Castlereagh ranked second only to Metternich as a European statesman. With the return of royal favour, Castlereagh's prestige and influence was thus reaching new heights.

" The body of the people, I do think,
are loyal still,"
But pray My L—ds and G—tl—n,
don't shrink
From exercising all your care
and skill,
Here, and at home,
TO CHECK THE CIRCULATION

OF LITTLE BOOKS,
Whose very looks—
Vile ' *two-p'nny trash,*'
bespeak abomination.
Oh ! they are full of blasphemies
and libels,
And people read them
oftener than their bibles !

A cartoon of Castlereagh, Sidmouth and Canning

7

Castlereagh and the
'New Diplomacy' 1816–22*

In 1885 an historian of the British Radical party expressed the
belief that Castlereagh had come to be viewed 'as the incar-
nation . . . of the principles on which despotic government were
based', not so much because of his responsibility for repressive
legislation at home, but because of his association with the
continental despotic powers. It is perhaps to be doubted whether
the unemployed Derbyshire puddler who exploded, 'Damn the
Prince Regent. Damn the Government. I'll kill Lord Castlereagh, before I settle, and roast his heart', was greatly swayed
by Castlereagh's attendance at European congresses, but among
the more sophisticated Castlereagh's foreign policy certainly
caused concern. Romilly, for one, in January 1816 feared that
British liberties — as well as those of Europe — might be
jeopardised by Castlereagh's alliance with continental despotism.[1] Furthermore, whereas in domestic policy Castlereagh
could claim to be representative of much upper-class opinion, in
his quest for a European Alliance he was acting almost wholly
alone. It is impossible to think of any British Foreign Secretary

* I have used the phrase 'New Diplomacy' to describe Castlereagh's
European policy as it is broader in meaning than Congress System or
Concert of Europe. The phrase can be justified in that Castlereagh
himself saw his diplomacy as something very different from that of the
past century (see below, p. 206), and it has the advantage of embracing
more than the occasional meetings of sovereigns and ministers in
formal conferences. Castlereagh intended that the new relationship
with the European powers should operate at all diplomatic levels and
at all times.

[1] Harris, pp. 163–5. Romilly, iii. 220–9.

o

who was so misunderstood and unsupported in one of the
fundamental principles of his policy. Thus Lord Colchester,
immediately after Castlereagh's death, expressed the hope that
Canning would 'support the interest and honour of the country
with a loftier policy than his predecessor'. Greville summed up
Opposition criticisms at the same time,

The result of his policy is this, that we are mixed up in the affairs of
the Continent in a manner which we have never been before, and which
entails upon us endless negotiations and enormous expenses. We have
associated ourselves with the Members of the Holy Alliance, and
countenanced their acts of ambition and despotism in such a manner as
to have drawn upon us the detestation of the nations of the Continent;
and our conduct towards them at the close of the war has brought a
stain upon our character for bad faith and desertion which no time will
wipe away, and the recollection of which will never be effaced from
their minds.

W. H. Fremantle thought the congress at Aix-la-Chapelle in
1818 'of all foolish measures the most so', and with Greville,
Holland and others he concluded that Castlereagh's infatuation
with the European despots could only be explained by the fact
that his head had been turned by association with so many
crowned heads.[1] Nor did his cabinet colleagues, apart from
Wellington, share his enthusiasm for European entanglements,
and his continental excursion in 1818 found them anxiously
perusing his despatches lest he should drag them into fresh
commitments.

Castlereagh's foreign policy after 1815 was thus one of the
most personal ever pursued by a British Foreign Secretary; the
fact that he was able to pursue so independent a line is, in part,
testimony to his prestige and influence in the cabinet and
Commons. It also indicates the comparative lack of interest in
foreign affairs on the part of his countrymen, and the ineffectiveness of those who did try to take an interest. This is not to say
that Castlereagh could ignore the cabinet, or the opinions of
Parliament and the public; as will be shown, these exercised no
mean restraint on his policy, and compelled him to proceed with
great caution. But the cabinet was susceptible to his charm,

[1] *Greville Memoirs*, i. 127–8. Fox-Strangeways, pp. 232–3. Buckingham, *Regency*, ii. 278–9. Colchester, iii. 256. See above, p. 160.

influence, and superior knowledge; Parliament could be managed by revealing as little of his policy to it as possible, and by exploitation of the majority's dislike of a Whig–Radical combination as an alternative ministry. If most members were insular, they were not disposed to inquire too closely into his policies providing they entailed no additional expense, and providing they did not associate Britain too openly with the despotic powers. In these circumstances it was not too difficult to escape the outraged protests of Whigs with liberal sympathies, and of indignant Radicals; such storms could often be left to blow themselves out in a sea of parliamentary apathy and inattention. Opinion outside Parliament gave him less concern, save when vitriolic newspaper articles against certain powers threatened to embarrass Britain's foreign relations.

These circumstances meant that his policy was practicable, but could not outlive his tenure of the Foreign Office. The only important figure to sympathise with his aims was Wellington, and he was never able to achieve the mastery of foreign affairs, the subtlety or discrimination to make him a possible successor to Castlereagh, even supposing the Foreign Office had ever been offered to him. Shortly before his death, Castlereagh informed the King that only they understood foreign affairs, an implicit recognition on his part that he had no possible successor. Castlereagh explained his policies to his diplomatic representatives abroad, and to his intimate assistants at home, but it is less clear how far he tried to instruct his cabinet colleagues in his objectives. His close friend, Wellington, had some understanding,[1] but it may well be that Castlereagh found his remaining colleagues' minds closed to his vision of great-power co-operation, and consequently contented himself with securing their consent rather than their approval. Certainly the perils of proselytising were brought home to him in 1818 when he wrote from the conference at Aix, 'I am quite convinced that past habits, common glory, and these occasional meetings, displays,

---

[1] Wellington was less discriminating than Castlereagh; note his military advice to the Austrians for the suppression of the Neapolitan revolt in 1821 (Webster, *Castlereagh, 1815–22*, p. 326), and his desire to paralyse British policy to appease the Russians and save the Alliance in 1822, see below pp. 228–9.

and repledges, are among the best securities Europe now has for a durable peace', or when he declared that the conference system seemed to him 'a new discovery in the European Government, at once extinguishing the cobwebs with which diplomacy obscures the horizon, bringing the whole bearing of the system into its true light, and giving the counsels of the Great Powers the efficiency and almost the simplicity of a single State'.[1] Remarks of this nature profoundly disturbed the cabinet, increased its insularity, and provoked additional warnings to Castlereagh against new commitments.

Castlereagh also made occasional efforts to demonstrate the value of diplomacy by conference in his parliamentary speeches, but the Opposition insisted that he was associating Britain with the despotic principles of the Holy Alliance. Out of blindness or deliberate intent, Castlereagh's critics often failed to distinguish between the Quadruple and Holy Alliances. Britain did not belong to the latter. But Castlereagh's critics were not interested in international co-operation; they were insistent that Britain should separate herself from the continental autocrats. They basked in a sea of vaguely liberal sentiment, and if some were genuinely fearful for British liberties, there were others who seemed to criticise for the sake of criticising. This deliberate refusal to understand Castlereagh's aims, coupled with the insularity of the majority of British politicians, left Parliament completely unreceptive to Castlereagh's laboured justifications of his policy. Long before Canning had succeeded Castlereagh at the Foreign Office he had shown his ability to use language which the Commons understood and liked. The contrast between the two in their parliamentary approach to foreign affairs was admirably demonstrated in their respective remarks on South American affairs in a debate of 11 July 1820. Both were defending the government's conduct, but where Castlereagh underlined his confidence in his allies and insisted that 'the honour of every individual power who was a party to that holy alliance . . . was untainted', Canning declared, 'He was as warm a friend for the extension of liberty and of liberal institutions throughout the world as his honourable and learned friend [Sir James Mackintosh] . . .' But who was likely to remember the qualification

[1] *C.C.* xii. 54–63.

that he would not support such sentiments at all costs, or hold it against Canning if he did ?[1]

In 1862 the young Lord Salisbury wisely noted that had Castlereagh addressed a few ringing phrases to the Commons, had he paid 'readier homage to the liberal catchwords of the day', he would have been less maligned by contemporaries and posterity.[2] This is only too true; he would have eased his own task, yet at the same time he would have been no nearer to — indeed, perhaps further from — convincing the British of the wisdom of his policy. Similarly one may regret his reluctance to take Parliament into his confidence, a reluctance which at times extended to downright secrecy and even duplicity,[3] yet without such tactics his foreign policy might have been wrecked or frustrated. In short, though one may note Castlereagh's inability to use the more public tactics of Canning, it is to be doubted whether they would have lightened his difficulties. In fact his policy of co-operation as far as was practicable with the other great powers in a mutual quest for European peace was dependent in Britain upon his own influence, ability and prestige, upon the acquiescence and apathy of his cabinet colleagues, and upon the ignorance and apathy of the majority of Parliament, reinforced by their fear of a Whig–Radical ministry. Backed by these circumstances, Castlereagh was broadly free to embark upon one of the most interesting experiments in British foreign policy, but an experiment that was doomed to die with his removal from office, and perhaps even to precede that removal were circumstances to change.

When the lengthy negotiations for the resettlement of Europe had at last run their course by November 1815, Castlereagh, after more than two years of careful study and personal experience of his allies, had decided to put his main trust for the future in occasional meetings of the leaders of the great powers.

[1] *Hansard*, new series, ii. 385, 392; iv. 1355–62, 1365–76; see also *Hansard*, xl. 498.

[2] *Quarterly Review*, Jan. 1862.

[3] For a comparison of the treatment of parliamentary and public opinion by Castlereagh and Canning, see the joint article by Webster and Temperley, *Cambridge Historical Journal* (1923–5), pp. 158–69.

The year 1815 had shown that little trust could be placed in the stability of the Bourbons of France; the revolutionary and Napoleonic threat to Europe and France remained, and the Quadruple Alliance seemed the only effective counter to that threat. But the years 1813–15 had also demonstrated the fragility of that Alliance; here was a most delicate plant which would require constant care and attention if the great deterrent against future French aggression was to be maintained. Practice had shown that only personal contact between the sovereigns and leading ministers of the powers could overcome the worst of their differences, and consequently Castlereagh, proceeding from the premise that war anywhere in Europe could lead to general war, and possibly to French hegemony, not to mention the possible overthrow of the existing political and social order, drew the conclusion that only regular meetings of great-power leaders promised to maintain sufficient allied unity to avert such perils. In the intervals between these meetings the Alliance was to be sustained by every possible diplomatic device and connexion.

Castlereagh clearly perceived that, if this allied unity were to possess real meaning and durability, diplomacy would have to be conducted in a spirit very different from that shown in the past — especially the recent past. Here, Britain could do no more than try to provide an example, and he consequently instructed his ambassadors that they should forget the techniques and standards of the eighteenth century, and disdain the petty intrigues and rivalries that characterised them. He agreed that British representatives must remain vigilant and well-informed, and place no 'blind confidence' in others, but he was convinced that on the whole the rewards that might result from sincerity and restraint would far exceed any possible dangers. Britain's greatest desire was peace; she was territorially satiated; her naval and economic lead over other powers had never been and never was to be so great.[1] Consequently Castlereagh could run

[1] Castlereagh's own concern for British sea power had been demonstrated by his quest for strategic bases at Vienna, and subsequently underlined by his jealousy of Russian naval ambitions in the Mediterranean, which he countered on at least one occasion by delicate diplomacy. See Webster, *Castlereagh, 1815–22*, pp. 462–4, and Bartlett, *Great Britain and Sea Power*, pp. 63–65.

certain risks in the belief that Britain would have ample time and space in which to take precautions should his expectations be disappointed. That he was taking a calculated risk is clear from his own remarks.

When I thus express myself with respect to the view of Russia, or indeed of any Court, I must be understood as not indulging that species of blind confidence which does not belong to the politics of any foreign State; but I wish to guard our missions abroad against the danger of accelerating, if not producing a conflict for influence between the two States. The existing state of European relations may possibly not endure beyond the danger which originally gave them birth, and which has recently confirmed them; but it is our duty, as well as interest, to retard, if we cannot avert, the return of a more contentious order of things; and our insular situation places us sufficiently out of the reach of danger to admit of our pursuing a more generous and confiding policy.[1]

To this end Castlereagh in the following years refused to be stampeded into counter-measures when alarmist reports of Russian intrigues in several capitals of Europe reached the Foreign Office, but he relied instead on personal appeals to the Tsar. On several occasions his confidence in Alexander's devotion to the Alliance was vindicated. Indeed, his policy was more hard-headed than it might appear, since firm language and hard bargaining were often employed, and his whole conception was backed by British power, and was based on British interests and on clear evidence that other European statesmen were disposed to co-operate.

A recent historian has claimed, 'The impressive thing about the behaviour of the Powers in 1815 is that they were prepared, as they had never previously been prepared, to waive their individual interests in the pursuit of an international system.'[2] The degree to which Castlereagh himself and his fellow statesmen were inspired by abstract, ideal and otherwise intangible motives may long be a matter for debate, but one and all they were impelled by the desire for peace, and what Castlereagh himself described as the desire for 'perfect security against the revolutionary embers more or less existing in every State of Europe'. Self-interest was the chief, if not the only form of

[1] Webster, *Castlereagh, 1815–22*, pp. 509–12. *C.C.* xi. 104–7.
[2] Hinsley, *Power and the Pursuit of Peace*, p. 197.

cement. Castlereagh was able to play upon the Tsar's fear of revolution and of Russian isolation in the uncertain post-Vienna world, as well as upon the Tsar's romantic attachment to the Alliance, and his evident delight in participating in these splendid international gatherings. Indeed, his enthusiasm had sometimes to be curbed and channelled away from still more ambitious forms of international co-operation, of which his Holy Alliance of 1815 was the most exotic but least harmful. The more cynical Metternich speedily became an enthusiast, for here was a form of personal diplomacy eminently suited to his talents and to the resources of his 'ramshackle empire', which was more formidable in the arts of entertainment and ceremonial than of war. Prussia had no dynamic figure who dared to defy the prevailing trend, and her cautious rulers were soon drawn nearer to the Alliance by fear of France and revolution. The French Bourbons were in no condition to think of foreign adventures in the years immediately following 1815; entry to the Alliance at first tickled French pride, and France was only taking her first tentative steps towards more ambitious and independent policies at the time of Castlereagh's death. There was thus a sufficient consensus for the 'new diplomacy' to be meaningful and effective in some, if not all circumstances. Castlereagh felt that a French intrigue in Buenos Aires in 1820 was sufficiently out of character with the diplomatic atmosphere of the post-war era to comment,

I am afraid that we must regard this affair as flowing from some of the dregs of that old diplomacy which so long poisoned the public health of the body politic of Europe, but which has happily in latter years been in great measure banished, at least from the councils of the Quadruple Alliance.[1]

The first major post-war international problem was that of France.[2] Although Napoleon was safely confined on the island of

[1] Webster, *Latin America*, ii. 9. In general for the above, see Webster, *Castlereagh, 1815–22*, pp. 1–73, 489, 509–12; Hinsley, pp. 199–211; *C.C.* xi. 104–7. As far back as 1716, François de Callières had advocated this type of diplomacy (*De la Manière de Négocies avec les Soverains*).

[2] The following discussion of the 'New Diplomacy' in operation is mainly drawn from Webster's *Castlereagh, 1815–22*.

St. Helena in the south Atlantic, there were doubts as late as 1818 as to whether the army of occupation could safely be withdrawn without precipitating a revolt against the Bourbons. On the other hand, it could be argued that the continued presence of this army annoyed the French, and weakened the Bourbons through their apparent dependence on foreign bayonets. This was the view of Wellington, the commander of this army, and his recommendation for an early allied withdrawal was approved by Castlereagh, who had always favoured leniency and conciliation as the surest means to encourage French restraint. But withdrawal would also reopen the question of European security against France, and for a time the British cabinet showed some interest in the possible formation of a special force on the frontier of the Netherlands. Nor could the allies lightly contemplate total evacuation when part of the French indemnity remained unpaid, and more particularly the question of numerous private claims against France for expenses and losses incurred during the wars remained unsettled. These private claims were nearly double the indemnity, and it was by no means certain that French credit would stand the strain of early payment. The British government was anxious for obvious political reasons to end this uncertainty; it was also hoped that a financial settlement would improve the stability of the international money market, and therefore Castlereagh and Wellington encouraged the efforts of the famous banker, Baring, to provide the funds for the extinction of these reparations. They similarly endeavoured to reduce the allied claims to more modest levels, and Wellington was finally accepted by the allies late in 1817 as the arbitrator in these matters. Another year was to pass before all the loose ends had been tidied up.

Progress towards a reparations settlement made an early decision on the army of occupation vital, together with allied agreement as to the future provision for the security of Europe. A meeting of allied sovereigns and ministers appeared the best way of grappling with these problems, and pressures in favour of a conference were increased by other European questions, such as the continuing revolt of the Spanish American colonies against the imperial power, and by the personal inclinations of the Tsar, Metternich, and Castlereagh. The latter, in particular, believed that such a meeting was desirable to dispel the accumulating clouds of suspicion, intrigue and rivalry, which were all too reminiscent of the old diplomacy. He personally had already been resisting pressure from his Ambassador in Paris to agree to counter-measures to his Russian colleague's efforts to influence the French government; similarly, although he was normally giving diplomatic support to the Austrian case in Germany against the designs of the Russians, he had firmly declined a proposal from Metternich for a union of the other powers against Russia. A conference would provide just that opportunity he required to test personally the sincerity of the Tsar and the depth of his continuing attachment, if any, to the Alliance. A clearer conception of the Alliance was also needed, not merely as a precaution against France, but to prevent recurrences of the efforts of Metternich and Pozzo di Borgo, the Russian Ambassador in Paris, to extend the competence of the Paris ambassadorial conference beyond the affairs of France to a general supervision of Europe, especially when revolution threatened.

Any difficulties Castlereagh may have had with the cabinet before the conference met at Aix-la-Chapelle in September 1818 can only be guessed at, but the wording of his instructions hint at the concern, which was subsequently to become explicit, lest Britain should become involved in further commitments. On the other hand, Castlereagh was able in the first place to suggest that the conference should be summoned under Article VI of the Quadruple Alliance — that is, the article which provided for periodic allied meetings — and later he was able to suggest that France should be invited to join the allied deliberations under Article VI, and so end her isolation in Europe. It was only during the conference itself that cabinet doubts at the long-term implications of Article VI began to express themselves. Perhaps one may be entitled to surmise that the rest of the cabinet, in Castlereagh's presence, were not able or willing to take a strong line in these questions, and it was only in his absence that real criticism made itself heard.

The conference of Aix-la-Chapelle began at the end of September 1818, and the outstanding problems with France were speedily settled. The army of occupation was withdrawn, the indemnity and reparation matters were soon cleared away, and though the Quadruple Alliance was secretly to be maintained against France, the latter was to be invited to attend the great-power reunions under Article VI. Castlereagh was also delighted to find that his belief in Alexander's loyalty to the Alliance had not been misplaced, that the Tsar did not approve of the efforts of some of his agents to promote a Franco-Russian alliance, and had resisted proposals designed, if not to separate Russia from her war-time allies, at least to increase her influence by traditional eighteenth-century methods. Unfortunately, the Tsar's enthusiasm for the Alliance was soon carrying him too far to the other extreme, and Castlereagh found himself caught between grandiose Russian proposals for the most far-reaching commitments by the great powers to each other and to Europe, and the growing insularity of the British cabinet freed from his restraining and guiding presence.

Alexander aspired to bind together all the states of Europe, great and small, 'in a common league guaranteeing to each other the existing order of things in thrones as well as in territories, all being bound to march, if requisite, against the first power that offended either by her ambitions or by her revolutionary transgressions'. Any such agreement would immediately wreck all British association with the other powers, and Castlereagh, to preserve his own limited conception of the Alliance, set out to defeat the Russian design with every diplomatic device he could muster. In his counter-suggestions he was careful to use high-sounding language that would appeal to the Tsar, without at the same time departing from his basic premise. In discussion he used all his debating talents to underline the impracticability of the Russian suggestions, and insisted that the guarantee in question implied 'the previous establishment of such a system of general government as may secure and enforce upon all kings and nations an internal system of peace and justice'. This was impossible. He reiterated the limited nature of the present obligations incurred under the Quadruple Alliance, and insisted that these could be supplemented only by the pragmatic decisions of individual states according to the circumstances of any one crisis, and by the interposition of the good offices of the allies. In down-to-earth, detailed argument of this sort the Russians had no champion worthy of Castlereagh. Nevertheless, he had often to confirm his position by private discussions with the Tsar, even giving courteous lessons in the interpretation of treaties, and in the implications of British parliamentary government. Metternich, less obviously, was also anxious to control the Tsar's itch for indiscriminate interference in the affairs of other states, though he was already becoming interested in more limited and controlled Russian assistance against possible future revolutionary outbreaks. Certainly he was attracted by a Prussian scheme for a European territorial guarantee by the great powers, but consideration of this was successfully postponed by Castlereagh *sine die*.

Though Castlereagh required no prompting from the cabinet to object to these Russian and Prussian proposals, despatches reaching him from London late in October reminded him that even the appearance of a concession to the allies could be misinterpreted in Britain. A new Parliament had been elected, and the cabinet correctly foresaw that its mood was likely to be more independent than its predecessor. The cabinet feared that the conference might result in new commitments, or at least conclude with a blaze of publicity as to its future intentions. Britain's continuing ties with her war-time allies had become known when the shadow of Napoleon had scarcely been removed from Europe; what had been approved then would not have been approved in the very different conditions of 1818, and the cabinet was anxious that Castlereagh should do all possible to avoid alarming Parliament. Castlereagh was also warned of rumblings of discontent within the cabinet, where Canning had begun to object to the allied reunions provided for by Article VI as 'new and of very questionable policy'. According to Bathurst, the cabinet did not agree with his criticisms, but it feared that Canning's arguments would delight many other people, and urged Castlereagh to avoid a public declaration of the allies' intention to continue this system of reunions. Although the cabinet professed no desire to abolish Article VI, it clearly had no great desire to see it invoked with any regularity. Liverpool, indeed, warned Castlereagh in October, 'The sixth article in the Treaty of Alliance, as well as some other stipulations in that treaty, could hardly have been adopted for the first time under such circumstances as the present.'[1] The cabinet ordered Castlereagh to agree to as little as possible that was new, publicly or in secret. Unfortunately for Castlereagh, the Tsar was intent on publicity concerning the admission of France to the concert, and to the continuance of the allied meetings, and, in order to smooth away Alexander's disappointment concerning his treaty of guarantee, Castlereagh felt that an appearance of concession, especially in high-sounding language, with some publicity, was necessary. He was, however, able to devise a compromise reasonably satisfactory to all, for, as he explained to the cabinet,

The eventual reunions are strictly limited to those interests that grow out of the transactions in question [i.e., the maintenance of peace by the existing treaties], and, instead of declaring any intention that such reunions shall be held at fixed periods, as the Sixth Article provides shall be the case, it is expressly declared that they shall be special, namely that they shall arise out of the occasion and be agreed upon by the five Courts at the time; in fact, no Power can be considered as pledged *a priori* to any meeting whatever.

Vague and non-committal as this was, such an agreement gave Castlereagh all that he required in the future. It satisfied the Tsar's itch for display without alarming British opinion; for Castlereagh it provided just that degree of flexibility he needed so that the Alliance would be invoked when only vital British interests were at stake. He hoped it would maintain 'a salutary impression of *surveillance*, of evincing to Europe that the Great Powers feel that they have not only a common interest, but a common duty to attend to; and that when the occasion shall call for it the Cabinets of these Powers may thus be brought into contact'. Meanwhile, of the other questions to be discussed at Aix-la-Chapelle, that of the revolt of Spain's American colonies was the most important. This can be more conveniently considered in a later section, though it is worthy of note here that Castlereagh's confidence in conference diplomacy was again vindicated. Not only were the rivalries of British and Russian diplomats in Spain smoothed over by the personal contacts between the Tsar and Castlereagh, but the latter was also able

[1] Yonge, ii. 345.

to persuade the other powers that allied intervention should be
limited to an offer of mediation in the person of the Duke of
Wellington. Castlereagh was successful on most other points of
interest to Britain, including the Tsar's suggestion of a maritime
league to act against the Barbary corsairs, who were said to be
terrorising the ships of many nations. Britain had no wish to see
a Russian fleet operating in the Mediterranean, and Castlereagh's
offer to accept the naval league only if a mutual right of search
against the slave trade were conceded has the appearance of
being a polite way of saying no. The French, for one, opposed
British claims to a right of search with all the power at their
disposal. Consequently the Barbary states were to be troubled
by no more than an allied delegation, a gesture which Castlereagh supported mainly to please the Tsar and promote allied
unity. As he told Melville, without such action 'we should have
left Russia in a state of discontent and separation'.[1]

Thus, in general, Castlereagh had every reason to feel well
pleased with his efforts at Aix. Controversial Russian and
Prussian proposals which would never have been accepted in
Britain had been argued away, or reduced to harmlessness;
British and European security against France had been maintained by the secret continuance of the Quadruple Alliance;
Article VI could be invoked if and when it seemed desirable to
hold further allied meetings. Castlereagh had been able to
confirm his belief that the Tsar remained highly susceptible to
his skill in argument in personal confrontations, and that
Alexander's enthusiasm for the Alliance could be relied upon to
arrest the tangential policies of his subordinates. Finally, he was
now convinced that there was no serious danger of a Russo-
French alliance, the most dangerous of all alliances to the peace
of Europe. As he informed Arbuthnot, 'all are gone home in
good humour and vowing eternal peace and friendship, so that
we shall be enabled to make our [arms] reductions with a good
conscience'.[2] This would be particularly welcome news for the
cabinet, with its fears of parliamentary pressure, and could be
used by Castlereagh as an impressive demonstration of the
value of his continued association with his old allies.

But there was to be no repetition of the Aix conference.

[1] *C.C.* xii. 59–60.   [2] Aspinall, *Arbuthnot*, pp. 12–13.

Castlereagh himself had attended his last international gathering, though he was making preparations to attend the conference at Verona at the time of his suicide in 1822. As will be shown later, the Alliance was by no means doomed until his death removed the one British statesman capable of maintaining British participation. But in the intervening years of 1819–21 events in Europe had underlined the precarious nature of the links between Britain and the continental powers, and had shown how tortuous a path Castlereagh was compelled to follow in order to preserve some vestige of allied unity. He had already received ample warning that few of his countrymen were agreeable to continental commitments, save for the purpose of increasing British security against France. On the other hand it had not been difficult for Castlereagh to use this limited commitment to justify his very considerable efforts since 1814 to solve other European questions, arguing that their solution would increase European and British security against France. Much could be achieved in this direction without undue publicity, and the matters in dispute had, on the whole, been of concern only to small minorities of British citizens. But outbreaks of revolution in several minor European states in 1820–1 could not be similarly treated, especially when on the one hand many of the rebels spoke the language of British constitutionalism and liberalism, and when on the other the autocratic powers of Europe tried to turn the Alliance into an instrument for the general suppression of revolution and political change. Vocal opinion in Britain either denounced these acts of counter-revolution, or favoured British neutrality and isolation; Castlereagh's efforts to preserve the Alliance in these circumstances found few sympathisers in Britain.

The basic principles that guided Castlereagh in his policy at this juncture were very simple, however complex and convoluted his diplomacy appeared on the surface. For the various European rebels he felt no sympathy; he had spent too much of his life fighting rebels of one sort and another. Britain herself was still in the grip of popular disturbances and political restlessness of unknown dimensions. Consequently he welcomed many of the repressive measures undertaken against this 'monster' of revolution. But this prejudice did not in fact dominate his policy.

His fundamental concern remained the peace and stability of
Europe, and this depended upon the continuance of unity and
harmony between the great powers. He saw that for the powers
to act in concert against the rebellious might impose too great a
strain upon their precarious unity. Action in concert would bring
the troops of some powers into the spheres of influence of
others; Russian troops in central and southern Europe could not
fail to alarm Austria, while the troops of any great power in
Spain or Portugal would threaten Great Britain. More pressing,
however, was the hostility in Britain to any appearance of
concerted action by the Alliance against rebellion. Castlereagh
feared that the image of the Alliance would become so tarnished
that British separation would be inescapable. It was imperative,
therefore, that action against the rebels should be taken only by
individual powers acting within their own spheres of influence.
Secret British government support of such action might be
possible, but Castlereagh also felt that in some circumstances
moderation on the part of the intervening power might have its
virtues. Indiscriminate action might antagonise the lesser states
within that sphere, weaken the influence of the dominant power,
and create instability there and consequently in Europe as a whole.

Castlereagh's task was therefore to reconcile the interests of
the great powers, avert any situation which would so arouse
British insularity and liberal sentiment as to wreck the Alliance,
and encourage all trends that promised peace and stability, even
if these included modest political concessions to constitutional
advance. To apply this policy in the face of revolution and disturbance in many parts of Europe at the same time was no easy
matter, as circumstances varied so sharply from place to place.
Simplicity of principle became highly complex in execution, and
it is not surprising that many contemporaries, both at home and
abroad, misunderstood his policies. It was, indeed, a long time
before Metternich began to understand Castlereagh's position,
despite the fact that of all European statesmen he was closest in
sympathy with him. At first he wrote of the inveterate egoism of
the English when Castlereagh refused him active support against
revolution, and then later came to the opinion that the weakness
of the Liverpool ministry was responsible for his caution. Only
gradually was Castlereagh able to show that there were limits

to the British commitment to the Alliance irrespective of the parliamentary strength or weakness of the cabinet.

Metternich's first moves against the supposed threat of revolution in Germany in 1819 received the secret approval of Castlereagh, the Prince Regent and the cabinet, though they were badly received in much of the British press. Castlereagh wrote, 'we are always pleased to see evil germs destroyed without the power to give our approbation openly', but he was soon adding reminders to Metternich that the latter might undo his good work if he intervened too openly and frequently in the internal affairs of south German states. A short-lived, vaguely liberal ministry in France in 1819 also alarmed the other powers, but Castlereagh hastened to reject proposals for a European clearing-house to watch events in France, and 'to aid generally in the maintenance of European repose'. He also restrained the desire of his Ambassador in Paris to exploit the Anglophil tendencies of the new French ministry. Nevertheless his own loyalty to the Alliance was continually offset by the warnings he was obliged to send to Metternich that Britain, as a parliamentary power, could not associate herself with any international counter-revolutionary actions. Castlereagh was hoping early in 1820 that Metternich would be able to visit Britain, so that he could fully explain his policy and problems in private conversations. But Metternich did not come; there was to be no personal meeting between them until the autumn of 1821. In the interval Metternich, persuaded that the revolutionary threat was becoming unmanageable, drew closer to the Russians for support, and was consequently driven nearer to the Tsar's interpretation of the Alliance to the detriment of his hitherto close and cordial relations with Castlereagh.

The international crises of 1820, with revolutions in Spain, Portugal and Naples, found Castlereagh with little time in which to develop his policy. He and the cabinet were becoming increasingly preoccupied with the great royal divorce question, and there also seemed a real possibility of the government's overthrow in that year. In these circumstances, British foreign policy had to be as uncontroversial as possible. Nevertheless, Castlereagh was able to make British policy crystal clear in his famous state paper of 5 May 1820, which was the British retort

P

to the proposals of other powers for a conference to discuss the revolution in Spain. The Russians and French, in particular, seemed to be drawing dangerously near to possible intervention in Spain. Either eventuality would be highly unpopular in Britain, while any great-power intervention in Spain would be contrary to the British interest in that country as a neutral buffer state on British trade-routes. The resulting state paper was probably mainly the work of Castlereagh, though it was discussed at length by the cabinet, and some of the stronger notes of emphasis may have been the work of the latter, especially of Canning. Much of what the paper enunciated had already been stated or implied; its novelties lay rather in tone and emphasis than in content, though it was odd to find Castlereagh writing that a conference, 'from the necessarily limited powers of the individuals composing it, must ever be better fitted to execute a purpose already decided upon than to frame a course of policy under delicate and difficult circumstances'.

At most Castlereagh was prepared to concede that the allies might individually warn the Spanish rebels against injuring their King or threatening the neighbouring state of Portugal, but the Quadruple Alliance had never been created to serve as 'an union for the government of the world or for the superintendence of the internal affairs of other States'. Admittedly the Alliance might discuss matters outside its original scope, but it should not take into its consideration as a matter of course every 'possible eventual danger'. Very significantly he drew attention to the constitutional difficulties in the way of British participation in a policy of intervention, and pointed out that autocratic and constitutional states could not feel alike on all subjects. He concluded with a promise and a warning, declaring that Britain had the 'last Government in Europe which can be expected or can venture to commit herself on any question of an abstract character. . . . We shall be found in our place when actual danger menaces the system of Europe : but this country cannot and will not act upon abstract and speculative principles of precaution'. In his application of this argument to the current crisis in Spain he insisted that rebellion in that country constituted no threat to the rest of Europe. One senses that, in this state paper, Castlereagh's prime object was to preserve the Alliance by demonstrating, without equivocation, precisely the point where Britain must part company with her allies unless they adopted his conception of mutual obligations. Esterházy, the Austrian Ambassador, noted in the spring of 1820, 'The British Cabinet wish, as the Duke of Wellington has often said to me, that the Alliance sleeps.'

Metternich, though uneasy at the prospect of leaving revolution unpunished, agreed with Castlereagh's opposition to intervention in Spain, and there was insufficient identity of purpose among the other powers for their alternative proposals to flourish. When revolution spread to Portugal in August 1820 none of the powers had any hesitation in acknowledging Britain's paramount interest and influence, and Castlereagh made good use of this recognition to deter the Spaniards from intervention, without at the same time pushing British action in Portugal beyond the tendering of advice for moderation and restraint to all parties. It was a policy of patience, inspired by the belief that the more overt British intervention became, the more unpopular it would become. But by judicious prompting he hoped to persuade the King that 'a system of unqualified reaction, would, . . . be extremely prejudicial to the King's, as well as to the general interest'. He also hoped to draw the revolutionaries towards a moderate, compromise constitution. In practice, Portugal stumbled from political crisis to political crisis for the rest of his lifetime, but it cannot be said that his tactics were any less successful than the more dramatic efforts of some of his successors. Castlereagh's hopes for Spain were similar, though here he had even less hope that British advice would be taken. Nevertheless, it is worthy of note that, with reference to both Portugal and Spain, his basic hope for the future lay not in the triumph of reaction, but in modest constitutional advance based on the ultimate recognition of all parties that this could be the only permanent solution to their rivalries. If neither country, in the long run, fulfilled his expectations, Castlereagh at least was able to contribute to the maintenance of positions of non-intervention by all the great powers, which was a greater British interest than the triumph of any particular political groups in the Peninsula.

Castlereagh's reaction to the Neapolitan revolt which broke

out in July 1820 was very different. Quite apart from his personal belief that Naples was well governed compared with Spain and Portugal, and therefore that the revolt was unjustified, he held that Italy lay within Austria's sphere of influence, and that consequently Austrian policy in that quarter must be supported — albeit discreetly. This was no personal reaction, for Esterházy received assurances from Canning, Harrowby and Bathurst of British sympathy from the outset.[1] As early as 29 July Castlereagh was able to assure the Austrians that Britain would not object to armed intervention in Naples should it be found necessary. There was a slight gesture to British constitutional sympathies, when his official despatch referred to the British government's anxiety to see 'the progressive advancement of rational liberty throughout Europe', but repeatedly in the disturbances afflicting Italy in 1820–1 Castlereagh subordinated any concern for or belief in modest constitutional progress to the interests and needs of Austria. The reason for this was quite simple. Castlereagh hoped that Britain's secret moral and diplomatic support would be sufficient to steel the Austrians to action without recourse to the Alliance or a conference. Such moves could only rouse passions in Britain; such moves also could only play into the hands of the Russians with their all-too-evident desire to meddle throughout Europe under cover of general guarantees and interventionist principles. High-minded and idealistic as the Tsar might possibly be in his motives, there was no knowing the mischief that might be unleashed, and certainly Britain's ties with the Alliance would never stand the strain. Invocation of the Alliance might also play into the hands of the French, the power whose influence in Italy Castlereagh dreaded more than any. Austria should therefore act alone in the interest of the preservation of the Alliance, and also of the balance of power, since the diminution of Austrian influence in Italy might not only open the door to others, but might also weaken her overall position in Europe.

Unfortunately Metternich's nature, as well as his appreciation of the revolutionary threat and Austrian vulnerability, forbade him to act on such bold advice. He agreed that action against

[1] Webster, *Castlereagh, 1815–22*, pp. 261–2. P. Schroeder, *Metternich's Diplomacy at its Zenith*, p. 47. Rolo, pp. 202–3.

Naples was essential, but he needed more than Britain's moral support. He needed the moral support of Russia to demonstrate to all Europe that, whatever the past actions of Russian agents, the Tsar was firmly behind the policy of repression, and that potential rebels could not look to Russia for comfort. Recent Russian policy had been full of ambiguities, and various Russian efforts to win friends in minor states had sometimes suggested not merely anti-Austrian objectives, but a genuine sympathy for liberalism. Metternich therefore needed a demonstration of the Tsar's true feelings, but he found he could not achieve this without agreeing to a full-scale allied conference, with the promise of loud-sounding allied declarations of principle, perhaps even of action, to follow. Metternich procrastinated and tried to obscure the differences with all the ingenuity his brilliance could devise, but to no avail. In the last resort, Metternich dared not act without Russia. With France also pressing for a conference, Metternich had no choice. It was not even certain that Castlereagh would survive the year as Britain's Foreign Secretary, and wild stories were circulating in Europe as to the revolutionary intentions of the Whigs and their Radical allies, should they secure office. When it became clear that Metternich was attempting to conceal the fact that a full-scale conference was intended, and that the British Opposition parties were becoming restless and suspected possible British involvement against Naples, Castlereagh and the cabinet had no choice but to limit British participation in the conference to the attendance of an observer. Their position became a little easier when the French decided on a similar course.

The conference of Troppau opened in October 1820. It began as a struggle for Alexander's mind between Metternich and Capo d'Istria, one of the Tsar's two Foreign Ministers. Metternich envisaged a limited role for the Tsar; that of high priest of the Alliance blessing the arms of Austria. But Capo d'Istria strove to rekindle the Tsar's passion to stand forth as the crusading, philosopher-king, entrusted with the task of leading all Europe into a new era of Christian monarchy, possibly reinforced by the grant of limited constitutions. Naples should be the first test case. Russian intervention on this scale, perhaps climaxed by the establishment of a Neapolitan con-

stitution, was viewed with horror by Metternich. In the end, the
victory lay with him, but at the cost of the invocation of general
principles and high-blown language so pleasing to the Tsar.
True, Austria could now act against the Neapolitan rebels with
Russian moral support, but at the cost of a general preliminary
protocol asserting that the Quadruple Alliance and other treaties
conferred upon the allies the right to take precautions against
revolutionary threats throughout Europe, and claiming an
ultimate right of coercion against any revolutionary state which
threatened the peace and security of others. As Metternich
foresaw, this concession to the Tsar robbed 'the world of its
tranquillity', and all his efforts to slip it through under the noses
of the British and French observers on 19 November came to
naught. It struck them like a bombshell.

Castlereagh himself was less surprised though no less angry.
He had sensed the drift of the negotiations at Troppau before
news of the protocol reached London. From 4 December, in
memoranda and despatches, and in interviews with the Russian
and Austrian Ambassadors he made his position abundantly
clear. He emphatically rejected all claims to a right of interference in the affairs of other states, save on the limited ground
of self-defence, which could never be defined in advance. He
warned that the protocol's claims would create a dangerous
precedent with which to jeopardise the liberties of Europe, as it
was impossible to rely on the benignity of future rulers. The
protocol might encourage some European rulers to rely upon
the Alliance rather than upon their own efforts to preserve their
thrones, and thereby increase the danger of revolution, or they
might let slip opportunities 'to accommodate themselves with
good faith and before it is too late by some prudent change of
system to the exigencies of their peculiar position'. Again
Castlereagh showed himself not averse to modest political
change on pragmatic grounds, and he concluded that the protocol
was contrary to international law, to the British constitution, to
common sense; nor could it be effectively implemented.

But Castlereagh was writing and speaking as much in sorrow
as in anger. His great counter-blast of 16 December was designed
for communication to Parliament should it become necessary,
but he told the Russian Ambassador that his heart bled at having

to write such a document. He reaffirmed his attachment to the Alliance; he spoke of his detestation of rebellion and secret societies; he did not even object to the aims and intentions of the allies with respect to Naples. There was more than a hint of regret in one remark that he was unable to attend the conference and use his influence with the Tsar to demonstrate how far the protocol had moved from the original purpose of the Alliance, to which Alexander had professed unswerving loyalty. He had told Esterházy in October that if only the allies would take account of 'the considerations due to our position, we will never refuse to take part' in certain questions outside the scope of the Alliance, but on which general action seemed necessary. But if the allies insisted on creating a super-state, if they strove to revise the eminently successful Alliance 'upon the exploded doctrine of *divine right* and of passive obedience', then Britain could not follow them. He concluded in a letter to his Ambassador in Vienna on 17 December,

It now rests with the three Courts to decide whether they choose to contend against the dangers of the times under separate banners : the choice is with them, not with us : they may contend upon the case as we propose without laying down disputed principles. We cannot adhere to their doctrine, and if they will be theorists we must act in separation upon matters not specifically provided for by Treaty, which seems an odd option for them to make in the present state of Europe. . . .[1]

The Troppau protocol was in fact superseded by the only slightly less objectionable Troppau circular, and the allies now moved to Laibach to meet the King of Naples and to prepare for the final denouement, the Austrian march against the rebels. Again, Castlereagh declined to be represented by more than an observer, but even so constant vigilance was necessary to guard against Metternich's efforts to implicate Britain and France in the allied denunciation of revolution. The substance of the Troppau circular was becoming public knowledge despite Castlereagh's warnings of counter-publicity on his part if this should take place. He recapitulated his own arguments in a diplomatic circular of 19 January 1821, which admitted only Austria's right to act in Naples, and that under gravest necessity in defence of her own security. He reaffirmed his support for the

[1] Webster, *Castlereagh, 1815–22*, pp. 298–306.

Alliance on other issues, and his determination to preserve the concert was as strong as ever, but the publicity which the document soon enjoyed earned Britain much popularity among the critics and enemies of the three eastern powers, especially in Italy and Spain. Nor was it well received by the Russians and Austrians. But of the Whig and Radical critics in the British Parliament, many agreed with Grey's verdict on the famous circular as no more than a 'cold and feeble' protest, and their suspicion of Castlereagh's policy was far from erased.

The parliamentary debates of February and March 1821 on Castlereagh's policy with respect to Naples, and his relations with the continental powers, reveal two main points. The government was in no danger of defeat in either House, and interest soon fell away. Furthermore, this took place despite the determination of Castlereagh to defend the conduct of Russia and Austria as far as it was practicable. Although this does not indicate parliamentary support — certainly not parliamentary enthusiasm — for his policies, it does underline that his policy was perfectly practicable in that members did not regard it with sufficient distaste or concern to outweigh their preference for the Liverpool ministry. Most defenders of the government, in fact, concentrated upon the need for perfect British neutrality, and made much of the Opposition's confused quest for an alternative policy which would not carry with it the dangers of war or exposure to the humiliation of complete ineffectiveness. Tierney had launched the Opposition on their irresponsible course on 23 January with an expression of delight at the promise of peace so badly needed to recoup Britain's battered finances, which he had instantly followed with a plea that Britain should defend small states from the aggression of others. Yet government exploitation of this confusion could not wholly hide the fact that Castlereagh's policy had been less neutral than he claimed. Nor could it conceal the fact that most speakers disliked and feared the 'Holy Alliance', and none was prepared to go so far as Castlereagh in his condemnation of revolution or his expressions of confidence in the conduct of the Austrians and the allies. Against this frankness on his part must be set his wholly inaccurate claim that he had never encouraged the Austrians to act against the Neapolitan rebels, or his verbal dexterity in proclaiming the virtues of non-intervention with one breath and asserting the reasonableness of the Austrian action with the next. Canning's forceful defence of neutrality and freedom was much more to the taste of members.[1]

The Russian Ambassador, Lieven, claimed that George IV and several members of the cabinet, in addition to Castlereagh and Wellington, assured him of their sympathy at this time. But European statesmen and diplomats continued to experience great difficulty in reaching a proper understanding of British policy. Gentz, indeed, believed that many of the British aristocracy, including Liverpool, 'had fallen prey to revolutionary doctrines and had abandoned sound principles'. Metternich was inclined to attribute Castlereagh's warnings to fear of Parliament, and it was in vain that Castlereagh pointed out to him that certain principles in the British political system were 'immutable', and that 'if the three Courts persevere much longer in the open promulgation of their ultra doctrines, they will ere long work a separation which it is the wish of us all to avoid'.[2] Nor did Castlereagh, even in Italy, wholly ignore the possibilities of cautious constitutional advance if it promised greater political stability on the side of monarchy, aristocracy and property. But Metternich and the Italian rulers would not listen to Castlereagh's tentative pleas on behalf of Piedmont, Naples and Sicily, and Castlereagh would not work with French and Russian diplomats who might have reinforced his recommendations. To have done so would have been contrary to his prior principle that Austria must dominate Italy for the good of Europe and the balance of power.[3]

By the middle of April 1821 the Austrians had suppressed revolution in both Naples and Piedmont; the cause of the diverging tactics of Metternich and Castlereagh was at an end, and the way was open to renewed co-operation between them.

---

[1] *Hansard*, new series, iv. 48, 742–95, 837–95, 1350–80, 1468–73; see also ibid., new series, v. 1220–60 for a further debate in June when less than 180 members were present, and Castlereagh was supported by 113 votes against 59.

[2] Sir A. Alison, *Castlereagh*, iii. 222–3 n.

[3] Schroeder, pp. 162, 244–8. A short-lived revolution occurred in Piedmont in March–April 1821.

In one sense the gap between them had never been very wide; Metternich had needed a demonstration of moral support from the Tsar against revolution, and to secure this he had been obliged to humour Alexander's taste for sweeping pronouncements of general principles. To these Castlereagh could never assent, and he feared that such proclamations would so provoke feeling in Britain that the Alliance would be wrecked. As he told the Commons on 21 June 1821, 'If we were to engage in a perpetual conflict of state paper against state paper, the councils of Europe would be resolved into a debating society, and all the links by which different countries were connected would be broken.' Short of support for these general declarations, Castlereagh gave Metternich all the support in his power. Unfortunately for Castlereagh, Metternich believed that this was insufficient; the ensuing tactical controversy exasperated both, not least because each believed that he was asking very little of the other. In the circumstances of 1820–1 the gap was unbridgeable, but once the Italian revolts had been suppressed the prospects of reconciliation were good.

True, revolution was still blatantly triumphant in Spain; another conference had been planned for 1822, and the Tsar's desire to apply the principles enunciated at Troppau and Laibach to the Iberian Peninsula was only too clear. But, much as Metternich disliked the Spanish revolutionaries, they constituted no direct threat to the Austrian empire, nor was Spain a region where he would be able to exercise a preponderant influence. For the Alliance to act in Spain would play into the hands of France, and perhaps of Russia; the threat to the European equilibrium was incalculable, and, once intervention had commenced, beyond Austria's power to control. From rather different points of view, therefore, both Castlereagh and Metternich were determined to leave the Spaniards to solve their domestic problems by themselves. As long as they could act in unison, their prospects of checking the Tsar in the name of the Alliance were considerable. The outbreak of a revolt at the other end of Europe likewise found Metternich and Castlereagh in close agreement, so that for the rest of 1821 circumstances generally were moving in favour of their renewed friendship and co-operation.

In April 1821 the Greek population of the Morea rose in revolt against their Ottoman masters. The vulnerability of the Ottoman empire had long been demonstrated by eighteenth-century Russian and Austrian conquests, by the partially successful revolt of the Christian Serbs in the early nineteenth century, and by the repeated contempt for the central authority shown by the more ambitious and energetic of the local Ottoman rulers. Ali Pasha, the 'Lion of Janina', had been at war with the Sultan since 1817, and it soon became evident that the Turks would not be able to bring this latest — the Greek — threat to their authority speedily under control. The Russians, in the past, had shown themselves quick to turn any Ottoman weakness to their advantage; there existed many outstanding differences between Russia and the Turks, and there was the further danger that the Russians might be drawn into the conflict through sympathy for the Greeks as co-religionists. On the British side, Pitt, ahead of his time, had shown some nervousness at the Russian advance as early as 1790, but it was Russian Near and Middle Eastern policies from 1801, reinforced by the activities of Napoleon from 1798, that had developed a serious British political and strategic interest in the Ottoman empire. Britain had similarly become interested in Persia as a bastion against Russia's further expansion, and, in contrast to the eighteenth century, Britain now displayed nervousness at Russia's naval interest in the Mediterranean. The relevance of the fate of the Ottoman empire to the British position in India and to British naval supremacy in the Mediterranean was becoming an important tenet in British policy. In 1815 Castlereagh had briefly sought the inclusion of the Ottoman empire in a European territorial guarantee until other considerations had made the whole guarantee concept impracticable.

Castlereagh's response to the Greek revolt was to urge restraint at both St. Petersburg and Constantinople. He warned the latter that Britain would not support the Turks were they to provoke a war with Russia. But Turkish counter-measures against the Greeks were already threatening to inflame Russian opinion. Russian trade was suffering from Turkish efforts to interdict Greek supplies; Russian feelings were outraged by Turkish atrocities such as the hanging of the Greek Patriarch

of Constantinople; finally, a short-lived revolt against the Turks
in their Danubian principalities had reopened the question of
respective Russo-Turkish rights in that region. By July 1821,
despite considerable initial Russian restraint, relations between
the two countries were near breaking-point. The British
Ambassador at Constantinople, Lord Strangford, was unable to
prevent the departure of his irate Russian colleague on 7 August,
though he may have contributed to his departure sound in wind
and limb. Meanwhile, both Castlereagh and Metternich were
devoting all their diplomatic ingenuity to the task of restraining
the Tsar. Much could be made of Alexander's devotion to the
Alliance, and his fear of revolution. Indeed, he was sufficiently
impressed by Metternich's warnings concerning the insidious
workings of the supposed Central Revolutionary Committee in
Paris to use the same argument against the bellicose Capo
d'Istria. Castlereagh made use of the Tsar's permission, given
to him when fraternal feelings were at their height at Aix-la-
Chapelle, to write to him personally in time of crisis. This was
useful, but on the whole Metternich's influence with the Tsar
may have been greater through his greater subtlety and tact.
Nevertheless, the styles of Castlereagh and Metternich were in
many respects complementary, and each was greatly indebted to
the other.

Castlereagh and Metternich, however, were not yet fully in
agreement, nor had they had time to repair all the damage to
their relations caused by the Italian revolts. Their understand-
ings of each other's positions was not complete, and Castlereagh
in fact opposed one of Metternich's first suggestions — an
allied conference of ambassadors in Vienna to deliberate, and
perhaps offer guidance on the question. Yet something more
constructive than Castlereagh's negative diplomacy at St.
Petersburg and Constantinople was clearly required. A personal
meeting between Metternich and Castlereagh was badly needed,
and the visit of George IV to Hanover as its new King provided
the perfect opportunity. This last meeting of Castlereagh and
Metternich in October 1821 was not remarkable for the measure
of agreement reached. This was very limited. What it did
establish was a closer understanding of their respective positions,
problems and policies. They were able to perceive that the

appearance of differing tactics was less important than the under-
lying quest for the same results. Both statesmen left Hanover
delighted with the outcome of their meetings, and this restored
harmony made the suicide of Castlereagh less than a year later
an even more shattering blow to Metternich in consequence.

At the time of their meeting, both St. Petersburg and Constantinople appeared a little more conciliatory than earlier in the
year. But there had come sombre warnings from the Tsar that
Russian public feeling might force war on him in the spring,
while an uncontrollable upsurge of Moslem fanaticism had
always to be reckoned with. Metternich and Castlereagh agreed
that complete unity of action on their part was impossible and
undesirable. Austria owed Russia a certain obligation following
the latter's conduct during the Italian revolts, while too close an
appearance of concert might provoke rather than restrain the
Russians. Both, according to the circumstances of their position,
should continue to try to restrain the Russians and Turks, and in
addition the aid of Prussia and France should be enlisted to the
same end. The individual dissent of all the great powers to a
Russian war with Turkey might have a decisive effect upon the
impressionable Tsar. The general appeal of the Alliance could
also be exploited. Efforts were also to be made to persuade the
Sultan to accept a moderated version of the Russian demands.

Metternich departed from Hanover claiming 'Mon entente
avec lord Londonderry est complète'. Castlereagh was equally
satisfied, but the task of averting war in the spring remained.
The months slipped by and the time was soon approaching when
campaigning in the Balkans would be possible. Preparations for
war continued in Russia, while diplomats strained every nerve
to extract a sufficient appearance of concession from the confusion, fatalism and fanaticism that prevailed in Constantinople
to persuade the Tsar that peace was still possible. Always there
remained the unpredictable personality of the Tsar himself, by
turns obstinate and impressionable, and throughout the winter of
1821–2 Metternich and Castlereagh dedicated themselves to
their desks, penning enormous despatches replete with every conceivable argument in favour of peace, and searching for the
vulnerable points in Alexander's character. They elaborated
upon the need for allied unity in the face of the revolutionary

threat in Spain, Portugal and Latin America, and perhaps even in France; they drew attention to every weakness — legal, moral and logical — in the Russian case. Metternich pointed out that Russian action against the Turks would divert the Tsar from his critical task in Europe and would play into the hands of the rebels. Castlereagh was more direct, questioning Alexander's premises, and attempting to demonstrate the moral iniquity of jeopardising the happiness and security of the present generation by seeking speculative benefits for the next. He doubted the capacity of the Greeks to set up a better government for themselves, and insisted that even if they could, a European war would unleash every adventurer and fanatic on the continent. He urged that the Greek question should be left to the healing hand of time.

Although Castlereagh's object was to demonstrate the dangers of Capo d'Istria's policy to the Tsar, the latter took some of his criticisms personally, so personally indeed that the British Ambassador dared not show Alexander one subsequent despatch lest it should increase his anger and resolve to fight. Metternich's smoother and more subtle approach was again perhaps the more effective, yet Alexander's awareness of British hostility could not fail to make Metternich's arguments more persuasive. In the long run this combined pressure was too much for the Tsar; he could not fail to be impressed by Russia's isolation, and this was disturbing both from the point of view of his doubts concerning the power of Russia and of his yearning for the fraternal atmosphere of the Alliance and its occasional conferences. He may also have been moved by the fear of revolution; certainly it provided him with an admirable face-saving excuse for his agreement on 19 February 1822 to further negotiations in Vienna. The current fear of revolution was such that Wellington in April 1822 was in favour of supporting the basic demands of Russia against the Turks lest war should result. He feared that such a war would wreck the conservative Alliance, and so unleash war and revolution in Europe as a whole. The destruction of Turkey in Europe would be a much smaller catastrophe.[1] Fortunately Castlereagh's nerves were stronger, his appreciation of the situation more

[1] *Wellington Dispatches from 1819*, i. 232–4.

realistic, and whatever his own reaction to the supposed revolutionary threat, he was able to use it as a means of furthering his own ends. Here was one more demonstration that Wellington lacked the diplomatic understanding and talent to succeed him.

From 8 March to 19 April 1822, as a result of the Tsar's retreat, a special Russian envoy was busily engaged in Vienna; his aim, Metternich's acknowledgement of the justice of the Russian claims to protect the Sultan's Christian subjects, and Austrian moral support if a Russo-Turkish war should ensue. The Russians also hoped to reduce Turkish authority in the Morea to a vague suzerainty. Metternich worked with great skill to persuade the Russian envoy, Tatischev, of Austrian sympathy, but at the same time he strove to confine Russian demands against the Turks to those which involved treaty rights alone, and above all to exclude the Greek question as an internal problem of the Ottoman empire. When Tatischev switched his ground, and sought an Austrian promise to break off relations with the Turks should the latter's stubbornness force a war on Russia, Metternich ultimately agreed, but effectively nullified the value of his promise by insisting that the other allies must make the same promise. Metternich had thus given the British a veto he knew they would use. His other concessions to the Russians were likewise more apparent than real, and he contrived to complete the diplomatic mesh he was weaving about Alexander with proposals for an ambassadorial conference in Vienna, or the advancement of the date for the allied conference which had been planned for 1822 at Laibach.

While Metternich flattered and tempted in order to delay and deceive, Castlereagh at first procrastinated and then opposed the Tsar with growing frankness. When his official reply to Russian requests for moral support was at last given at the end of April, he, like Metternich, but more bluntly, opposed the inclusion of the Greek question in Russia's dispute with the Turks. He also complained that there were some elements in Russia which were planning, if not the expulsion of the Turks from all of Europe, at least Greek autonomy under Russian protection. His frankness was perhaps encouraged by growing British public interest in the crisis, part of this feeling being genuinely pro-Greek, but far more was anti-Russian. Castlereagh's difficulty, as he pointed out to a more understanding Metternich, was that he could not publicly pursue the policy which he believed to be most effective in restraining the Tsar, namely to obstruct him by exploiting his devotion to the Alliance. As it was, a brief parliamentary defence by Castlereagh of his relations with the continental powers in May provoked a fierce and loudly applauded retort from Mackintosh.[1] Castlereagh feared that public hostility to the Alliance might compel him to repeat the stand which Britain had taken during the Conference of Laibach. Nevertheless, he assured Metternich that the reality of Anglo-Austrian co-operation would continue beneath the surface. In any case, the uncompromising British refusal to support any Russian move against the Turks served Metternich's purpose admirably; it drove the uncertain Tsar closer to Vienna.

Metternich and Castlereagh were also greatly aided in April 1822 by the grudging and belated agreement of the Turks to their military evacuation of the Danubian principalities, the last outstanding Russian claim based on treaty rights. Anglo-Austrian diplomatic pressure had been reinforced by deteriorating relations between the Ottoman empire and Persia, and difficult as the Turks remained in the eyes of Castlereagh and Metternich, Russia's diplomatic freedom for manœuvre had been seriously circumscribed. The Tsar's refusal to advance the date of the intended conference was consequently not a setback; indeed it probably facilitated Castlereagh's decision to attend a pre-conference meeting to be held in Vienna in September. War, in any case, had been averted in 1822. But Castlereagh was already laying plans for 1823. The instructions which he prepared for the meeting at Vienna — instructions that he was never to use — showed that he was prepared to recognise the Greeks as belligerents, though 'with caution and without ostentation, lest it should render the Turks wholly inaccessible to our remonstrances'. In addition, he was prepared to contemplate the possibility of agreeing to the employment of British good offices — though nothing more — to secure an amnesty for the Greeks, assurances of protection for persons, property and religion, and even in 'the creation of a qualified Greek

[1] *Hansard*, new series, vii. 626–38.

The Congress of Vienna

Government'. This was an interesting possibility, since Metternich was to show considerable interest in a similar idea in 1823. At Vienna Castlereagh might have been able to use this idea of a degree of Greek autonomy to draw the Tsar more closely to Britain and Austria. The point is hypothetical, but it demonstrates that Castlereagh's Alliance diplomacy was far from bankrupt.

In fact Castlereagh's last act in the Greek drama was to despatch a sharp protest to Constantinople against the Turkish massacre of the Greek population on the island of Scio. Such episodes could only complicate his quest for agreement with the Tsar. But his suicide on 12 August threw the whole situation into the melting-pot, firstly because Wellington, who attended the conference at Verona, was not equal to the task of seeking an allied policy concerning the Near East, secondly because his successor at the Foreign Office — Canning — was not interested in an allied approach to the question, and thirdly because Metternich abandoned his existing policy for closer relations with Russia in the confident expectation that no new British Foreign Secretary would or could follow Castlereagh's policies. Metternich had insisted that Castlereagh's presence at some part of the forthcoming allied talks was essential, and there is good reason to suppose that he would have been happy to follow Castlereagh's lead on most questions, including the Greek issue. Not all Wellington's prestige as a general, nor his sympathy for the Alliance, could persuade Metternich that he was an effective substitute; indeed, he frequently ignored the Duke at Verona, and dismissed much of his diplomacy with contempt.[1] Such a relationship with Castlereagh would have been inconceivable.

Although the Greek question was not a major matter at the 1822 conference, within a year Metternich was to confess that it had passed beyond the control of diplomacy. Without the support of Castlereagh he was not prepared to expose himself to Russian hostility; all his instincts impelled him to run for shelter

---

[1] Rolo (*Canning*, p. 208) comments on Castlereagh's death, 'There could hardly have been a more awkward time for a change of master at the Foreign Office.' See also Schroeder, pp. 204–5, and Webster, *Castlereagh, 1815–22*, p. 488.

beneath the Tsar's wing. In consequence Britain could no longer look to Metternich as a supporter of non-intervention in Spain. Metternich, in fact, excluded Wellington from some of the crucial discussions on Spain at Verona, and relied on his own diplomatic skill to try to devise an appearance of allied control in the event of French intervention in Spain. In this he was not very successful, and the following year the French were to tear his diplomatic cobweb to shreds, not least because they could exploit the division between Austria and Britain. Again one can do no more than speculate on the outcome had Castlereagh lived to attend the conference. Castlereagh's own instructions concerning the Spanish problem refer only to the need to secure the safety of the Spanish and Portuguese royal families, and to the importance of maintaining the principle of non-intervention. How he would have resisted the Tsar's desire for some dramatic act against the Spanish revolutionaries, how he would have obstructed the ambition of several French ministers and diplomats to intervene in Spain, is far from clear.

One of the main Russian motives for interest in Spain arose from the hope that the Spanish question might break the Anglo-Austrian understanding. Given Metternich's faith in Castlereagh, this Russian expectation might well have been disappointed. Castlereagh may also have hoped that his intended visit to France before the conference would prove remunerative. Here the key figure was the French Prime Minister, Villèle, whose intentions at this time are still a matter for debate among historians. With Villèle's support for the British policy the Tsar would once again have been isolated. Castlereagh had also reason to hope that the Tsar would still prove susceptible to his personal influence and appeals. Finally, the rather longer references by Castlereagh in his instructions to Greece and Spanish America possibly indicate that he hoped to use these questions as the main topics for discussion, and that if the Russians or French proved difficult over Spain, Britain's greater freedom of manœuvre over those regions might be exploited.[1] Again, one cannot be sure, and to speculate further would be absurd. But the point can surely be made that Castlereagh's presence at the conference of Vienna–Verona would have been

[1] See below, p. 250.

more significant than that of Wellington, that Castlereagh's policies were far from bankrupt, even within the context of the Alliance, and that his death was a matter of profound European significance.

All the strengths and weaknesses of Castlereagh's foreign policy are thus high-lighted by his death. To a great extent it was based on his personal relationship with other statesmen and rulers. So long as he was in office in Britain, his presence or influence could be profound. The French Ambassador in Britain, Chateaubriand, believed that the Anglo-Austrian connexion, which was based essentially on the personal relationship of Metternich and Castlereagh, had profoundly restricted French freedom of action. Russian diplomats believed the same, and were striving to circumvent it in 1822. Metternich's faith in Britain was wholly centred in Castlereagh. But the emergence of new personalities in other states was a constant menace to Castlereagh's policy; the death of Alexander or the fall of Metternich could have been a disaster. He had made — perhaps he could make — no preparations for the future in Britain. In Britain his ability to pursue his highly personal policy was based on his own prestige in the cabinet and in the Commons, and on the detestation of the majority of members of Parliament for a Whig–Radical government. His Near Eastern policy depended in no small measure on British sentiment remaining anti-Russian rather than becoming pro-Greek. His whole policy owed much to his ability to operate free from prying eyes. It was only with some difficulty that he was able to agree to attend the pre-conference meeting at Vienna. Above all it was imperative that no revolution in Europe should break out that would compel Metternich to turn to Russia and the policies of the Troppau–Laibach era, or that any events should take place which provoked British feeling against the supposed purpose of the Alliance. Castlereagh's whole policy was thus precariously based. Yet the aftermath of Troppau–Laibach had demonstrated its resilience; criticism in the British Parliament had not yet seriously impeded his policy, whatever its effect upon Castlereagh's future image as a statesman; the approach of the Vienna–Verona conference does not suggest impending disaster. On the contrary, the events of the summer and autumn of 1822 underline the fact that

Castlereagh's death, in so far as it is possible for an individual to influence the course of history, was a matter of profound international significance. In foreign affairs his suicide marked the end of an era, especially in British policy.

8

Castlereagh and the Wider World

Momentous and time-consuming as Britain's relations with the European great powers may have been from 1814 to 1822, those with the non-European world were also of great significance. Although many of these matters fell within the competence of the President of the Board of Control or the Secretary of State for War and Colonies rather than of the Foreign Secretary, Castlereagh's tenure of the Foreign Office witnessed considerable progress towards the later nineteenth-century position when a large proportion of the business of the department was concerned with non-European matters. Quite apart from the projection of European rivalries to the wider world, British foreign policy had to take account of the pressure from the anti-slave-trade movement, and from various British commercial interests in search of new and secure markets. The colossal expansion of British trade was to carry British representatives into many unlikely parts of the world, and give rise to an immense variety of questions. Although the Far East was still mainly the preserve of the East Indian Company, under the supervision of the Board of Control, Dutch activity in the East Indies led to the involvement of the Foreign Office soon after 1815. Africa, as yet, attracted comparatively little interest, save for the question of the slave trade, and it was left to the Americas to draw the attention of the Foreign Office in large measure. Here, on the one hand, Britain was still learning how to live at peace with her ex-American colonists, while on the other she was trying to restore peace between Spain and her rebellious Latin American colonists. More seemed to be at stake than Britain's commercial interests, important as they were, since the outcome of these questions might, in the long run at least, influence the Atlantic balance of power to the advantage or detriment of Britain. Castlereagh sought peace in the New World, not only to promote British trade, but to maintain or increase British power and security. A further Anglo-American war would weaken Britain's position in Europe; other states might turn the confusion in Latin America to their advantage. The various permutations of hypothetical developments all led to one conclusion — peace was Britain's prime interest.

Castlereagh's early attitude to the United States gave little hint of his later anxiety for better relations.[1] His policy in 1812 revealed no originality save that his tone was less overbearing than that of his predecessors. This in itself was an advance, for past British neglect of elementary courtesies had often given offence. During the war itself Castlereagh combined a steady defence of Britain's interests, especially her maritime claims, with a cautious eye for a promising opening towards peace negotiations.[2] Many circumstances were responsible for the slow progress towards such talks, but finally in August 1814 British and American commissioners met at Ghent. Castlereagh's intentions at this point are by no means clear, save that his representatives at Ghent interpreted his instructions far more literally than he intended, and adopted an uncompromising tone which he disliked. In particular they failed to probe American determination and intentions. In his instructions Castlereagh had demanded that all American forts on or near the Great Lakes should be destroyed, and all American warships should be excluded from the Lakes. He also made some sizeable territorial claims. But these demands were not his last word, and already Castlereagh had shown some interest in the possibility of mutual Anglo-American disarmament on the Lakes. Probably British cabinet opinion was not yet ripe for so radical an idea.[3] Both Castlereagh and Liverpool soon showed themselves disposed to make concessions to secure peace, even before the failure of the latest British military moves in North America was known.[4] In any case, European questions were beginning to absorb most of

---

[1] See above, pp. 108 ff.   [2] Perkins, *Castlereagh and Adams*, pp. 22 ff.
[3] J. M. Callahan, *American Foreign Policy in Canadian Relations* (1937), p. 76.
[4] Perkins, pp. 122, 141.

Castlereagh's attention and energies, and the peace negotiations with the United States were increasingly supervised by the cabinet rather than by the Foreign Secretary. As autumn gave way to winter, American firmness, the cost of the war, pressure for economy from the British public, and the continuing great-power rivalries and tensions in Europe all helped to create a British readiness to accept a compromise peace. Castlereagh had good cause to welcome the conclusion of peace at Ghent in December 1814, since news of this event reached him in Vienna at the height of the Saxon crisis.[1]

The Treaty of Ghent brought peace, but it solved none of the basic causes of the war. It was regarded by many, especially in the United States, as no more than an armistice.[2] During the Hundred Days, Castlereagh watched American policy carefully, and tried to avoid provocation. Once the European scene permitted, he became increasingly disposed to grapple with some of the outstanding issues in earnest. This was not a simple task, since feeling ran high on both sides of the Atlantic. American xenophobia competed with British arrogance, and it was fortunate that both governments were intent on restraint. British Radicals and many businessmen were also champions of a *détente*, and as early as April 1815 Mr. Hart Davis had told the Commons, 'Peace with America, then, was the natural policy of this country . . .' As for Castlereagh, he proceeded without haste, and made no dramatic concessions, but his purpose was clear. Allied disputes in the winter of 1814–15, the apparent vulnerability of the Bourbons in France, the probable weakness of some of the other monarchical governments in Europe, and the likelihood of further allied dissension can have left him with little doubt of the value of good relations with the United States. Repeatedly until the 1870s British politicians referred to the danger of American exploitation of British embarrassments in Europe, a fear which led to occasional demands for a three-power naval standard.[3] Castlereagh may also have pondered the lesson of the War of 1812; namely the difficulty of inflicting decisive as

[1] See above, pp. 141–2. For the negotiations as a whole, see Perkins, pp. 58–133.

[2] Ibid., pp. 161 ff.

[3] Bartlett, *Great Britain and Sea Power*, pp. 71, 125, 214–15, 274–6.

opposed to damaging blows against so distant and vast a country, not to mention the difficulty and cost of protecting British colonies and shipping against such an opponent. Furthermore, there was emerging on the British side — and it was extending to government circles — a growing recognition of the importance of American raw materials and the American market to the British economy. Both Liverpool and Castlereagh were to display some awareness of this fact over the next few years. On the other hand, Canada's economic importance to Britain did not justify a heavy arms expenditure for her protection, while the British West Indies were resuming their important economic ties with the United States. There were therefore many strong reasons and pressures impelling Castlereagh towards a policy of conciliation towards the United States.

As usual, Castlereagh relied heavily on good personal relations. Bagot, the British Minister in Washington until 1819, and Richard Rush, the American representative in London from 1817, greatly reinforced his efforts.[1] Rush's predecessor, John Quincy Adams, soon to become Secretary of State, was too proud and sensitive for a real bond to develop between him and Castlereagh. Adams at first described the latter as 'cold, but not absolutely repulsive', and even after a degree of mutual respect had developed, Adams remained true to the principle, 'Timeo Danaos, umquam donas ferentes'. Nevertheless, his residence in London coincided with the American initiative which led finally to the Rush–Bagot Agreement of 1817. This provided for the laying up of most British and American warships on the Great Lakes. Castlereagh, after an initially cautious response, did much to impress the cabinet with its possible advantages, especially in the realm of economy. Although the much publicised undefended North American frontier does not date from 1817, but rather from the 1870s, this was nevertheless an important step forward, and whatever the debt of the Agreement to the desire for military economy by both governments, Castlereagh and others are deserving of praise for the way in which they exploited this interesting and novel opportunity.[2]

[1] Perkins, pp. 202–6, 215–19.

[2] C. P. Stacey, 'The Myth of the Unguarded Frontier, 1815–71', *American Historical Review* (1950–1), pp. 1–18. Perkins, pp. 240–4.

Positive action did not always characterise Castlereagh's conduct towards the United States. Often he relied upon time and soft words to smoothe away seemingly intractable problems, but it was his readiness to compromise where compromise was possible, and to bear with patience difficulties that might have provoked a lesser man that made his Fabian tactics so profitable. All these tactics were to the fore in 1818–22 when Anglo-American relations were frequently discussed. With Adams as Secretary of State from 1817, American policy took a more positive turn, and in the summer of 1818 the able Albert Gallatin was sent to join Rush in a major effort to clear up outstanding fishery, commercial, boundary and other questions. Castlereagh, who had prepared much of the groundwork for these talks, remained in the background, and he was in any case much preoccupied with the approaching conference at Aix-la-Chapelle.[1] On many points agreement was impossible, but the commercial convention of 1815 was immediately extended for ten years. The Newfoundland fishery dispute was resolved by the permanent grant of a limited area where the Americans might fish and cure their catch. The 49th parallel was extended from the Lake of the Woods to the Rocky Mountains, but the British desire to enjoy free access to the Columbia River necessitated a temporary compromise west of the summit of the Rockies. This region was declared open to the subjects of both countries for the next ten years, without prejudice to the sovereign claims of either. The north-east frontier also proved insoluble for the moment, and the 7,500,000 disputed acres were not finally apportioned until 1842. The British also agreed to submit to arbitration American claims for compensation for slaves carried away by the British during the War of 1812, the matter being finally settled in 1826 with a British payment of $1,200,000.

On the other hand, the vexed question of American trade with the British West Indies remained as insoluble as ever. The British wished to reserve to themselves the profitable triangular trade between Britain, the United States and the West Indies both on account of its profits and of the stimulus that it gave to British shipping. The principles of the Navigation Acts and

[1] Perkins, pp. 259–82.

mercantilism were still sacrosanct. American shipping, confined
to a direct trade between Britain and the United States, was at a
serious disadvantage; a determined effort was therefore made to
open the West Indies to American shipping. The case was
pressed by diplomatic means, and by increasingly effective
economic reprisals. In 1818 the British were disposed to
concede some of the American claims; the latter's ships should
be admitted to the islands to trade in some commodities only,
and with British shipping continuing to enjoy certain preferential
rights. These concessions were finally rejected as inadequate by
the Americans, and in 1819 Rush presented himself before
Castlereagh with a demand for complete reciprocity in trade.
Castlereagh replied that such a demand would 'effect an entire
subversion of the British colonial system', and proceeded to
lecture the unfortunate diplomat on the principles of British
eighteenth-century mercantilism. But where diplomacy had
failed, American economic pressure proved more persuasive. A
series of measures introduced between 1817 and 1820 gradually
strangled trade between the United States and British colonies
in America, so destroying the British triangular traffic. The
colonial economies were also injured, and various interests were
soon bringing pressure to bear on the government. Castlereagh
had opposed the American claims with a massive imperturbability, but Robinson, with others, was gradually converting the
cabinet to the view that concessions were necessary. These were
finally granted in 1822. Throughout, Castlereagh emerges merely
as the spokesman of the cabinet; his own position, if any, is not
known.[1]

One of the unresolved causes of the War of 1812 was the
question of impressment. The end of the war in Europe enabled
the issue to be dropped at Ghent, but it was too likely a cause of
future conflict to be permanently ignored. The United States
government soon showed its willingness to consider limiting
service on American ships to American subjects in the hope that
Britain would abandon her claim to impress supposed British
subjects on American ships. Bathurst, on the British side,

[1] G. S. Graham, *Sea Power and British North America, 1783–1820*
(1941), pp. 216–31. F. L. Benns, *The American Struggle for the British
West Indian Carrying Trade, 1815–30* (1923).

encouraged discussion on these lines, and Castlereagh also showed some interest. Several members of the cabinet were, however, strongly opposed, and Castlereagh moved very discreetly. Ultimately Bathurst and Castlereagh were able to secure assent to a series of proposals which were so hedged by qualifications that the Americans were discouraged, and negotiations broke down during Castlereagh's absence at Aix-la-Chapelle. Castlereagh himself finally closed the question with a remark more prophetic than he can ever have dared to hope, 'Time will do much more than we can.'[1]

But if Castlereagh was several times reduced to the hope that time would solve problems which were beyond him, he did his best to ensure that time was given its chance. He therefore ignored several outbursts of British public and press opinion hostile to the United States, notably in 1818 when he damped down an explosion of British feeling following the execution of two British subjects in Florida who were accused of inciting Indian tribes against the Americans. Castlereagh was content to try to gain credit by pointing out to Washington how delicate the situation might have been without his restraining hand. In the same year, and again in 1821, he refused to protest against American moves to strengthen their claims to the Columbia River, moves which ultimately proved premature. Meanwhile, Castlereagh's restraint ensured the continuance of the ten-year compromise already noted, to the great advantage of the North West and Hudson's Bay Companies' fur traders in the basin of the Columbia. Old alliances with the Indians were abandoned; likewise the British claim to navigate the Mississippi. Castlereagh was a most ardent practitioner of his own advice to Gallatin and Rush, 'Let us, in short, strive so to regulate our intercourse in all respects as that each nation may be able to do its utmost towards making the other rich and happy.' Unlike many of his class, he refused to allow conservative dislike of American republicanism, or alarm at British Radical admiration for the United States to influence his conduct.[2] His real opinions of the Americans he kept to himself. He was, according to

[1] Perkins, pp. 253–8, 268–75.

[2] He was not quite alone in this among the British governing class. See Perkins, pp. 197, 403.

Bradford Perkins, the first British Foreign Secretary, to accept the reality of American independence.[1]

The task of transforming Anglo-American relations had, of course, been scarcely begun by 1822. Much rivalry and hostility persisted, and would explode into future crises of some significance. Much of Castlereagh's work had been negative, but in his emphasis upon the beneficent influence of trade he was far-sighted indeed. Increasingly over the next half-century, 'Old Kingdom and new republic shared an unprecedented community of interests.'[2] The two economies were intensely interdependent; American cotton, British goods, capital, labour and technical knowledge brought the two countries close together, so that in July 1851 *The Times* could comment, 'For all practical purposes the United States are far more closely united with this kingdom than any one of our colonies. . . .' If shipping magnates such as Jeremiah Thompson, little-known Lancashire entrepreneurs, a host of bankers, dealers and agents from both countries provided the main positive impulse behind this traffic, politicians and diplomats helped to smoothe and prepare the way. Although Castlereagh was associated with the decision in 1818 which led to Anglo-American economic warfare over the West Indies, he was also a member of the government which was beginning to grope its way towards a freer commercial system from 1817, and he several times expressed his sympathy with that objective in the Commons.[3] It is worthy of note that Castlereagh, the bugbear of British reformers, was much admired and praised at the time of his death in the press of the United States.[4]

Castlereagh's policy towards the United States was not all sweetness and honey. If he was anxious for peace, he was also determined to draw limits round this burgeoning republic. Canada was safe for the moment; a temporary compromise had

[1] Ibid., p. 2.
[2] F. Thistlethwaite, *The Anglo–American Connection in the early Nineteenth Century* (1959), p. 4.
[3] *Hansard*, xl. 500, and see above, pp. 192–3.
[4] Lane Poole, *Stratford Canning*, i. 334. Perkins, p. 303.

been reached concerning the Far West; but the crumbling American empire of Spain was also attracting Yankee interest. The United States as a commercial and shipping rival could not be ignored; her republican institutions might prove dangerously attractive to the Spanish American rebels, and who could calculate the political and economic consequences. Canning was later to argue — how seriously it is not clear — that for the United States to prosper through trade with Latin America would increase her maritime threat — both mercantile and naval — to Britain. Certainly Britain had no intention of permitting the increase of American power — political, strategic or economic — in the Caribbean if she could possibly avoid it. Castlereagh himself pointedly remarked concerning a dubious rumour in 1820 of the possible sale of Spanish Santo Domingo to King Henry of Haiti, 'I should prefer *Blacks* to *Americans*.'[1] British fears of an American bid for Cuba lay not far distant.

As will be seen later, Britain had comparatively little to fear from the United States as a trading rival among the states of Latin America. But Castlereagh's interest in the establishment of monarchies in the ex-colonies arose in part from fear of American republicanism, while he followed American territorial expansion towards the Caribbean and Central America with the closest attention and with a ready eye to opportunities to slow or stop the process. In the first ten years of the nineteenth century the United States had acquired Louisiana and West Florida, and were clearly intent on East Florida, from whence they would be able to menace one of the main British shipping routes from Jamaica. During the War of 1812 there had existed some vague British hopes that they might be able to prevent this further advance, but from 1815 Florida was written off, and the best that could be hoped for was a satisfactory Mexican frontier for Spain in exchange. In addition, Castlereagh pointed out to Washington that the British had as much territory as they could manage. 'Do you only observe the same moderation. If we should find you hereafter pursuing a system of encroachment upon your neighbours, what we might do defensively is another consideration.' But his main purpose was to avoid a collision between Spain and the United States; he urged the Spaniards to

[1] *Bathurst MSS.*, p. 485.

surrender East Florida, and vainly offered British mediation in 1817–18. The latter was declined by Washington, but his pressure upon Spain probably contributed to the latter's gradual retreat and surrender in 1819–21. Castlereagh was able to gain no territory for Mexico, but he could hope, for the moment at least, that the Americans had been deprived of all excuse for further expansion in the area.

Meanwhile the United States was also involved in the question of Spanish American independence, but here there were many other considerations in British policy as well.[1] When Castlereagh had become Foreign Secretary in 1812, he found Britain in alliance with Spain against Napoleon, but with British trade benefiting considerably from the revolt of many of Spain's Latin American colonists. His predecessor had been conducting a delicate balancing act between Spain and the colonists, and fortunately the Spaniards had been willing to wink at the illicit trade in their preoccupation with the struggle against France. The Spanish American rebels, for their part, were heavily dependent for their revenue on customs dues, mostly paid by British traders. The British government, however, were becoming increasingly impressed by the advantages to be gained from a restoration of peace in that continent; peace would improve trade, ensure supplies of specie from Mexico, ease Britain's relations with Spain, and eliminate the threat from France and the United States. The financial embarrassments of the Spanish Regency provided an opening, and in May 1811 British mediation was offered. Britain sought a cessation of hostilities, a general amnesty for the rebels, the grant of virtual self-government to the colonists, and the opening of trade with Spanish America to all nations — though with a fair preference for Spain. Britain would also guarantee the final settlement. But the Spaniards insisted on the continuance of their trade monopoly, and also an assurance of British military aid against the rebels should the mediation fail. This was the position that Castlereagh inherited in 1812.

[1] On Britain and Latin America, see especially Webster, *Latin America*, W. W. Kaufmann, *British Policy and the Independence of Latin America* (1951), and J. F. Rippy, *Rivalry of the United States and Great Britain over Latin America* (1929).

He was to enjoy no better fortune than his predecessor in persuading the Spaniards to accept Britain's terms, and as the French position in Spain deteriorated and finally collapsed, so Spanish hopes of crushing the rebellion in Latin America revived. In vain Castlereagh tried to shake the Spanish insistence on their trade monopoly by pointing to British liberal practice in India, and more especially to the boom in British trade with their ex-colonists in North America. The influence of Cadiz, the great centre of Spanish trade with their colonies, over the Cortes was too strong, though the Spanish government later tried the bait of special trade advantages to Britain in return for active British aid against the rebels. This was an impossible condition, but in any case Castlereagh was convinced — and the Board of Trade was emphatic — that Britain required no special preference for the development of her trade in Spanish America. Her position as a mediator would be destroyed were she to accept special privileges. He later claimed that Britain had 'always recommended the commerce of South America to be opened to all nations upon moderate duties with a reasonable preference to Spain herself as the best means of settling that country in connection with Spain'. To accept the Spanish offer would be short-sighted and self-defeating, though whether the terms which Castlereagh pressed on Spain would have permanently satisfied the colonials, had they been accepted, is another matter. As it was, discussion of the British mediation offer gained valuable time; time during which the Spaniards permitted British trade with their colonies, time during which British relations with both Spain and the colonists were eased, and British and Spanish efforts could be concentrated on the defeat of France.

Unofficial British aid to the rebels continued, and British diplomats occasionally reminded the Spaniards that circumstances might soon compel them to have closer dealings with the rebels. This threat could be used to try to impress the value of British mediation on Spain, but in private Castlereagh confessed that 'this is an act of the most grave and serious responsibility which nothing but an overriding necessity could justify, and the consequences of which upon the Alliance in Europe, and consequently upon the war, it is difficult, if not impossible to anticipate'. The expulsion of France from Spain in 1813 created a new situation. The Spaniards were now in a better position to act against the rebels, and in fact proceeded to do so with some success until 1817. Britain's freedom of action was also increased, but Castlereagh continued to move cautiously, despite pressure from certain British trading interests, and from sections of the Opposition in Parliament. As a conservative he disliked rebels; as Foreign Secretary he was preoccupied with establishing a new order in Europe, and to have acted precipitately in favour of the rebels might have wrecked his hopes for the Alliance. In short, his approach to Spanish American problems was of a piece with his overall foreign policy; his belief that Britain's power was such that she could dispense — for the moment at least — with eighteenth-century methods, that moderation in pursuit of political or economic objectives would prove more rewarding.

Consequently in July 1814 British traders had to be content with an Anglo–Spanish treaty which promised no more than a share of the Spanish American colonial trade should the Spaniards ever abandon their monopoly. Britain, for her part, promised to give no aid to the rebels. But Castlereagh could not stop there, since there remained the danger of a rebel appeal to the United States and of a Spanish appeal to the other European powers. Castlereagh wished to confine the struggle to Spain and her colonists, with Britain ever-ready at the ring-side to mediate and to exploit any chance of a peaceful settlement. The mediation offer was therefore renewed in December 1815, though with little hope of early acceptance, and Britain's view of the question was firmly presented in Washington and in the various European capitals in the hope that such a statement would be sufficient to prevent their intervention.

Castlereagh's veiled warnings to the United States, and his efforts to impress them with the solidarity of the Alliance on this question were not always taken seriously. American restraint down to 1821 owed much to the desire to settle the Florida question. Disagreement on Latin American policies existed within the United States government, so that Adams' continuing caution is not surprising.[1] In the end charges of subserviency to Britain helped to prod the American administration slowly towards recognition of some of the new Latin

[1] Perkins, pp. 299, 302.

Robert Viscount Castlereagh by Hugh Douglas Hamilton

American states by the beginning of 1822. Even then, Adams was anxious to reassure Castlereagh and to avoid any appearance of a provocative policy. Probably these hesitations arose mainly from a general respect for the power of Britain, and from the innate caution of Adams rather than from any diplomatic ingenuity on the part of Castlereagh. Whatever the cause, it was clearly to Castlereagh's advantage that it was not until May 1822 that the United States began to make provision for the appointment of missions to the new states.

The Spaniards, meanwhile, having failed to tempt Britain with offers of commercial concessions at the end of 1815, had turned to the other European powers, and had found the Russian Ambassadors in Madrid and Paris particularly responsive to their pleas. Castlereagh's inquiries at St. Petersburg, his warnings of August 1817 that any European intervention might wreck the Alliance, and his insistence that Britain would never use force against the rebels checked these moves so decisively that his action at this time has been acclaimed as conclusive in removing all possibility of European intervention in the struggle for Latin America.[1] With the crucial battles for Chile and New Granada being fought out in 1817–20, it was of the utmost importance to the Spanish American cause that Spain should be unable to draw on outside help at this juncture. Castlereagh's protests of August 1817 required some reiteration at later dates, not least in February 1818 when the Russians began to display some interest in a boycott of Spanish American trade. Castlereagh's protest was worthy of Canning in a later period, but his concern for the Alliance prevented the publication of a document which would have done much to improve his reputation with contemporaries. He asked his allies.

Upon what principles of law and morality could England rely, to legitimise her participation in the slightest act of constraint such as it is desired to exercise against these peoples . . . by what right could she force a population, which had freed itself because its government was oppressive, to place itself once more under the domination of that same government?[2]

[1] Webster, *Latin America*, i. 14. See also *English Historical Review*, xl. 35 ff., and xli. 583 ff.

[2] Webster, *Castlereagh, 1815–22*, pp. 413–15.

R

The idea of economic sanctions was not at once quashed, and was revived by Russia and France at the congress of Aix-la-Chapelle in company with proposals for allied mediation. Spain had appealed to the Alliance for assistance, and some of its members were also moved by the fear that unless the rebels were crushed, the influence of the United States, republicanism and perhaps Jacobinism would increase in the area. It was Castlereagh's aim at the congress to render these proposals innocuous, while preserving the Alliance for its own sake, and to impress the Americans with its unity. Although in October 1816 he had speculated on the possibility of allied mediation forcing upon Spain 'some more liberal and practicable system in South America',[1] he appears to have had little hope of such a result in 1818. His objectives were now essentially negative. He submitted to his allies an immense document, containing no less than 43 queries as to the wisdom and practicability of the forms of allied intervention proposed. As tirelessly, he argued his case with the Tsar's ministers, and when this failed he made a dramatic appeal to the Tsar himself, condemning his ministers' contemplation of the possible use of economic sanctions if the allied arbitration failed. Again he pressed the Tsar's ministers — this time successfully — to stop the anti-British activities of their Ambassador in Madrid. The sum total of these efforts was to persuade the allies — by an overwhelming flow of logic which concentrated mainly on practical considerations, avoided matters of principle, and continually sought common ground — that the mediation should be entrusted to one allied commissioner to prevent any confusion or jealousy, that this commissioner should be the Duke of Wellington, that there should be no threats or guarantees, and that the terms should be those suggested by Britain in 1812.

Having achieved this, Castlereagh was content to sit back and wait on events. As he probably anticipated, the Spaniards were not interested in mediation on these terms. But the other powers had been brought into line, and the struggle in Spanish America would be left to develop after its own fashion. It is not clear when Castlereagh began to feel that the independence of the Spanish American states was inevitable. As early as November

[1] *C.C.* xi. 307–9.

1818 Liverpool remarked that some of the colonies could never return to Spanish sovereignty; at most, they would accept Spanish princes as their kings.[1] Six months later Esterházy thought that an ultimate separation was certain.[2] Nevertheless, in 1819 Britain strengthened her neutrality in the struggle with a new Foreign Enlistment Act, and Castlereagh continued to maintain the appearance of a desire to see Spain and her colonies reconciled. Perhaps this was still his hope, for on the terms which he had in mind, the colonies would secure almost complete self-government, freedom to trade with all nations, and all without weakening the Alliance or facilitating the spread of republicanism. The realisation that this might not be possible had already led him, as early as September 1818, to speak favourably to Lieven of monarchical regimes in Spanish America. Events soon compelled him to take this possibility more seriously. On the one hand, there was the growing measure of public sympathy in Britain for the Spanish Americans, not to mention the mounting commercial interests.[3] On the other hand, Castlereagh could not rely on Adams' caution for ever, and in 1820 a French conspiracy to secure the election of a French Bourbon prince to a throne in Buenos Aires came to his attention. Castlereagh was highly indignant, and followed his protest to Paris with an assurance to an unofficial Columbian representative in Britain that the British government would recognise the independence of any colony that proclaimed itself a monarchy. This was in July 1820. The success of the rebels in recent months, and the outbreak of revolution in Spain seemed to make separation inevitable, and for Castlereagh the problem was fast becoming one of timing and method.

In 1821 the Spaniards, despite their hopeless military position in South America, still refused to compromise. By 1822 American recognition of some at least of the new states was imminent; the commercial agitation in Britain could no longer be ignored, while the absence of any official relationship between the ex-colonists and Britain was creating various legal and

[1] *C.C.* xii. 76–78.
[2] R. Rush, *A Residence at the Court of London, 1819–25* (1845), i. 80.
[3] *Hansard*, xl. 482–3. Canning at this time (May 1819) was rather unhappily defending the government's policy of neutrality, xl. 533–4.

practical difficulties. A Columbian threat to close its ports to the ships of nations who failed to recognise its independence was not taken very seriously, but circumstances as a whole necessitated some form of commercial recognition of the new states. The revision of the Navigation Acts in 1822 provided a convenient and discreet way of doing so, and afforded Castlereagh further time in which to prepare for full recognition. As he warned the Spaniards on 28 June 1822.

His Catholic Majesty must be aware that so large a portion of the world cannot, without fundamentally disturbing the intercourse of civilized society, long continue without some recognized and established relations; that the State which can neither by its councils nor by its arms effectually assert its own rights over its dependencies, so as to enforce obedience and thus make itself responsible for maintaining their relations with other Powers, must sooner or later be prepared to see those relations establish themselves from the over-ruling necessity of the case, under some other form.[1]

Castlereagh had already taken his first steps, beginning in the spring of 1822 with overtures to France designed to ensure that she would act in concert in all political and commercial matters relating to the Spanish colonies. He spoke of his reluctance to see revolutionary governments multiply, and of his determination to recognise them at the last possible moment. The French declined his overture, but Castlereagh refused to despair, and he continued to explore the possibility of monarchical regimes in Spanish America, and also to seek the adoption of 'common sentiments' by all the great powers, though without creating impediments to the independent discretion of Britain. In particular, he saw in the approaching European conference the perfect opportunity to establish such a consensus, and he began to lay careful plans accordingly. In the instructions which he prepared for himself he noted concerning the colonies which had completely ousted the Spanish power that recognition had become a matter of time and method rather than of principle. Although he included no reference in these instructions to monarchical institutions, it is surely permissible to surmise that Castlereagh would have raised the matter had it seemed opportune at the conference. It is also possible that he would have raised the

[1] Webster, *Latin America*, ii. 388.

same question with Villèle, the French Prime Minister, on his way to Vienna, but it is anyone's guess whether he would have secured the latter's support, especially as Louis XVIII seemed highly reluctant to do anything that would detract from the authority of his brother sovereign, Ferdinand VII of Spain. All that is certain is that the suicide of Castlereagh deprived Europe of the one statesman who might have carried through the question of recognising the Spanish American colonies on a European basis.

Sir Charles Webster has claimed[1] that in the affairs of Spanish America Castlereagh's skill as a diplomat is to be seen at its best. There is much truth in this contention, as can be seen in his handling of the European interest in the question in 1817–18. Yet his debt to Adams' caution, to the Tsar's determination to abide by the Alliance, and to British naval and economic power must also be acknowledged. In particular, British trade was able to look after itself to a great extent by reason of its indispensability to the Spanish Americans. The United States were powerful shipping rivals, but they had little to offer in the way of products of their own other than flour and coarse cotton fabrics, and many of their exports to Latin America were in fact re-exports of British goods. Only in Cuba did they outstrip British sales; only in Columbia did they run the British a close second. They had little capital to invest, whereas British goods, credit and capital were even better protectors of British interests than the royal navy save in the most anarchical of circumstances.[2] Castlereagh himself noted that even if Spanish rule were re-established, British goods would still enter Spanish America in large quantities as contraband. Consequently, despite the agitation of some British commercial interests, for most of the period he was able to act with political considerations prominent in his mind. His Spanish American policy was therefore influenced by his dislike of rebels, and of republicanism, by his desire to maintain the Alliance and to leave the struggle to be decided by the Spaniards and the rebels themselves. Had it been otherwise, he might well have moved towards a policy of recognition much earlier than he did.

[1] Webster, *Castlereagh, 1815–22*, p. 408.
[2] H. S. Ferns, *Britain and Argentina in the Nineteenth Century* (1960), pp. 86, 92. But see also pp. 96 ff.

Castlereagh repeatedly made use of Britain's economic lead over other nations as a justification for his policies of restraint upon various issues. This has sometimes given rise to the criticism that he neglected commercial matters.[1] Napoleon, for one, professed astonishment at Castlereagh's failure to press Britain's commercial interests at the peace settlement. Castlereagh did, indeed, weigh the pros and cons of a commercial treaty with France in August 1814, and he concluded that British trade required no special preference (outside the British empire), and that equality of opportunity for all nations would prove most conducive to the prosperity of all. In general in 1814–15 he was reluctant to press British commercial interests lest his political objectives should be injured. The equilibrium of Europe, and British security throughout the world were his prime aims, and he feared that to pursue purely commercial objectives would merely incur odium and weaken Britain's moral position. British trade would flourish without artificial aids.[2] This did not mean that economic interests were wholly neglected, and between 1813 and 1815, for instance, he had displayed considerable activity in the defence of British trade against Russian jealousy and exclusionist policies. When the British Ambassador followed the Tsar on his European campaigns, Castlereagh raised the embassy Secretary, Lord Walpole, to the status of Minister Plenipotentiary, mainly to protect British trade, and the Foreign Office continued to follow the matter with keen attention until the Russians relaxed their restraints in June 1815.[3] But one of the most striking instances of Castlereagh's interest in trading questions occurs at a later period in connexion with Dutch policies in the East Indies. Here one can see a steady evolution from his primary concern in 1814 to create a strong Netherlands barrier to the French — which was to be assisted by the return of the Dutch East Indies — to the position in 1822 when the British government, including Castlereagh, were seeking an agreement with the Dutch to

[1] See especially a speech by Brougham, *Hansard*, xxxv. 1036–9, and Nicolson, pp. 259–61.

[2] *Hansard*, xl. 499–500. But this certainly was a period of rising European and American tariffs.

[3] Renier, pp. 183–6.

protect British economic interests in the East Indies.

Castlereagh's policy in 1814 was greatly assisted by the comparative lack of British commercial interest in the East Indies, and by the refusal of the main authorities of the East India Company to countenance such interested parties as did exist. Britain did not even seek the station or post in the archipelago which she had repeatedly demanded before 1802.[1] In the long run, however, it was too much to expect that Anglo-Dutch relations in the East Indies could be settled as easily as this. Many treaty rights and claims were already in dispute, whilst in general Dutch pretensions in the huge archipelago were too vast and vague to be accepted without question by a stronger power, whose subjects' quest for new markets was unceasing, and was stimulated by the post-war depression. In addition there was the growing British trade with China, which passed through the Straits of Malacca. Already it required protection from the swarming local pirates, and it was soon to be contended that the political pretensions of the Dutch in the area were so extensive as to constitute a potential threat to this through traffic.

The interest and interference of the Foreign Office was gradually evoked, and at the end of 1816 — in response to warnings from the committee of London shipowners that the Dutch might revert to their pre-war policy of exclusion in Java— it secured a Dutch promise to give previous warning of any such move. A year later the Foreign Office began to explore the possibility of a consular appointment at Batavia to protect the growing British trade. The main initiative for a change of policy came from the East, where Sir Stamford Raffles and other merchants were able to impress the Governor-General, Lord Hastings, with the dangers of the exclusive ambitions of the Dutch, so that he authorised Raffles's famous expedition which resulted in the occupation of Singapore in January 1819. This move was a matter of some embarrassment to the British government, which was thinking in terms of a diplomatic approach to the Dutch. Castlereagh hoped to secure from the Dutch 'some explicit avowal of [their] views and pretensions',

[1] N. Tarling, *Anglo-Dutch Rivalry in the Malay World, 1780–1824* (1963), pp. 71–74, 133.

and was hoping to discover 'by what rules of intercourse the Netherlands Government proposes to consider the rights and authority of that state to be restrained or modified towards the subjects of other powers frequenting those seas'. Britain could not assent to a 'practical exclusion' or 'permissive toleration' of her trade, nor could she expose her China trade to the danger of all the military and naval keys to the Straits of Malacca being in the hands of the Dutch. Castlereagh wished to leave the Dutch in no doubt that Britain would prefer to protect her interests in concert with the Dutch, and by means of commercial agents and facilities alone, but if the Dutch aspired to a position in the East Indies similar to that enjoyed by Britain in India, 'the day cannot be far off when naval stations in those seas will involve both in unnecessary expense and when commerce will be sought thro' dominion and dominion thro' the intrigues and disputed titles of the endless sultans that abound in those seas. . . .'[1]

The Dutch promptly disclaimed any aspiration to the establishment of a general supremacy, but this left untouched the multitude of treaty rights which they claimed in the area, and which the British believed, when added together and when their full potential was weighed, to be 'nearly equivalent to a universal sovereignty'. The India Board believed that it would be too difficult and dangerous to challenge these rights on general or particular grounds, and favoured negotiation on the basis of mutual concessions. Such an approach led gradually to recognition of the value of some permanent British possession in the Straits as a lasting guarantee for the future. British mercantile pressure made it all the more necessary for the government to seek some solution, and negotiations actually began in July 1820 with Canning — President of the Board of Control — as the main British representative. A permanent station in the Straits was one of the main British demands, a point particularly emphasised by Castlereagh when he attended one of the meetings. To this the Dutch were firmly opposed, though some progress was made in the question of improving trade relations on a reciprocal basis. The negotiations were suspended in August 1820, as the British desired to obtain

[1] Ibid., pp. 104–5, extracts from Castlereagh's letter of 13 Aug. 1819.

further information on Singapore from Hastings. This involved a long delay, which was further prolonged by the parliamentary distractions of Castlereagh. It was not until Canning had succeeded him at the Foreign Office that the negotiations were resumed, and finally reached a satisfactory conclusion, including British possession of Singapore in 1824.

Castlereagh was not always to the fore in the negotiations that took place between 1816 and 1822, and much of the work was handled by his Ambassador at The Hague, or by Canning and the India Board. But Castlereagh's massive letter of 13 August 1819, already quoted, underlines his own involvement in the question, and there is no evidence to suggest that he was in any way responsible for any delay or weakness in British policy in defence of her commercial interests in this part of the world. There is, however, ample evidence of his customary desire to proceed by tact and conciliation if possible, and a definite reluctance until the middle of 1820 to involve the British government in additional territorial and financial responsibilities.[1] By comparison with some later periods, the defence of British trading interests may seem lacking in drama and forcefulness, but much of this difference arises from different circumstances. Nor has the Palmerstonian policy at the other extreme been without its critics, and it is clear that Castlereagh's tactics suited the temper of his cabinet colleagues, as well as being complementary to his overall objectives in foreign policy.

Castlereagh's desire to tread softly is again apparent in his handling of that important question, the slave trade. In 1805–6 Castlereagh had opposed the agitation for the abolition of the British slave trade on the ground that it could not be effective or wise to do so when other powers would be able to continue the traffic.[2] Once the act had been passed, Castlereagh, by his own logic, had a practical interest in exploring the possibility of international suppression. In the debates leading to suppression he had always professed sympathy with the cause, and as early as 1805 Wilberforce had given him credit for his very efficient enforcement of an order in council forbidding the traffic with recently conquered colonies. By 1811 the British part in the

[1] Ibid., pp. 81–138. Philips, *East India Co.*, pp. 230–5.
[2] *Cobbett's Parliamentary Debates*, ii. 546, vii. 588–90.

slave trade was more or less at an end, and Wilberforce and his supporters were soon turning to the question of international abolition. It is not clear how far Castlereagh's early pressure on Sweden and France was forced on him by the British abolitionists, but he was undoubtedly impressed by the outburst of feeling in Britain in the spring of 1814, when his failure to wring immediate abolition from the French was much criticised. At the same time, he feared that the outcry would make his task more difficult, since it might provoke the French into a nationalist stand, and encourage other powers to believe that Britain would make concessions on other issues in order to win support for abolition. Nevertheless, although he never appeared to become emotionally involved in the question, and appeared to consider it essentially as a matter of practical politics, he was continually on the alert to exploit every opening to promote abolition.

It was not Castlereagh's diplomatic skill but Napoleon's return from Elba and his interest in presenting himself to Europe as a liberal that led to the immediate abolition of the French slave trade. This still left the question of enforcement, and all Castlereagh's efforts at Vienna in 1814–15 could secure no more than a joint declaration condemning the trade. This was of little value, and Castlereagh strove to reach agreements with all slave-trading nations whereby they would not only agree to abolish the traffic, but would also agree to some form of joint enforcement. In any system of enforcement, the British navy would be the main instrument. To this, few states would readily assent, for reasons of national pride, and also from long memories of British exercise of the right of search in time of war. No progress, in particular, could be made with the French towards any form of joint enforcement, while Castlereagh's efforts to build on the sympathy of a section of American opinion in favour of a limited reciprocal right of search from 1817 were equally unsuccessful.

The smaller states were more vulnerable to British pressure. The Dutch and Scandinavians had agreed to abolition by 1815, and in 1818 the Dutch agreed to a reciprocal right of search and detention, with a mixed commission to adjudicate on seizures. In 1814 Spain was vainly offered a colony in return for immediate and complete abolition, but she proved vulnerable to a later British threat to withhold subsidies and to impose a commercial boycott, and promised total abolition over the next eight years. In the meantime Spanish slave trading was to be confined to the region below latitude 10° North. These concessions unfortunately meant little, and the Spanish slave trade continued to grow. The British reply was to use naval action even south of the agreed line, and Castlereagh also made it clear that British mediation between Spain and her colonies would depend upon abolition. The Spaniards began to weaken, and with Castlereagh restraining Wilberforce and his friends lest the Spaniards should be tempted to raise their price, he secured a treaty in 1817 which abolished the traffic north of the equator immediately, and the remainder from 1820. The British also secured a limited right of search. Portugal had promised to abolish the slave trade gradually from 1810, but the trade was too lucrative and well established for much reliance to be placed in a pious expression of this type. At Vienna Castlereagh coaxed immediate abolition north of the equator from the Portuguese, and also a promise of final abolition after eight years. In return, Britain modified the treaty of commerce of 1810, which was unduly favourable to Britain, and made financial arrangements which were worth nearly one million pounds sterling to the Portuguese. But it was not until late in 1817 that this agreement could be implemented, coupled with a limited right of search.

Nevertheless, despite these achievements there were still too many loopholes in the situation as a whole, and the trade continued to flourish. One estimate puts the proportion of slaves liberated from ships sailing from West Africa as low as one in eight between 1808 and 1848. The traffic with Brazil was at its height in 1848, and it would seem that the establishment of an anti-slave trade regime in Brazil in 1850 and the victory of the North in the American Civil War were the decisive circumstances that brought the trade to an end.[1] Yet Castlereagh's place in the British efforts to defeat the trade — however limited in their results — is a worthy one. Wilberforce, from 1815 onwards, spoke of his efforts in the warmest terms: 'He

---

[1] C. Lloyd, *Navy and the Slave Trade* (1949), pp. 117, 139–48. For Castlereagh and the slave trade in general, see Webster, *Castlereagh, 1815–22*, pp. 454–66 etc.

really takes much pains for the cause.' True, he found Castlereagh 'a fish of the cold-blooded kind', and sometimes found the latter's insistence on tactical considerations at the expense of enthusiasm dampening and frustrating. In the long run, however, he was driven to acknowledge Castlereagh's superior political and executive skill, and to agree that he had done all possible to promote the cause.

9

Suicide and Conclusion

In the winter of 1821–2 Castlereagh seemed at the height of his powers. In retrospect it may be possible to detect occasional symptoms of the approaching disorder of his mind, but most of his admirers would have agreed with Croker that he seemed better than ever. With Liverpool still recovering from his domestic tragedy of 1821, and with the recent shadow of royal displeasure slowly lifting, Castlereagh's authority was at its peak. Above all, Croker was impressed by his bearing and manner — imperturbable and aloof as Mont Blanc. Many others had commented upon this tremendous outward calm. Bamford had noted his 'handsome but immoveable features'; Caulaincourt had found him 'just and passionless', and Cornwallis described him as 'so cold that nothing can warm him'. Indeed, Salisbury thought that 'It was this impassibility which worked so badly for his fame'. Yet such coldness did not permeate all his character, and much of it was the result of conscious effort on his part. The occasional glimpses that exist of him in his youth suggest an expansive and volatile temperament, and there were occasions in later life when his emotions broke through to the surface. Part of his apparent coldness arose from shyness and diffidence in a large company, especially among strangers. Princess Lieven did not meet him until he was famous, yet she noted, 'It is strange how timid he is of society, as if he were just beginning'. Yet the discovery of a common interest with a stranger was a great tongue-loosener, as for instance when he found that a foreign diplomat shared his passion for sheep-breeding. Public speaking did not come easily to Castlereagh,

259

and according to Huskisson Castlereagh and Liverpool 'both took ether, as an excitement, before speaking'.[1]

Some inkling of the explosive forces that lurked beneath that impressive exterior may be gathered from his heated — and in the last resort unreasoning — demand for satisfaction from Canning in 1809. There was the occasion in June 1818 when Castlereagh insisted on attending the Westminster hustings to vote for the government candidate. Greville observed, 'he was hooted, pelted, and got off with some difficulty. His lordship's judgement was not very conspicuous on this occasion; . . .'[2] According to the American Minister, Rush, when the Thistlewood conspiracy to assassinate the whole cabinet over dinner at Lord Harrowby's was discovered, Castlereagh was in favour of allowing the dinner to proceed, with the cabinet, armed to the teeth, lying in wait for the conspirators.[3] In 1820 Castlereagh was hooted out of a London theatre at the height of the Queen's Affair for his supposed part in the divorce, and upon several occasions he displayed such a contemptuous disregard for danger, even to the point of courting it, as to suggest a desire to find some release from the emotional strait-jacket in which he had enfolded his public self.

The real Castlereagh was to be found at his desk, or in private conversation with individuals or with handfuls of political figures. Alternatively, he was to be found at his pleasant rural retreat at North Cray, sixteen miles from London, dividing his time between official work and entertainment, more relaxed gatherings of his friends, watching the progress of his merino flock and flower gardens, and delighting generally in country life.[4] Rush found him more at ease and light-hearted in these surroundings. Visits to Cray prompted reflections on the pleasures of English society at its best — delightful and informal, so perfect as to appear quite natural. All the emphasis was on grace, with the extremes muted; the conversation neither superficial nor profound, neither contentious nor dull. Castlereagh's house in London, No. 18 St. James's Square, was much more ornate and less relaxed, and seems to have expressed

---

[1] Fay, *Huskisson and his Age*, p. 72 n.   [2] *Greville Memoirs*, i. 55.
[3] Rush, *London, 1819–25*, i. 289.
[4] Leigh (pp. 222–30) gives a good description of life at Cray.

the personality of his wife rather than himself. Castlereagh's taste in clothes was often admired for its restrained dignity, whereas his wife was always liable to provoke comment by such eccentricities as wearing her husband's Garter in her hair. In public Castlereagh had the appearance and manner of the great aristocrat; tall, slender, handsome, aloof, he almost stole the show at George IV's Coronation. The elusive, inner man, however, is to be found in the simpler surroundings of North Cray, or delighting in the non-public part of his official responsibilities.[1]

Castlereagh's great pleasures in life were essentially those of the open air : gentleman farming, shooting, sailing, riding or walking. He was a keen musician, and in his youth at Cambridge he had proved himself an excellent Classical scholar, but contemporary politics, the art of warfare, and some aspects of modern science attracted him more. In 1805, as Secretary of State for War, he was seriously interested in the possibility of attacking French ports with the new Congreve rockets. To all outward appearances his marriage to Lady Emily Hobart was a great success; they dreaded separation, and Lady Emily accompanied him on several of his foreign journeys. Yet they made an odd pair, the voluminous and over-dressed Emily, for all her kindness and good nature, seeming to some people too superficial a character to achieve a profound relationship with her more complex and introspective husband. Lady Bessborough said of her, 'there is a look of contented disregard of the cares of life in her round, grey Eye, that makes one wonder if she ever felt any crosses or knows the meaning of the word anxiety'. She appeared to treat all things, great or small, as of equal value; socially she was not a success, and politically her quarrel with Lady Conyngham was an embarrassment. A French witness, who had been rather amused by Lady Emily's continual fussing around her husband, subsequently wondered whether she had possessed a deeper understanding of him than people gave her credit for. The absence of children, and Castlereagh's loss of his own mother in early childhood may help to explain the relationship.[2]

[1] Rush, *London, 1819–25*, i. 176, 179–81. Countess Brownlow, *The Eve of Victorianism* (1940), pp. 39, 100–3.

[2] Webster, *Castlereagh, 1812–15*, pp. 7–10, and *Castlereagh, 1815–22* p. 34.

Such was the personality that began to disintegrate in 1822, to the astonishment of contemporaries, who had marvelled so often at his courage, level-headedness, and air of unconcern. His physical health had been less good from 1819, with recurrent periods of gout, but it was his jealousy and suspicion of Peel in 1821 which gave perhaps the first hint of approaching mental strain. The parliamentary session of 1822 was one of the most strenuous of his career, the main cause being a fall in wheat prices, which inevitably lessened the loyalty and trustworthiness of the country gentlemen. There were also disturbances in Ireland, and not even the presence of Peel and Huskisson on the government benches in the Commons could appreciably relieve Castlereagh's responsibilities. Meanwhile, the burden of the poorly organised Foreign Office remained as heavy as ever. Castlereagh's private secretary, Planta, complained bitterly of the burden of work, and though one can hardly argue from the evidence that Castlereagh's growing mental instability was caused by overwork alone, it cannot be discounted. Canning himself later said the work of the Foreign Office with the lead in the Commons was 'too much for any man'.

Castlereagh's condition varied sharply in the last weeks of his life. As late as 3 August Sidmouth found him cheerful and full of life at Cray. Princess Lieven, on the other hand, believed she detected signs of mental strain as early as May, and from this time it was remarkable how he turned to people, even comparative strangers like Lord Tavistock, and described his fears and troubles. This need to commune with others was most uncharacteristic. From June his handwriting began to deteriorate, and was soon almost illegible; at times he became irritable and expressed doubts as to his competence to manage affairs at home or at the forthcoming conference.[1] At the very end he began to suspect that old friends — even his wife and so close a friend as Wellington — were conspiring against him, and on 9 August he showed clear signs of insanity in the presence of Wellington and George IV. He also expressed the fear that he was about to be denounced in public as a homosexual, but since he seemed to imagine conspiracies on all sides, this particular piece of evidence need not be taken very seriously — at least,

[1] Yonge, iii. 193 n. Sidmouth, iii. 409–10.

not on its own. His condition deteriorated quickly during the next two days, which he spent at North Cray. Precautions were taken against suicide, but on the morning of 12 August Castlereagh remembered or found a small knife in the drawer of a washstand. He severed the carotid artery in his neck, and died instantly.

There has been much speculation as to the cause of this suicide, including the possibility that Castlereagh was being blackmailed for an act of homosexuality which he did not commit, but the true circumstances of which would be exceedingly difficult to prove. The main evidence is slight, and is partly derived from Castlereagh's own remarks. Castlereagh, however, imagined conspiracies of all kinds against himself in his last days. It has been suggested that Lord Clanwilliam, Castlereagh's Parliamentary Under-Secretary for Foreign Affairs, possessed some information. He certainly wrote to Sir Charles Stewart immediately after the event, 'I believe I have omitted nothing; there is only one subject on which I have still something to say, the ideas upon which his imagination dwelt during the various moments of his delirium. I reserve these for the conversations, which I shall have with you when we see one another again.'[1] This may or may not mean anything. Wellington claimed to have made a careful investigation of the blackmail theory, and insisted there was nothing to it. Even if there were, it would still not be proven that this was the only cause of the suicide.[2]

Castlereagh was buried in Westminster Abbey, but as the coffin was borne into the building, jeering and hooting broke out in some sections of the watching crowd. Estimates as to the number involved vary between Lord Clancarty's twenty at most and *The Morning Chronicles*'s 'thousands'. It is clear, however, that his death was welcomed by many; Radicals found it 'a ray of hope in the midst of blackest darkness'; the villages of Saxfield and Hambledon were reported to have rung their bells

---

[1] Webster, *Castlereagh, 1815–22*, p. 486 n.

[2] H. M. Hyde (*The Strange Death of Lord Castlereagh* (1959), pp. 182–90) gives a full account of the blackmail theory. See also Leigh, pp. 346–68, who suggests melancholia, and Aspinall, *Hobhouse*, pp. 88–93, which draws attention to 'an hereditary trait' in the family of Castlereagh's mother.

s

in jubilation. *The Times* explained the insults at Castlereagh's funeral in rather more general terms.

It was because the people regarded Lord Londonderry as an instrument or an author of much public wrong — of manifold political abuses — of grievous national and individual suffering — of a system of government disgraceful abroad, at home insupportable — as a conspicuous member of an Administration essentially odious.

But the Radical *Scotsman* was in no doubt — a worse minister could not exist.

In our minds, then, the name of Castlereagh . . . will long be connected with tyranny abroad, and all that was slavish and oppressive at home . . . We believe conscientiously that he has done infinitely more injury to England in the course of his administration, than the best who remain behind him can redress in a century.

Its obituary was so popular that it was reprinted within a month.[1]

For the government, on the other hand, Castlereagh's death seemed a shattering blow. Liverpool felt that they had lost their 'right arm'; to Eldon the loss seemed 'quite irreparable'. Yet ministries have survived worse shocks, and in this case the politician to fill the void was fortunately to hand, if only the ultra-Tories could bring themselves to accept him. For Metternich's 'malevolent meteor', George Canning, had not yet left to become Governor-General of India; he was about to enter upon the inheritance which he thought had been rightly his in 1809. Castlereagh was undoubtedly irreplaceable in one sense, for no one could provide complete continuity in the conduct of foreign affairs. In ability and experience of foreign affairs, Canning was alone fit to succeed him as Foreign Minister. But Canning neither knew nor cared to know Castlereagh's innermost thoughts on the conduct and development of British policy in 1822. Although practice showed that they were in rough agreement as to British interests in Spain, Portugal, Latin America and Greece, and although their analyses of Britain's world interests did not differ fundamentally, a considerable gulf existed between them as to the means by which these objectives could best be pursued. Where Castlereagh rested his hopes on

[1] *The Scotsman*, 17 Aug. and 14 Sept. 1822. Note also Creevey, ii. 47, Martineau, i. 286–7, and Harris, pp. 163–5.

the Alliance, Canning believed that Britain could disengage herself from continental affairs and become 'a spectatress'. In any case, the same means would not have been open to Canning even had he wished to adopt them. Castlereagh's techniques owed much to ten years' cumulative experience at the Foreign Office, and to the personal relationships he had established with foreign diplomats and potentates over the same period — in particular with Alexander I and Metternich. The latter saw at once that Castlereagh could have no immediate successor. There could be no heir to this sort of personal influence and experience. In this sense Castlereagh's death was the end of an era.

Thus whatever the continuity in aim, Canning's style of diplomatic conduct was bound to be very different. Not for him the pressing desire to preserve the unity of the great powers if at all practicable and consistent with British interests; not for him the reluctance to publicise one's diplomatic quarrels or triumphs. Above all, Canning gave British foreign policy a positive, exciting, patriotic, even liberal appearance, which would have been an anathema to Castlereagh. And differing methods led, to a certain extent, to different results, for Britain's relations with all leading powers could hardly be so generally cordial when the tone of British diplomacy was so strident and positive. Contrary to his wishes, Canning failed to maintain Anglo-American relations at the friendly level finally achieved by Castlereagh, while the ultimate measure of co-operation achieved with Russia and France over the Greek question in 1826–7 was prefaced by the suspicions and recriminations of 1823–5. Canning's diplomatic brilliance and fertility is plain for all to see, but Castlereagh's more ponderous and pedestrian tactics made for a quieter international scene.

An earlier chapter maintained that no similar break was created in the conduct of domestic affairs by Castlereagh's death. True, one must concede that Castlereagh's continuance as Leader of the House would have made the projection of a more liberal image by the government more difficult. Although Canning had been prominent in the defence of the repressive measures of the period 1817–19, his retirement from public office for two years, and his apparent sympathy for Queen Caroline, not to mention the popular *éclat* he was ultimately able to give to his foreign policy, were circumstances all greatly in his favour. He could, in consequence, live down even his opposition to parliamentary reform. As Harriet Martineau wrote of him, 'He must be the hero.'[1] In this sense, therefore, the death of Castlereagh was an important gain to the Liverpool ministry. But beyond that, the only measure associated with the Liberal Tories and concerning which there is evidence that Castlereagh made difficulties, is the resumption of cash payments. If Castlereagh is unlikely to have deserved positive credit for any of the reforming measures of the 1820s — apart from Catholic Emancipation — there is no reason to suppose he would have been an obstacle. Indeed, with his gift of management, he might have been an asset.[2]

Castlereagh's suicide, therefore, probably had more effect on the future development of British foreign rather than domestic policy. But it is necessary to turn now from this hypothetical consideration to an analysis of Castlereagh's place in British history. Contemporaries were in no doubt of his importance, though they disagreed as to whether he was a champion of order, or a suave enemy of freedom and progress. The historian, however, would perhaps be best advised to seek the security of common ground as his starting-point before venturing into the mire of controversy. Expletives and encomiums still impede his path, yet critics and eulogisers broadly agree as to his skill as a politician. Only in the highest arts of parliamentary debate was he seriously deficient. His great strength lay in private discussion, where rhetoric was at a discount, and where patience, tact, logic and industry were decisive. Wilberforce, for one, came to prefer written communications with Castlereagh, so persuasive was the latter in personal meetings.[3] Castlereagh pulled well in harness with the rest of the cabinet, though outside it he was too inclined to rely on his own efforts, and was too

---

[1] Martineau, ii. 145. But note *The Scotsman's* opinion of Canning on 7 Sept. 1822. 'For some time he has incurred less public obloquy than some of his party. But let him not mistake the cause. It is partly in compliment to his supposed insignificance in the cabinet — and partly that the remorselessness and atrocity of Lord Castlereagh threw the weaker voices of his character into the shade.'

[2] See above, Chapter 6.   [3] *Wilberforce*, iv. 304.

little disposed to delegate.[1] This proved both an administrative and parliamentary weakness, though not a vital one. As Melbourne remarked, he shuffled through the business, 'nobody knew how'. There was also widespread contemporary agreement concerning the 'manifest mediocrity of his genius', as *The Times* of 13 August 1822 put it. *The Annual Register* complained of his lack of intellectual distinction, the absence of the slightest tinge of scholarship or literature in his parlance. *The Traveller* concluded, 'It is idle to talk of Lord Londonderry as a great man, . . . [but a] man, who so long, and with a degree of credit among his own party, held power against enemies and rivals, must either have had some striking qualities, or that host of smaller virtues, which, as Bacon well imagines it, "makes up a fortune".' It was indeed through this 'host of smaller virtues' that Castlereagh made the most of the opportunities given to him to become the most effective and influential British politician of the period 1812–22.

Castlereagh owed his political advancement — apart from his own abilities — to his family background, to useful family connexions, and to the fatal political mistakes of the one individual on the same side of the House as himself of outstanding calibre. Had Canning acted with more discrimination he might have occupied the Foreign Office during the momentous years between 1812 and 1815. With still more discrimination, he might have led the government in the Commons ten years earlier than he did. Instead, the more pedestrian Castlereagh held both responsibilities, though with what gains and losses to Britain and to Europe none can tell. Earlier, and perhaps with a similar debt to the political choice of Thomas Grenville, Castlereagh had held the first place in the Irish House of Commons, and had been the most important individual in the onerous task of effecting the Union of the Parliaments. Nor are the intervening years from 1801 to 1812 without their interest, for Castlereagh's periods out of office were interspersed with responsibility, first for India, and later for the detailed conduct of the war against Napoleon. But Castlereagh's prominent place in British history arises mainly from the opportunities opened to him by the political errors of Canning between 1809 and 1812.

[1] *Croker Papers*, iii. 189–90.

Castlereagh explained his political philosophy to the Tsar in 1821 in one of his more fluent passages. He wrote, 'if a statesman were permitted to regulate his conduct by the counsels of his heart instead of the dictates of his understanding, I really see no limits to the impulse, which might be given to his conduct, upon a case so stated'.[1] Castlereagh was certainly faithful to this precept for most of his career, and he owed much of his success at home and abroad to his intense political realism and pragmatism. Nevertheless, there were important limits to his objectivity, and it is necessary to attempt a definition of the political and social concepts which guided his conduct. In particular, it is desirable to explain his attitude to political change, since this profoundly influenced his domestic and foreign policies.

The essentially moderate nature of Castlereagh's interest in parliamentary reform in Ireland as a young man has already been explained, though he was sometimes subsequently twitted by the Opposition benches at Westminster for his apparent change of opinion. Castlereagh boldly retorted that,

notwithstanding the events of the last twenty-five years which had been by no means calculated to encourage the general principle of parliamentary reform, under the circumstances in which the Irish House of Commons then stood, he should again support parliamentary reform.[2]

Castlereagh had never been very specific in the early 1790s as to the type of parliamentary reform he had envisaged for Ireland, but his main complaint then had been directed against the control of Parliament by a narrow clique of aristocrats, and he had favoured increased representation for the respectable and propertied classes in general. He would have been hard pressed to explain just where the ignorant masses ended, and the solid, respectable sections of the community — who were worthy of a voice in the conduct of affairs — began. He was, however, convinced that the British House of Commons adequately represented all worthy sections of opinion in Britain, as he had good cause to remember following the government defeats over the Orders in Council and the renewal of the income tax. In a

---

[1] Webster, *Castlereagh, 1815–22*, p. 376.

[2] *Hansard*, new series, iv. 617.

brief explanation of his own political beliefs in January 1821, he insisted that a government should possess the confidence of King, Parliament, and the 'rational' part of the community. Concerning the latter, he asserted that it 'always made its sentiments as distinctly and intelligibly felt in that House as if the wildest plan of reform that was ever proposed had been adopted'.[1]

All this was perfectly conventional; the stock arguments of champions of the unreformed Parliament. Castlereagh's half-brother indeed described him as a resolute opponent of parliamentary reform. Moreover it is certain that rebellion in Ireland, the French Revolution, violence in Britain, and the fear of further violence and even rebellion in Europe and Britain had strengthened his social and political prejudices. But despite his bias in favour of the aristocracy and squirearchy, he frequently showed his awareness of the importance of trade and industry, and the need for a successful government to respond to some at least of their demands. More than this, in Ireland in the 1790s he had displayed a growing recognition of the value of attracting new groups to assist in the defence of the old order — in this instance, wealthy Catholics and Presbyterians. It is true that here also he betrayed the limitations in his outlook, in that he demanded too much from them in the way of subservience, and he also exaggerated the ability of Catholic aristocrats to control co-religionists of lower social status. The political solution was too limited, and it did not touch the more important social and economic problems in Ireland. Yet, for all its limitations, Castlereagh's move reveals a flexibility that separates him from the truly reactionary Irish aristocrat. His insistence on a certain degree of discrimination in the punishment of Irish rebels points to a similar conclusion.

In British politics there is slight evidence in the same direction, and it is worthy of inclusion in order to question the old description of Castlereagh as the driving force of Ultra-Toryism, and to underline his pragmatism as a politician. His remarks on the possibility of constitutional change in July 1817 were not wholly negative. He remarked, 'it would be dangerous to yield to any but gradual improvement, arising from, and dictated

[1] Ibid. 58.

by experience'. Such a remark to Parliament from a shrewd politician may, of course, mean little, though it is in interesting contrast to Wellington's blunt negative in 1830. Castlereagh's great critic, Lord Holland, thought that he had perhaps not wholly forgotten the principles which he had professed in 1790, while his conduct in the initial stages of Lord John Russell's agitation for the disfranchisement of the corrupt Cornish borough of Grampound in favour of an unrepresented northern city provoked some interesting comment among his political opponents. Sir Robert Heron wrote : 'We all expected to be treated with derision. Sir Henry Ward was supposed to be ready, and Canning evidently so. Suddenly Lord Castlereagh yields this question, as far as it goes, of radical reform.'[1] Castlereagh, on this occasion, was careful to exclude the question of principle, save the one already established by Parliament that corrupt boroughs should be disfranchised. But he agreed that it would be difficult to disfranchise Grampound in favour of the neighbouring areas which were already well represented, and stated that he personally was in favour of transferring the seats elsewhere 'to the general representation of the country'. He refused to commit himself, and emphatically discountenanced any general parliamentary reform, but his reply had pleased the Opposition. Castlereagh's later insistence that the Grampound franchise should be thrown into the hundred suggests that the cabinet felt he had gone too far, and certainly Eldon and Wellington were opposed even to the disfranchisement of Grampound. In the end the seats went to the county of Yorkshire, and not Leeds as Russell had demanded.[2]

The impression that Castlereagh was more flexible than the Ultras is further confirmed by his attitude to political change on

[1] A. and E. Porritt, *Unreformed House of Commons*, i. 86–88. Thomas Grenville (*Dropmore MSS*. x. 452) and Lord John Russell (*Recollections*, pp. 39–41), however, thought Castlereagh not very favourable, and Russell recalled that Castlereagh was co-operative only so long as the disfranchisement was in favour of the neighbouring hundred. This opinion does not fit in very neatly with the evidence from *Hansard* — see below, note 2.

[2] Feiling, pp. 323–4. Spencer Walpole, ii. 278. *Hansard*, xli. 1091–1122, new series, i. 489–95, iv. 1074.

the continent. Although he repeatedly expressed his horror and dislike of radical or violent change, he admitted that moderate change might often be conducive to greater political stability in the country in question, and might therefore contribute to the peace of the area as a whole. He tried to view the French and Spanish constitutions in this light, and his hostility to even moderate constitutions was most acute in those areas where he feared their existence might antagonise a major power, and perhaps weaken the delicate fabric of European peace which was his main objective. It is not enough to claim that his expressions in favour of constitutions arose from fear of the British Parliament; equally it would be wrong to attribute to Castlereagh any strong interest in constitutions *per se*; the crucial test was the practical one of European peace and stability. A similarly cold intellectual approach is to be seen in many other of his policies, and not least in his conversion to support of Catholic Emancipation in Ireland on the grounds of its political utility, but his refusal to press for its accomplishment against adverse political circumstances. He had opposed the abolition of the slave trade as impractical, and had worked assiduously for its elimination internationally because British opinion was insistent. With the same absence of emotion he bowed to the demand that Christian missionaries should be admitted to India, and to a limited extent he might have agreed to small changes in British parliamentary representation if the demand were sufficient, and the results likely to be in accord with his wishes. It is worth remembering that the fall of the Wellington ministry in 1830 was hastened by its inability to conduct a skilful tactical retreat in the face of mounting public discontent. Castlereagh may have been a Tory, but he was not an Ultra.

It is clear that one must look for little creativity in Castlereagh's conduct of internal affairs. Even in the passage of the Irish Union, despite his important contributions to the detail of the measure, his role as a manager and manipulator of men and interests was more important. He bowed to those demands which he found tolerable; in his lifetime he even bowed to some which he disliked intensely, but in no case was he driven to the wall by any movement which would have undermined his political principles. His flexibility as a politician was therefore never fully tested; the limit of his concessions under real pressure never revealed. Instead, at the political level, he was permitted to conduct modest, and mostly ineffectual experiments, while in economic matters his blend of the traditions of eighteenth-century model landlordism, which he had imbibed from his family in Ireland, with a working knowledge of the principles of *laisser faire* sufficed to maintain an uneasy balance between the contending interests of land and trade in Britain. Neither got out of hand, despite the economic crises from 1811 to 1822, nor did the massive discontents of the poor. Castlereagh was therefore free to shuffle along in his undogmatic and essentially uncreative way, making a concession here and there, contributing a little to the expansion of British trade, and threatening to erect no major obstacles when demands for new government fiscal policies became overwhelming. Save in the contribution of diplomacy to the improvement of trade it was an unremarkable performance, yet it helped to preserve the government's position until the great economic trends of the nineteenth century became clearer, and it even helped to anticipate some aspects of the final verdict.

Castlereagh thus falls far short of the arch-villain, the arch-tyrant, conjured up in the overheated minds of radical young poets. They attributed a diabolical genius to him that was far beyond his capacity. Indeed, Castlereagh rose superior to the Whig charge of mediocrity — as far as domestic politics were concerned — mainly by reason of his executive skill, his ability to influence and manage people, his acute sense of realism, his political courage and resolution. In the main he responded to events rather than took the initiative; within the limits of his political philosophy he showed no little flexibility; but his real strength lay in the execution of policy.

Castlereagh's place in British foreign and imperial politics before 1812 was not spectacular. His influence upon events in India was modest, while his share in the conduct of the war against Napoleon — without being marked by any real victories — showed the value of hard work and common sense. He did much to improve the strength and mobility of Britain's forces, he helped to advance the fortunes of Britain's best general of the war, and he did something towards the formulation of a more coherent British strategy, which resisted the temptation of irrelevant side-shows. But it was as Foreign Secretary from 1812 that Castlereagh earned a prominent place in Napoleon's post-war reminiscences. Indeed, of all his leading opponents Napoleon was most critical and contemptuous of Castlereagh, an inverted form of testimony as to his crucial part in the final overthrow of the Emperor. For he undoubtedly was mainly responsible for smoothing away the quarrels of the allies sufficiently to enable them to overthrow Napoleon in 1814, and to prevent the conclusion of a compromise peace which might have left Napoleon with sufficient power to throw Europe into yet another state of war within a few years. Historical argument of this sort is not susceptible to practical demonstration, but the potentiality of the allied divisions is there for all to see, even if the precise value of a restraining personality cannot be determined. Castlereagh then proceeded to exert a profound influence in favour of a European peace — both before and after the Hundred Days — that would satisfy most of the aspirations of the great powers, and leave not even France with an invincible sense of grievance. The years 1814–15 were the peak of Castlereagh's career, and no value judgement can alter the practical importance of the creation of a European balance of power which lasted broadly undisturbed for nearly half a century. Castlereagh was not the only architect, but he was the main one; the design may not have been pleasing to all, it may have had a rather old-fashioned look, but it proved one of the most durable structures of its type ever erected.

Nevertheless, in many ways Castlereagh's foreign policy during the last seven years of his life is more interesting, if less lasting and successful. During this period Castlereagh undertook a policy so distinctive and original that it is unlikely that any other British politician of his time would or could have attempted it. It was, in fact, one of the most ambitious foreign policies ever attempted by a British minister, not least because it was actively supported by so few of his countrymen. They were apathetic, or reluctantly bowed to his superior knowledge, or they were openly hostile and critical. Few understood his real purpose. Criticism of this policy, as well as admiration, has persisted even from Castlereagh's greatest twentieth-century admirers. Thus Sir Charles Webster has argued that 'he failed to associate his ideas with the deepest emotions of his age'. Castlereagh's interest in international conferences has been criticised for his failure to include the smaller powers, and for the absence of an institutional framework. It has been contended that he relied too much on himself and on personal relationships, and that his work was doomed to failure in the near future even if his guiding influence could have been retained beyond August 1822. Indeed, Webster concludes that Castlereagh attempted an impossible task, that he failed in much that he set out to do, but that one cannot fail to admire the nobility of his aims, the industry and ability with which he pursued them, and his success in reconciling his policy with overall British interests.[1]

It is certainly true that Castlereagh failed to comprehend the future political development of Britain and much of Europe; in the long run he exaggerated the viability of a policy designed to preserve a monarchical-aristocratic order, moderated and strengthened here and there by modest concessions to other responsible and respectable sections of society. He failed to see that these concessions would be insufficient in the long run to satisfy the new aspirants for political power. Both he and Canning allowed the shadow of republicanism to encourage a fruitless quest on their part for the establishment of monarchies in Spanish America, where it was soon proved that Britain had no reason to fear the economic or political consequences of the emergence of republics.[2] Nevertheless, Castlereagh did not allow his fear of revolution to carry him so far as Wellington, whose advice on the Greek question would have paralysed British policy in favour of Russia. Nor should Castlereagh's failure to foresee future political developments be given too much weight, for liberal and nationalist movements in Europe were too weak to provide the basis for a new political order during Castlereagh's lifetime. This is not to say that Castlereagh's response would necessarily have been more liberal had circumstances been different, but it does underline that his was not a form of conservatism which flew blatantly in the face of facts.

In 1814–15 British and European society was emerging from a traumatic experience. One had to be very young, restless,

---

[1] Webster, *Castlereagh, 1815–22*, pp. 490–505.
[2] Some Latin American politicians were equally misled.

discontented or idealistic to wish for further change and up-
heavals at such a time. The weight of influential opinion in
Britain was all in favour of peace, economy and increased trade.
British crusading zeal was limited to the abolition of the slave
trade. Castlereagh set out to create a world at peace, so that
men of property and status might sleep quietly in their beds, so
that men of business might grow rich, and so that the masses
might live in modest comfort within their appointed station in
life, free from the political or moral temptations of agitators and
high wages. There have been worse visions of the world.
Castlereagh believed that to achieve these objects Britain could
not withdraw to her island and empire fortress. He had seen
how near the allies had come to war over Saxony in little more
than six months after the first overthrow of Napoleon; he had
seen little more than six weeks later the contemptuous ease with
which Napoleon had ousted the Bourbons of France. The
rivalries of the continental powers and vulnerability of certain
European states to revolution threatened to expose Europe yet
again to the dangers of 1793–1815, and so jeopardise all that the
strongest interests in Britain desired — namely peace and
prosperity. In this precarious situation, Britain could not opt
out.

He did not allow fear of revolution to dominate his policy. In
fact he committed Britain only to the exclusion of Napoleon from
power in France. Otherwise he judged revolution in terms of its
threat to the peace of Europe, and in accordance with his efforts
to delimit the spheres of influence of each of the great powers to
its own satisfaction and in accordance with the overall European
balance of power. If dissension between all or most of the great
powers could be avoided, there lay the best guarantee of the
peace and stability of Europe. If he paid little attention to the
interests of the smaller powers in this process, it is hard to see
how he could have served their interests better by promises or
expressions of sympathy which neither he nor they could have
backed or utilised with material power. Castlereagh also believed
that many, though not all British interests, could best be
promoted through a policy of co-operation with the other
powers. Even in the New World, where he sought to exclude
the influence of the other great powers, he emphasised the

merits of compromise and conciliation, and was clearly contemplating some form of international approach to the problem of recognising the independence of the Spanish colonies at the time of his death. Above all he argued the merits of a new type of diplomacy, inspired by mutual trust and co-operation. He tried to exploit the personal relationships which he had established with the leading European political figures in 1814–15; relationships which he utilised in his personal correspondence with them, in his talks with their representatives in London, and more dramatically in meetings with them. Some parts of this system were being applied to Anglo-American relations as well.

Although Article VI of the Quadruple Alliance was mainly his work, he actually attended only one conference after 1815, though he was preparing to attend a second at the time of his death. He made no attempt to give greater precision to Article VI, and the conferences were in fact arranged on an *ad hoc* basis. He came to see, in practice, that these conferences could be an embarrassment as well as an asset to his policy; whatever his original intention with respect to Article VI, his conference policy became increasingly pragmatic. Consequently his interest in such meetings should not be allowed to eclipse the other components of the 'new diplomacy'. The whole was a series of expedients, based upon the exceptional opportunities for personal contact created by the exigencies of war. Great as Castlereagh's enthusiasm for the 'new diplomacy' undoubtedly was, and despite the suggestion of permanence in Article VI, it would be unhistorical to attribute to Castlereagh the sort of conceptions that inspired the League of Nations and United Nations.[1] Equally, to emphasise the absence of institutions, rules and regulations, the exclusion of the small powers, and its dependence on personal relations as crucial sources of weakness for the conference system is to miss the main point. Formal institutions had no place in his scheme. The 'new diplomacy' and the conferences were a product of personal relationships; without

[1] It is true that Castlereagh once wrote of the conferences as a 'new discovery' (see above, p. 202), and seemed to bubble over with enthusiasm at the idea, but in practice his use of this new diplomatic instrument was very cautious. Compare his attitudes in 1818 and 1822 with those of 1820–1.

the latter, the former might never have been created at that time.[1] As for continuity, Castlereagh could neither guarantee his own successor, nor those of his counterparts in Europe. He was never explicit on the point, but it is possible that he saw that these relationships were an unexpected and perhaps never-to-be-repeated bonus in the conduct of foreign policy at a critical time. Here was an opportunity to be exploited rather than a permanent system to be created.[2]

Earlier chapters have endeavoured to prove that Castlereagh's 'new diplomacy' was by no means a bankrupt policy at the time of his suicide, however uncertain the future. The same chapters have also attempted to show that no vital British interests were sacrificed in the process, and that the only practical alternative to Castlereagh's policy would have been one of greater aloofness from European affairs. Such a policy would probably have so weakened Austria's position in Europe, and increased the Russian and French freedom of action, that more positive British action would soon have been called for. Was not Canning driven to work with Russia and France in 1826–7 as the best means of controlling them? Castlereagh preferred to try to anticipate such an eventuality by working with all the powers, and by resorting to definite alignments only as a last resort, and then as discreetly as possible. The risks that would attend either policy were diminished by Britain's financial, economic and naval power, but Castlereagh's course had the added merit of trying to keep the international temperature low, and of trying to prevent crises reaching flashpoint in the first place. In the highly charged atmosphere following the Napoleonic wars this seems the more constructive approach, and even if the need for precautions against a resurgent revolutionary or Napoleonic France was passing by the 1820s, the same methods could be employed as a possible — though not infallible — means of

[1] For a brief account of the personal nature of the conference system see Metternich's *Memoirs* (London, 1880, i. 172–3), cited by Schenk, pp. 125–6 and notes.

[2] This is not to deny Castlereagh's place in the evolution of international organisations, but one must try to see his ideas in the context of his own period, and it is clear that his concern was with personal relationships — not institutions.

restraint on Russia and the more limited ambitions of Bourbon France.

Some historians have contended that Castlereagh's policy was doomed to failure because of the lack of British public support, and because of the basic incompatibility of Britain and her despotic allies. Yet it is doubtful whether lack of public support constituted an immediate threat to Castlereagh's policies in 1822. Castlereagh himself seemed indispensable to the Liverpool ministry for as long as he lived; the Liverpool ministry in its turn seemed indispensable to King and Commons in the circumstances of the early 1820s. Castlereagh's freedom of action in foreign policy was based essentially on these conditions. It is true that, when in 1820–1 fear of revolution in Europe threatened to turn the Alliance into a general instrument of repression, Castlereagh was in danger of falling into the ideological gulf thus created between the despotic powers and British opinion. But the crisis had passed; the Alliance came to serve British interests in the Near East well in 1822, and Canning was obliged to find a substitute for the Alliance to maintain British influence in the Greek question a few years later. One cannot say whether Castlereagh at Vienna–Verona and later could have used the Alliance to prevent French intervention in Spain in 1823, but Canning could find no better substitute. There was no inevitable impediment to co-operation between a constitutional state and reactionary powers in these circumstances. The immediate threat to Castlereagh arose not so much from British opinion as from the type of continental crises that might arise, and the reaction of the continental statesmen to such crises. Thus rebellion in Italy or Germany tended to unite Austria and Russia, but rebellion in the Iberian peninsula or Greece tended to draw Metternich and Castlereagh together. Consequently there remained considerable opportunities for profitable co-operation within the Alliance without provoking effective opposition from the British public. At the same time, the danger of another 1820–1 — or even worse — was always present, and the Alliance might be torn apart at any time. Yet even the collapse of Castlereagh's Alliance policy in his lifetime would not necessarily have condemned it. One of the tests of statesmanship is surely the utility of a policy at a given time, provided such a policy does not carry with it unacceptable penalties or limitations on future action.[1] Castlereagh's 'new diplomacy' can be defended both on grounds of immediate utility, and on the ground that it was imposing no mortgage on the future. It is clear that Castlereagh used the Alliance; he was not ensnared and entrapped in it. One has only to study his Spanish American policies to see how he moved in and out of the Alliance context according to his needs.

If the above arguments be accepted, it is clear that Castlereagh's achievement in foreign policy between 1815 and 1822 was an impressive one. Although these years fall short of the period 1814–15 in accomplishment, they form a fitting and complementary sequel. True, there were momentary failings in execution: in conception, Castlereagh's policy sometimes betrays his limitations in outlook and imagination. The historian, with the advantages of hindsight, may smile a little at the exaggerated hopes and fears, at elaborate precautions against receding dangers, at other human weaknesses. So much energy and ingenuity expended upon the task of making the world safe for aristocracy may even seem distasteful, but seen in the circumstances of his time and background the overall achievement remains a diplomatic masterpiece. The 'new diplomacy' must always stand as a rare example of intelligent exploitation of strength — of enlightened self-interest which perceived the subtle inter-connexions and interactions between British interests and those of Europe. The system was even extended to a lesser degree to the New World, where Britain's ex-American colonists were treated with a greater measure of tact and conciliation than they had hitherto experienced at the hands of a British Foreign Minister.

Although Castlereagh's name is often associated with the growth of international institutions, the limited nature of his international experiment is plain for all to see. His most far-sighted act was probably his determination to conciliate the United States. He quickly outgrew the speculative enthusiasms

---

[1] The Hoare–Laval pact of 1935 is a classic example. It seems to me that the late Professor Temperley exaggerated 'the dangers' attendant upon Castlereagh's secret diplomacy. See *Cambridge Historical Journal* (1938–40), pp. 1–3.

T

of his youth, and though his attitude to Catholic Emancipation or freer trade may be described as forward-looking, the inspiration behind them was mainly his keenly pragmatic and realistic approach to politics. It was as a practical politician that he excelled, smoothing away causes of dissension, drawing men together, forcing them to face facts, and steeling them to action. He was one of the most effective men of business of his time, and it is in this context that his career in relation to Irish, British, or European politics should be viewed.

Bibliographical Note

Although the author has not consulted unpublished material, it is necessary to draw the reader's attention to the following primary sources. The primary material for the study of Castlereagh's career is abundant, but scattered. Although Sir Charles Webster found the most important evidence for his two studies of Castlereagh's foreign policy in the Public Record Office in London, the value of his work was enhanced by his visits to the leading archives in Europe to study, in particular, the reports of foreign ambassadors from London. Similarly, Bradford Perkins, to give but one recent example, in his studies of Anglo-American relations down to 1822, has placed the student of Castlereagh in his debt by his researches in American archives. Consequently, although further research is unlikely to modify the overall interpretation of Castlereagh's foreign policy, many interesting sidelights may yet emerge from the archives of lesser states, both in Europe and elsewhere. One would like to know more about Castlereagh's relations with Spanish, Portuguese, Neapolitan and Spanish American diplomats, and intriguing figures such as Miranda and Pozzo di Borgo. The study of such evidence is likely to be rewarding in view of the emphasis which Castlereagh placed upon personal relations and contacts, on private explanations and gentle hints. To enumerate the possible sources for a comprehensive study of Castlereagh's foreign policy could therefore extend to a list of many national and state archives, and of the private papers of the leading statesmen and diplomats of the period.

In domestic affairs the situation is simplified geographically, but still raises extensive problems. In Irish matters, the Londonderry Papers, the Camden and Pelham Papers, and various other obvious sources have been thoroughly explored, but much of interest might well emerge from the private papers of Irish members of Parliament who were approached by Castlereagh and others during the preparations for the passage of the Act of Union. Similarly, it would be interesting to have more Catholic and Presbyterian accounts of Castlereagh's negotiations with them from 1798 to 1801. Equally

281

for British politics after 1812, when Castlereagh was Leader of the Commons, the papers of great borough owners, possibly also of some leading government backbenchers, might well reveal something concerning the management of Parliament at this time. Of all aspects of Castlereagh's career this is the least studied, yet some understanding of his success here is essential in order not only to understand Castlereagh's influence in the Commons, but also to explain his independence as Foreign Secretary. Despite the invaluable studies by Mr. D. Gray and Mr. R. Glover, monographs upon the Pittites between 1806 and 1812, and upon Castlereagh's tenure of the Secretaryship for War between 1807 and 1809 would be most welcome. The papers of leading politicians, the War Office Records and other military sources could usefully be consulted for this purpose.

The following is a list of the main sources consulted by students of the career of Castlereagh, or those whose work on other themes throws light upon his conduct.

Public Record Office, London : Foreign Office and War Office Records; Irish State Papers; Pitt Papers.

British Museum, London : Liverpool, Ripon, Peel, Huskisson, Vansittart, Melville, Aberdeen, Stratford Canning, Lieven, Pelham, Perceval and Wellesley Papers.

India Office Library.

State Paper Office, Dublin, and Public Record Office, Belfast.

Royal archives at Windsor Castle.

University Library, Cambridge : Pitt Papers.

John Rylands Library, Manchester : 2nd Earl of Chatham's Papers.

Mount Stewart and Londonderry House : Londonderry Papers.

Sandon Hall, Staffs. : Harrowby Papers.

Bayham Abbey : Camden Papers.

Apsley House : Wellington Papers.

County Record Office, The Castle, Exeter : Sidmouth Papers.

W. L. Clements Library, Ann Arbor, Michigan, and County Hall, Kingston-on-Thames : Goulburn and Melville Papers.

Harewood House, Leeds : Canning Papers.

A list of the main works relating to Castlereagh and aspects of his career.

Alison, Sir A., *The Lives of Lord Castlereagh and Sir Charles Stewart* (1861).

Aspinall, A., *Lord Brougham and the Whig Party* (1927); 'The Cabinet Council: 1783–1835', *Proceedings of the British Academy,* xxxviii. 145–252; *The Correspondence of Charles Arbuthnot* (1941); *The Letters of George IV: 1812–30* (1938); *The Diary of Henry Hobhouse* (1947).

Barnes, D. G., *George III and William Pitt* (1939).

Bathurst, *Report on the MSS. of Earl Bathurst* (Historical MSS. Commission, 1923).

Bemis, S. F., *John Quincy Adams and the Foundations of American Foreign Policy* (1949).

Brock, W. R., *Lord Liverpool and Liberal Toryism* (1941).

Brougham, Lord, *Historical Sketches of Statesmen who flourished in the Time of George III* (1839–43).

Buckingham, Duke of, *Memoirs of the Courts and Cabinets of George III* (1853–5); *Memoirs of the Regency* (1856); *Memoirs of the Court of George IV* (1859).

Buckland, C. S. B., *Metternich and the British Government from 1809 to 1815* (1932).

Burne, Col. A. H., *The Noble Duke of York* (1949).

Colchester, Lord, *The Diary and Correspondence of . . .* (1861).

Creevey, T., *The Creevey Papers* (1903), ed. Sir H. Maxwell.

Croker, J. W., *The Croker Papers* (1884), ed. L. J. Jennings.

Crouzet, F., *L'Économie Britannique et le Blocus Continental* (1958).

Dangerfield, G., *The Era of Good Feelings* (1952).

Dropmore MSS., *The Correspondence of William Wyndham Grenville* (Historical MSS. Commission, 1892–1910).

Feiling, Sir K. G., *The Second Tory Party, 1714–1832* (1938).

Foord, A. S., 'The Waning of "The Influence of the Crown" ', *English Historical Review* (1947), lxii. 484–507.

Fortescue, Sir J. W., *History of the British Army* (1899–1930); *British Statesmen of the Great War* (1911).

Fox-Strangeways, G., *Further Memoirs of the Whig Party, 1807–21* (1905). *See also* Holland.

Fremantle, A. F., *England in the Nineteenth Century, 1801–10* (1929–30).

Fyffe, C. A., *Modern Europe* (1886).

Gash, N., *Mr. Secretary Peel* (1961).

Glover, R. G., *Peninsular Preparation* (1963).

Graubard, S. R., 'Castlereagh and the Peace of Europe', *The Journal of British Studies*, Nov. 1963, pp. 79–87.

Gray, D., *Spencer Perceval* (1963).

Greville, C. C. F., *The Greville Memoirs* (1938), ed. L. Strachey and R. Fulford.

Gulick, E. V., *Europe's Classical Balance of Power* (1955).

Gurwood, Col. G., *The Dispatches of the Duke of Wellington, 1799–1818* (1835–8).

Hassall, A., *Castlereagh* (1908).

Hinsley, F. H., *Power and the Pursuit of Peace* (1963).

Holland, Lord, *Memoirs of the Whig Party during my Time* (1852–4). *See also* Fox-Strangeways.

Hyde, H. M., *The Rise of Lord Castlereagh* (1933); *The Strange Death of Lord Castlereagh* (1959).

Johnston, E. M., *Great Britain and Ireland, 1760–1800* (1963).

Kissinger, H., *A World Restored, 1812–22* (1957).

Kraehe, E. E., *Metternich's German Policy*, (1963).

Lane Poole, S., *Life of Stratford Canning* (1888).

Lecky, W. E. H., *A History of Ireland in the Eighteenth Century* (1892).

Leigh, I., *Castlereagh* (1951).

Londonderry, 3rd Marquis of, *Memoirs and Correspondence of Viscount Castlereagh* (1848–53).

McDowell, R. B., *Irish Public Opinion, 1750–1800* (1944); *Public Opinion and Government Policy in Ireland, 1801–46* (1952).

Mackesy, P., *The War in the Mediterranean, 1803–10* (1957).

Malmesbury, Lord, *Diaries and Correspondence of 1st Earl of . . .* (1845).

Marriot, Sir J. A. R., *Castlereagh* (1936).

New, C. W., *The Life of Henry Brougham to 1830* (1961).

Nicolson, Sir H., *The Congress of Vienna* (1946).

Pares, R., *George III and the Politicians* (1953).

Perkins, B., *Prologue to War, England and the United States, 1805–12* (1961); *Castlereagh and Adams, Britain and the United States, 1812–23* (1964).

Philips, C. H., *The East India Company, 1784–1834* (1940).

Plumer Ward, R., *Memoirs of . . .* (1850), ed. E. Phipps.

Porritt, A. and E., *The Unreformed House of Commons* (1909).

Renier, G. J., *Great Britain and the Establishment of the Kingdom of the Netherlands, 1813–15* (1930).

Rippy, J. F., *Rivalry of the United States and Great Britain over Latin America, 1808–30* (1929).

Roberts, M., *The Whig Party, 1807–12* (1939).

Rolo, P. J. V., *George Canning* (1965).

Romilly, Sir S., *Memoirs of the Life of . . .* (1840).

Rose, J. Holland, *Pitt and the Great War* (1914).

Ross, C., *Correspondence of Charles, 1st Marquis Cornwallis* (1859).

Rush, R., *A Residence at the Court of London, 1819–25* (1845).

Schroeder, P. W., *Metternich's Diplomacy at its Zenith, 1820–3* (1962).

Sidmouth, Lord, *The Life and Correspondence of Henry Addington . . .* (1847), ed. G. Pellew.

Temperley, H. W. V., and Penson, L. M., *The Foundations of British Foreign Policy, 1792–1902* (1938).

Thompson, E. P., *The Making of the English Working Class* (1963).

Twiss, H., *The Public and Private Life of Lord Chancellor Eldon* (1844).

Walpole, Sir Spencer, *A History of England from 1815* (1890).

Webster, Sir C. K., *The Foreign Policy of Castlereagh, 1812–15* (1931); *The Foreign Policy of Castlereagh, 1815–22* (1925); *The Congress of Vienna* (1937); *British Diplomacy, 1813–15, Select Documents dealing with the reconstruction of Europe* (1921); *Britain and the Independence of Latin America, 1812–30* (1938).

Wellington, 2nd Duke of, *Supplementary Dispatches and Memoranda of the Duke of Wellington* (1858–72); *Dispatches, Correspondence and Memoranda of the Duke of Wellington from 1819* (1867–80). See *also* Gurwood.

White, R. J., *From Waterloo to Peterloo* (1957).

Wilberforce, R. I. and S., *Life of William Wilberforce* (1838).

Yonge, C. D., *Life and Administration of Lord Liverpool* (1868).

Ziegler, P., *Addington* (1965).

Index

PRINTED IN GREAT BRITAIN BY ROBERT MACLEHOSE AND CO. LTD
THE UNIVERSITY PRESS, GLASGOW